ARCHAEOLOGY, NATION, AND RACE

Archaeology, Nation, and Race is a must-read book for students of archaeology and adjacent fields. It demonstrates how archaeology and concepts of antiquity have shaped, and have been shaped by, colonialism, race, and nationalism. Structured as a lucid and lively dialogue between two leading scholars, the volume compares modern Greece and modern Israel – two prototypical and influential cases – where archaeology sits at the very heart of the modern national imagination. Exchanging views on the foundational myths, moral economies, and racial prejudices in the field of archaeology and beyond, Raphael Greenberg and Yannis Hamilakis explore topics such as the colonial origins of national archaeologies, the crypto-colonization of the countries and their archaeologies, the role of archaeology as a process of purification, and the racialization and "whitening" of Greece and Israel and their archaeological and material heritage. They conclude with a call for decolonization and the need to forge alliances with subjugated communities and new political movements.

Raphael Greenberg is Professor of Archaeology at Tel Aviv University. He has conducted numerous excavations and published widely on the Bronze and Iron Age Levant and on the social and political contexts of archaeology in Israel/Palestine. His book *The Archaeology of the Bronze Age Levant* won the G. Ernest Wright Award and the Biblical Archaeology Society Publication Award.

Yannis Hamilakis is Joukowsky Family Professor at Brown University where he teaches archaeology and Modern Greek Studies. He has published widely on archaeological theory, politics of the past, decolonization, archaeology and the senses, and the Neolithic and Bronze Age Aegean. His *Nation and Its Ruins* won the Edmund Keeley Book Prize, was shortlisted for the Runciman Prize and has been translated into several languages. His edited book, *The New Nomadic Age*, was among the best books of 2019 as listed on *Artforum*.

Advance Praise for *Archaeology, Nation, and Race*

This is one of the most interesting and thought-provoking archaeology books that I have read in a long time. It is truly a meeting of two deep-thinking minds – Yannis Hamilakis musing on Greece and Rafael Greenberg musing on Israel. Universally regarded as two of the most thoughtful, intellectual, and politically active archaeologists working today, both with impeccable credentials, one couldn't ask for two more devoted and opinionated (in a good way) scholars, who don't fear to speak their minds and advocate for the causes that they hold dear.

- *Eric H. Cline, George Washington University*

We get to eavesdrop on two accomplished archeologists as they discuss the high stakes of the interplay of nationalism with notions of antiquity. This comparison of the Israeli and Greek instances is ultimately about the meaning of archeology itself, as a discipline that is no less concerned with the present than it is with the past.

- *Katherine Fleming, New York University*

National archeology stands out as a field in which politics is both uniquely dominant and entirely suppressed. Two top experts offer a frank discussion of archeology's role in the history of nationalism in their respective countries and of its costs. They uncover the various manners in which archeology functions as both a means and an end in struggles of liberation and conquest, which are often driven by spatial imagination and fantasies no less than by material aspirations. A must-read for anyone interested in archeology, in ancient and modern Israel and Greece, and in critical thinking about nationalism. This is a uniquely original contribution to the ever-urgent question: who owns the past?

- *Ishay Rosen-Zvi, Tel Aviv University*

These two scholars provide fascinating insight into how and why archaeology has been a critical tool in building two very different nations – Greece and Israel. Using conversation rather than dry exposition, Greenberg and Hamilakis also show that science, no matter how entangled with religion and nationalism, can upset our narrow ideas about history. An essential book for anyone curious about the way we create our past to control the present – and future.

- *Andrew Lawler, Author of* Under Jerusalem: The Buried History of the World's Most Contested City

Archaeology, Nation, and Race is a serious pleasure – a smart, wide-ranging, and spirited conversation, not just between two highly knowledgeable and thoughtful interlocutors, but between the Hellenic and Hebraic, local and global, seen and unseen, dead and living. Greenberg and Hamilakis each come steeped in the particulars of the national archaeologies to which they've devoted their lives; both are also deeply open, and committed to challenging themselves and the cultural and political assumptions that surround them. This book has a refreshing urgency about it.

- *Adina Hoffman, Yale University, author of* Till We have Built Jerusalem: Architects of a New City

Two leading scholars have a fascinating conversation comparing the contribution of archaeology to the mythical constitution, racialization, and crypto-colonialism of Israel and Greece. Shedding new light on the Eurocentric models of Hebraism and Hellenism, they conduct a masterful critique of purification and idealization, and invite us to envision a decolonizing scholarship that forges activist alliances.

- *Vassilis Lambropoulos, University of Michigan*

It may seem paradoxical that it should be archaeologists who unravel the ideological underpinnings of global modernity, but Greenberg and Hamilakis are uniquely qualified to perform this long-overdue task of conceptual excavation. Taking the twin cases of Greek and Israeli nationalism – and emphasizing their sometimes unexpected and even shocking commonalities – they deploy a disarmingly dialogical format to expose the intersections of race, antiquity, territoriality, and cultural hegemony in a formulation that the world has, for far too long, largely taken as the natural order of things.

- *Michael Herzfeld, Harvard University, author of* Subversive Archaism: Troubling Traditionalists and the Politics of National Heritage

Archaeology, Nation, and Race

Confronting the Past, Decolonizing the Future in Greece and Israel

RAPHAEL GREENBERG

Tel Aviv University

YANNIS HAMILAKIS

Brown University

CAMBRIDGE
UNIVERSITY PRESS

CAMBRIDGE
UNIVERSITY PRESS

University Printing House, Cambridge CB2 8BS, United Kingdom

One Liberty Plaza, 20th Floor, New York, NY 10006, USA

477 Williamstown Road, Port Melbourne, VIC 3207, Australia

314–321, 3rd Floor, Plot 3, Splendor Forum, Jasola District Centre,
New Delhi – 110025, India

103 Penang Road, #05–06/07, Visioncrest Commercial, Singapore 238467

Cambridge University Press is part of the University of Cambridge.

It furthers the University's mission by disseminating knowledge in the pursuit of education, learning, and research at the highest international levels of excellence.

www.cambridge.org
Information on this title: www.cambridge.org/9781009160230
DOI: 10.1017/9781009160247

© Raphael Greenberg and Yannis Hamilakis 2022

This publication is in copyright. Subject to statutory exception
and to the provisions of relevant collective licensing agreements,
no reproduction of any part may take place without the written
permission of Cambridge University Press.

First published 2022

Printed in the United Kingdom by TJ Books Limited, Padstow Cornwall

A catalogue record for this publication is available from the British Library.

Library of Congress Cataloging-in-Publication Data
NAMES: Greenberg, Raphael, author. | Hamilakis, Yannis, 1966– author.
TITLE: Archaeology, nation and race : confronting the past, decolonizing the future in Greece and Israel / Raphael Greenberg, Tel Aviv University, Yannis Hamilakis, Brown University, Rhode Island.
DESCRIPTION: Cambridge ; New York : Cambridge University Press, 2022. | Includes bibliographical references and index.
IDENTIFIERS: LCCN 2021048058 (print) | LCCN 2021048059 (ebook) | ISBN 9781009160230 (hardback) | ISBN 9781009160254 (paperback) | ISBN 9781009160247 (epub)
SUBJECTS: LCSH: Archaeology–Political aspects. | Archaeology–Social aspects. | Archaeology and history. | Race. | Nationalism. | Imperialism. | Ethnoarchaeology. | Excavations (Archaeology)–Political aspects–Israel. | Israel–Antiquities–Political aspects. | Excavations (Archaeology)–Political aspects–Greece. | Greece–Antiquities–Political aspects. | BISAC: SOCIAL SCIENCE / Archaeology
CLASSIFICATION: LCC CC75.7 .G7412 2022 (print) | LCC CC75.7 (ebook) | DDC 930.1–DC23/eng/20211207
LC record available at https://lccn.loc.gov/2021048058
LC ebook record available at https://lccn.loc.gov/2021048059

ISBN 978-1-009-16023-0 Hardback
ISBN 978-1-009-16025-4 Paperback

Cambridge University Press has no responsibility for the persistence or accuracy of URLs for external or third-party internet websites referred to in this publication and does not guarantee that any content on such websites is, or will remain, accurate or appropriate.

To Giorgos Hamilakis (1933–2021), an archaeophile
To Moshe Greenberg (1928–2010), rodef shalom

Contents

List of Figures	*page* ix
Preface	xiii

1	Introduction	1
2	The Colonial Origins of National Archaeologies	8
3	Archaeology in the Crypto-Colony	42
4	Archaeology as Purification	75
5	Whitening Greece and Israel: Nation, Race, and Archaeogenetics	109
6	Decolonizing Our Imagination	151
7	Conclusion	180

References	185
Index	209

Figures

2.1 The Parthenon as drawn by George Wheler. . . . . *page* 13
2.2 Yigael Yadin and Israel's first prime minister, David Ben-Gurion, peer into a storage pithos from Canaanite Hazor, presumed to have been destroyed by the first Israelite settlers c. 1200 BCE. 27
2.3 *Gehazi* (1940s), a now-lost sculpture by Yechiel Shemi (1922–2003), created in a Near Eastern idiom that characterized the "Canaanite" movement in mid-20th-century Israel. 34
2.4 Upper register of the "elephant mosaic" from the Huqoq synagogue, 5th–6th centuries CE. 35
2.5 Moses Lilien's masthead for the journal *Altneuland* (1904). 38
3.1 British troops on the Acropolis, during the battle of December 1944. 50
3.2 The Oriental Institute tympanum, illustrating, at center, the passing of the torch of knowledge from the Orient, left, to the Occident, right; note the pyramids and minarets in the background at left; the Acropolis and skyscraper at right; and the archaeologist at far right. 61
3.3 A Greek postage stamp, issued in 1913 to commemorate the 1912 military campaign. 67

3.4 The director of the American School of Classical Studies at Athens B. H. Hill (with the white suit) on the visit to Asia Minor to locate a suitable site for excavation (c. 1921). 69

4.1 A protest tent in Silwan's al-Bustan neighborhood. 77

4.2 Sara Netanyahu with American and Israeli officials, political donors, and settlers in an archaeological tunnel beneath Silwan, June 2019. 85

4.3 A photograph of the Propylaia on the Athenian Acropolis taken by Bonfils (c. 1865–70), showing the medieval tower a few years before its demolition. 94

4.4 Extreme purification and the revenge of animality: the new, concreted-over Acropolis. 96

5.1 Photograph from Yadin's popular book on the excavations at Hazor, with the caption "A girl from North Africa felt 'at home' operating the two grinding stones, which are over 3,000 years old." 112

5.2 The Venetian Bembo fountain in Candia (Heraklion) in Crete, with the embedded Roman statue painted black, in a photograph taken in 1900–1902. 120

5.3 The front plate from A. Korais's *Salpisma Polemistirion* (Unknown artist, Paris, 1801). Note the fragmented antiquities and the papyrus with the word OMHPOC (Homer) upon which the human figure, the personification of enslaved Greece, stands. 124

5.4 View of the exhibition, *Sculpture Victorious: Art in an Age of Invention, 1837–1901* (held at Yale Center for British Art, New Haven, 2014), showing Hiram Powers' *The Greek Slave*, 1847. 127

5.5 The *Virginian slave* by John Tenniel, published in the *Punch* magazine in 1851. 129

5.6 Eugène Delacroix, *The Massacre at Chios* (1824) 132

List of Figures

5.7 Eugène Delacroix, *Greece on the Ruins of Missolonghi* (1826) 133
5.8 Screenshot from the webpage of the Greek neo-Nazi party, Golden Dawn (August 3, 2017)........... 146
6.1 A soap factory of early 20th-century Ludd. 160
6.2 Moria, Lesvos: the largest refugee camp in Europe, following its destruction by fire in September 2020........ 166
6.3 Rubble in the midst of heavily reconstructed ruins: Fragments from Muslim tombstones on the Acropolis. 174
6.4 Ruins of Qadas Village in northern Palestine/Israel. 177

Preface

This dialogic encounter is the by-product of a seminar that we taught jointly at Brown University in the spring of 2020 titled "Archaeology, Materiality, and National Imagination in Israel and Greece." At the time, we sensed that such comparative endeavors, in teaching and research, are rare, and that there was a lot to be gained from a side-by-side examination, beyond what we had each done on our own. After concluding the course and reading our students' papers and online feedback, we engaged in a series of lockdown-induced video discussions in which we summed up what we had learned in preparing this course, what the class had raised in discussions, and what new insights had emerged. As the subject has never received sustained attention, we thought that these insights would be of interest to students of nationalism, archaeology, and the politics of the past, both in the countries we study and beyond them. We have, therefore, edited our discussion, extended our research of certain topics, expanded on a few salient points, and added references, leaving the dialogic structure intact to highlight our hope that this is the beginning of a discussion rather than its conclusion.

Our ambition is to go beyond well-rehearsed schemes of archaeology and nationalization, and provoke each other to explore themes that are rarely explored and brought into the foreground, partly because they are too difficult or because they are too sensitive or even explosive, epistemically and politically. We therefore begin, after presenting our individual paths to a critical archaeological stance in Chapter 1, by exploring the relation between the origins of archaeology and emerging Hellenic and Zionist nationalisms in Chapter 2, extending the discussion to the enduring impact of imperial structures in 20th-century national archaeologies and to the long history of Jewish–Hellenic entanglement, especially with respect to the idealized individual and national body. In Chapter 3 we discuss the important – but rarely acknowledged – role of archaeology in the constitution of Greece and Israel as contemporary crypto-colonized states that serve as buffer zones for the West and as staging-grounds for assertions of Western cultural values. In Chapter 4 we explore the concept of purity and the processes of purification in their archaeological as well as broader national and religious expressions. Chapter 5 examines the inherently racialized premises of colonial–national modernity and recent ancient DNA studies, juxtaposing them with the contradictions and fluidity inherent in "Greek" and "Israeli" identities. In Chapter 6 we reflect on archaeology as decolonizing action: What is it in archaeology itself – in its origins, in its methods, in the way archaeologists think and act – that must be reimagined and redesigned? Our short conclusion, Chapter 7, sums up the broader themes that emerged throughout this exploration and ends on an optimistic note, celebrating the revolutionary potential of matter, its ability to endure, to surprise us, to resist.

The value of this dialogic endeavor lies not only in the juxtaposition and comparative exploration of two national archaeological projects, something which has never been attempted previously, but also in its constitution of a space "in-between," a space that has gained its individual autonomy beyond our own respective preoccupations, a fertile terrain and a field from which several "lines of flight" (to recall Deleuze) could be attempted: grounded in decades of research and reflection, we offer a wide range of thoughts, refracted through the contemporary moment. We hope that what has emerged in this in-between space, in this autonomous territory, will be of interest well beyond archaeology and anthropology more broadly, and the specific national contexts. We also hope that these thoughts and ideas will find their own flight paths, to re-emerge in other discussions and projects in the years to come.

Preface

We thank the Joukowsky Institute for Archaeology and the Ancient World, the Center for Middle East Studies, the Program in Modern Greek Studies, and the Program in Early Cultures at Brown University which supported our course, Sam Kimball, who transcribed the original dialogue, and the students of our seminar for their passion, enthusiasm, and dedication: Sara Al-Rabiah, Ana González San Martín, Jacob Leiken, Jinette Jimenez, Sam Kimball, Rebecca Mandelbaum, John Metz, Kelley Tackett, Sunshine Wu, Parker Zane. Three anonymous referees provided very useful feedback and advice, and a number of friends and colleagues read and commented on earlier versions, showing us what care, love, and attention mean when dealing with one's ideas and writing: Michal Aviad, Hannah Bernick, Vangelis Calotychos, Maria Choleva, Michael Herzfeld, Vassilis Lambropoulos, Eva Mol, Felipe Rojas, Gideon Solimani. An invitation by the British School at Athens to give a seminar on March 8, 2021, came at the right time offering us encouragement and further food for thought: we are grateful to the many hundreds who attended, to its director, John Bennet, for the invitation, and to its staff for facilitating the event. Our editor at Cambridge University Press, Beatrice Rehl, embraced this project enthusiastically from the beginning and shepherded it into production with care and professionalism. We are thankful to various archives and publishers who gave permission to reproduce illustrations and to various friends who facilitated the whole process: Katerina Athanasaki, Tawfiq Da'adli, Jodi Magness, Yannis Nikolopoulos, Donald Rallis, Konstantinos Thanasakis, Natalia Vogeikoff-Brogan. Finally, Yannis Hamilakis would like to thank Avgoustinos and Spyros at the bookshop "To Lemoni" in Athens who, in the middle of a long lockdown and with the libraries closed, worked hard to find every book he requested. It proved once again how valuable, indeed indispensable, small independent bookshops are ...

Jerusalem and Sitia (Crete), August 2021

CHAPTER 1

Introduction

In which we each present a brief intellectual autobiography and the path that led us to this dialog.

YH: I propose we start with a brief word about our respective standpoints, then move on to explore the origins of the two national projects and the links to archaeology. From there we will proceed to the other themes we have selected for a sustained discussion: The notions of the crypto-colony and crypto-colonization, the idea of purification and its expression in the fields of material heritage and archaeology, the logic of race and its entanglement with the emergence of archaeogenetics, and finally, our struggles for decolonization. Rather than opting for a generic comparison, we have decided to focus instead on specific phenomena, at play in both national contexts. Do you want to start?

RG: I came to archaeology, as a boy, in an entirely physical way, joining an excavation in the Old City of Jerusalem in the autumn of 1970. As a child of Jewish-American immigrants, I suppose digging was a way of connecting with my new surroundings. When I eventually returned to archaeology as a graduate student (after completing a degree in literature), I discovered that there were many recent immigrants studying alongside me. This is something I've noticed ever since: Many of the students that I studied with, and many of the students currently in my classes, were not born in Israel. Clearly, archaeology offers an outsider a way of bonding with a new place: There is something about the physicality, the camaraderie, being out in the sun and dirt, that answers a need – perhaps for rebirth. At the same time, there's something equivocal about this connection; it is mediated and evades direct interaction with contemporary people. That's probably my starting point, apart from the things that I guess most archaeologists share – being attracted to old stuff and a little bit romantic about the past.

Archaeology in Israel in the late 1970s and early 1980s was more of a craft and a vocation than an independent intellectual discipline; you might call it "applied history." Our studies were focused on the accumulation of expertise and on method, and we were measured by our endurance and our initiative, blending the German tradition of acquisition and systemization of data with the British tradition of enterprise. We took pride in our impassive scientific gaze, and although I was politically active as a student, sensitive to the political contexts in which excavations took place, I was certain that archaeology transcended all that. As I have mentioned to you on several occasions, introspection was never the strong suit of Israeli archaeology; we were simply enjoined to "dig the right way." Even if I was aware of political dissonance at an excavation, I did not see where it intersected with practice. This came about later, after I was already doing my own research and running my own excavations, especially when I started working for the Israel Antiquities Authority (IAA).

IAA excavations are conducted in the public domain, far away from the sequestered academic framework: They're out in the world, in communities, in people's yards – and it is there that you face the most fundamental questions: Who owns the past? What is the archaeologist's claim to it and what is the source of their authority? Working in salvage archaeology, that is, on excavations made necessary by infrastructure and construction projects, forced me to question and confront the structures of authority and coercion within which I worked, and the values embedded in interpretation. Issues of conscience that might have been obscured by the façade of academic respectability while I was a student, presented themselves in a very stark way. And as I became more independent as a scholar, I realized that my convictions had to be backed up by action, within my organization and outside of it. If, as a student, I clung to the belief that science should be kept free of politics, archaeological praxis

Introduction

taught me that science was structured by the social and political context – whether it was the structural violence of military occupation, the agendas of those who funded our work, or the identity and status of the archaeologists themselves.[1] This was my route to thinking about the impact and the deployment of archaeology in society, beyond academic questions, and, as a critical position, it has often led me to uncomfortable confrontations with colleagues and governmental bodies, both during my time in the IAA and in my academic career in a public university.

More recently, after becoming involved in the Rogem Ganim community project in my own, West Jerusalem, neighborhood, after initiating the creation of the "alternate archaeology" group (now called Emek Shaveh) in Silwan, and after participating in the discussions on decolonizing archaeology across the discipline and around the globe, I found myself increasingly intrigued by the deep roots of archaeology in colonialism and racism, and by the demand to rebuild archaeology on entirely new foundations.[2] This is one of the things that brought me to Brown, to our joint project of examining the context of archaeology in the two regions that can be viewed as "ground zero" for the development of the discipline in the context of Western modernity and nationalism. Spending 2019–2020 in the US, the year of covid, the murder of George Floyd, and the political entrenchment of white nationalism, provided an extraordinary background to our discussion, bringing home its importance and encouraging me to educate myself on the nature of systemic racism and inequality.

What about you?

YH: My way into archaeology was similar to yours, in some respects. I was born and raised in Crete, surrounded by Bronze Age ("Minoan") ruins, so archaeology was very much present in my life. My father, who passed away as we were completing this book, also used to be an amateur archaeophile, and although neither he nor my mother had any formal education beyond primary school, he was an avid reader and admired learning. The very few books that we had at home were often about archaeology, especially local archaeology. I remember, for example, the copy of Paul Faure's *Everyday Life in Minoan Crete*. But I was reading much literature at the time, both

Greek and world literature, and I wanted to study it at the University, but did not get the grades for it. So, I ended up in archaeology, which had lower entry requirements compared to literature, by accident. Yet, I decided to give it a serious go, especially in the later years of my undergraduate degree. At first, I found it difficult to see its relevance: Archaeology was then, in early-mid 1980s and in that context, mostly classical archaeology; the rest was prehistory or Byzantine art, and, therefore, of much less significance to the national imagination and Greek academic culture. We were told that the founder of archaeology was Winckelmann, the iconic 18th-century, German Hellenist and art historian who, ironically, never set foot in Greece but who established a framework for appreciating and studying ancient Greek art. This was a framework based on biological/organic principles of birth, maturity and decline, on geographical and environmental determinism and on cultural hierarchies, a scheme still venerated by many scholars. There was no debate on the complex nature of his work nor on its problematic facets.[3] The permanent positions in archaeology (this was at the University of Crete) had been occupied mostly by classical archaeologists, trained in the German tradition. At that time, like you I was already politicized, and I could not really see any direct relevance to what was happening in the world or to what interested me as a political being. I was also disheartened by the lack of any explicit theoretical reflection or critique on the epistemology and politics of archaeology.[4]

It was only in the last two years of my undergraduate studies that I started seeing some connection because it happened that I attended some broader and more theoretical courses, mostly to do with what we call prehistory, which were exploring other facets of human experience beyond conventional and formalistic art history, such as economy and society. These were courses offered mostly by younger, female professors often on precarious contracts, and I was incredibly lucky to have had the chance to learn and get inspired by them. That's why I decided to give it a go, and then got seriously into it. The practical, physical aspect of it, however, was there from the beginning, and it always fascinated and attracted me, and I was taking part in archaeological surveys and excavations from the first year.

Introduction

So, the interest in the political dimensions of archaeology was there, but academically it was not, at the beginning, a very important part of my research.[5] It gradually became so, and it helped that the degrees in Greece were broad, allowing you and, in fact, requiring you to take courses outside archaeology and outside ancient studies, including courses on modern and contemporary history. And I was always fascinated by anthropology, although I had no formal training in it. The unconventional courses I referred to, taught by people such as Katerina Kopaka or Antikleia Moudrea-Agrafioti at the University of Crete and several people at the University of Sheffield (during my postgraduate studies), nurtured this fascination. My work on the politics of archaeology started as a kind of sideline, a secondary interest or a kind of an activity you do in your free time, alongside your mainstream study and research. But it progressively became more and more important, and I realized early on that it cannot really continue being an add-on, it needed to become central. So, I eventually did the work on nationalism and more recently on other, related matters, on colonialism and colonization. The warm reception of *The Nation and its Ruins*, which was published in 2007, encouraged me to continue.[6] Ethnographic work was also important for me from early on, and while at the beginning it was mostly in the tradition of ethnoarchaeology, I eventually developed it into what we now call archaeological ethnography, defined as a shared space of multiple encounters, an explicitly political enterprise.[7] My graduate studies and work abroad helped me in some ways to take some distance from the habitual routines of nationhood, develop critical, personal and intellectual reflexivity, and articulate more clearly the conditions of coloniality for archaeology and for society more broadly. It eventually led me into redefining the archaeological as a transdisciplinary field in which the epistemic and the philosophical, the aesthetic and the sensorial, and the social and the political are all prominent.

Even the work that had to do with seemingly "non-political" topics, such as the archaeology of the Bronze Age for example, had to confront the critical history and the entrenched traditions of scholarship, in other words the epistemology and the political economy of archaeological practice. To give just one example, how could I have studied the Bronze Age of Crete (the "Minoan" period, the focus of my doctoral dissertation) without interrogating and historicizing terms and schemes such as palaces, kings and queens or the assumed naval supremacy of the "Minoans" in the writings of people such as Arthur Evans? Or without examining their link with British imperial and colonial history, monarchical politics, and European modernity?[8] So again I was led, through another route, back to the politics of archaeology. I came to realize early on that whatever you do in archaeology is political, whether you accept it or not.

As for my interest in Israel and Palestine and the politics of archaeology there, it stemmed from a comparative impulse, trying to situate the Greek case in a broader context: So I came across books such as the ones by Neil Silberman and Nadia Abu El-Haj, and later your own articles and those by Palestinian colleagues.[9] But it was also a contemporary political impulse in terms of what was happening in that region, and a theoretical impulse because I saw that some of the thoughts and ideas, for example on the links between national ideologies and religion, were already developing within the discussion of Israeli archaeology. I realized that such thoughts had wider applicability, beyond the case of Israel and Palestine. That is why I started following these discussions and continue to do so, and that's why I embarked with great enthusiasm into our teaching and writing collaboration.

RG: Well, there are some curious similarities in our paths (like our shared beginnings in literature), but also differences in context, in training, and in our intellectual predilections; it will be interesting to see how they play out. Let's move on to the first part of our discussion, on the origins and trajectories of our respective national archaeologies.

Notes

1 Greenberg 2015.
2 See, e.g., Bruchac 2014; Lydon and Rizvi 2010; Mignolo 2011.
3 Winckelmann's work is much more interesting and complex than it is usually assumed, and its mechanistic use within traditional archaeology does not do justice to it. See, amongst others, Harloe 2013; Potts 2000.

Introduction

4 See for a short critique, Hamilakis 2000.
5 A key early article was the one published in collaboration with Eleana Yalouri: Hamilakis and Yalouri 1996.
6 Hamilakis 2007; the Greek translation appeared in 2012, the Turkish in 2020, and the Macedonian in 2021.
7 Hamilakis 2011a. Initial writings on archaeological ethnography were developed in collaboration with Aris Anagnostopoulos: Hamilakis and Anagnostopoulos 2009.
8 See Hamilakis and Momigliano 2006 and Papadopoulos 2005, Varouchakis 2017, amongst other writings.
9 Abu El-Haj 2001; Silberman 1990; Yahya 2005, amongst others.

CHAPTER 2

The Colonial Origins of National Archaeologies

In this chapter we discuss the origins of Greek and Israeli archaeology in 19th-century concerns that accompanied European colonialism, the relation of archaeology to emerging Hellenic and Zionist nationalisms, and the enduring impact of imperial structures in 20th-century national archaeologies. We conclude with a brief consideration of the place of archaeology in the long history of Jewish–Hellenic entanglement, especially with respect to concepts of the idealized body.

YH: In terms of origins, we might start by exploring to what extent these two national projects are different or similar, given their chronological asymmetry, with Greece being a case of early nationalism that emerged mostly in the 18th and early 19th centuries, and Israel being a later phenomenon that led to the formation of a nation-state in the middle of the 20th century. Yet, the shared heritage of the Ottoman Empire is an echo that can be still heard in both areas. What are your thoughts on that?

RG: It might be surprising to realize that these two cases had such different starting points, considering how they appear to converge with time. If I backtrack for a moment, I proposed our course to you when I visited Brown a few years ago because when I first read *The Nation and Its Ruins*[1] I was struck by certain analogies with Israel, whether in the obvious attempt by the modern nation-state to forge links with antiquity or in the remarkable similarity in the public

The Colonial Origins of National Archaeologies

standing of leading archaeological figures such as Manolis Andronikos and Yigael Yadin, and I thought, "that's strange, nobody has said much about this before." Then this year, once we started looking at the origins of the two national archaeological projects, I began to hesitate: Perhaps they did not take the same route after all? Greek national sentiment preceded political Zionism by many decades, and while archaeology was a prominent part of Greek nationhood, Zionism was slow to enlist antiquities to its nation-building project. And yet, somehow, the integration of archaeology into statist projects of the 19th and 20th centuries did ultimately bring the two cases into convergence, or homogenized them, in a way that is probably worth figuring out.

If we go back to the early 19th century, Greek nationalism was already well in the making, but the emergence of modern Zionism, much less the idea of its fulfilment in Palestine, was still distant. As many scholars have discussed, the original, early interest in the archaeology of the Holy Land or Palestine came from the West, from Christianity, from Britain and Germany and France, and it was very closely aligned with 19th-century imperialism, colonialism, orientalism, and mid-19th-century concerns about the survival of canonical cultural and religious texts in the face of the onslaught of modernity.[2] And although some of the same people who promoted archaeology in the 19th century were inserting the Jews into the colonial equation, as possible agents of a modern revival of a land seen widely as desolate, political Zionism did not yet exist; European Jews had not yet crystallized their own approach either to the land or to the nation, and certainly not to archaeology. The Jews of central and western Europe had only just been invited – or invited themselves – to the project of Western modernity, and the project of fulfilling that modern destiny in Palestine was only a blip on the horizon. The national idea took root much later, and that may be quite different from the Greek experience.

Another issue is the significantly different starting point of archaeology itself in the two countries. The antiquities of Greece were there to be seen, as ruins and works of art, prominent and marked. Sometimes they were obscured by later structures, and we will talk about that later, but they were nonetheless visible. In Palestine, in the

Holy Land, the sites that had been so vividly imagined by millions, constantly depicted in European art, and attested in Jewish texts barely had a presence in the countryside. For a new class of mainly Protestant travelers and scholars, the very map of the country had been distorted by clerical ignorance. Authentic antiquities were obscured by centuries of conflict and ruination (even living villages were perceived as ruins), and they were disappointing when they were occasionally "recovered." I would like to read a passage by George Adam Smith, a historical geographer who wrote an important study on Jerusalem around the turn of the 20th century. It is about reimagining ancient Jerusalem:

> He who would raise again the Essential City must wait for the night, when Jerusalem hides her decay, throws off every modern intrusion, feels her valleys deepen about her, and rising to her proper outline, resumes something of her ancient spell. At night, too, or early in the morning, the humblest and most permanent habits of her life may be observed, unconfused by the western energies which are so quickly transforming and disguising her.[3]

Here is a romantic striving for an essence that cannot be seen but can only be sensed. You have to turn off the lights. You have to wait till darkness for this city of the imagination to emerge again. The effect of centuries of decay was a common trope in the early archaeology of Palestine: The past is not going to give up its secrets easily, and when it does, there will not be much to look at; it will have to be largely recreated in the mind.

That said, it has become increasingly clear to me that 19th-century colonialist archaeology in Palestine, limited as it was, made cardinal contributions to the later emergence of the Jewish national project and its archaeology. First, the modern, dispassionate archaeological gaze of the philologist, the surveyor, or the excavator led to a complete reconceptualization of Palestine: It was no longer merely a destination for pilgrims but a potential resource that was to be studied, rehabilitated, and eventually incorporated in empire. Under archaeology's gaze – as elsewhere in the Near East – the past became the most important asset the land had to offer, while the present (including both Ottoman rulers and Muslim, Christian, and

Jewish subjects) was relegated to the status of an encumbrance. Second, archaeology provided a telos, a direction to time, and a promise of progress; the sense that the land was awaiting its destiny under worthy proprietors. Third, the Bible could safely be retained in modernity as the core of a shared Western "Judeo-Christian" tradition: The great discoveries in Mesopotamia and Egypt had, by and large, validated biblical history, while nothing discovered in Palestine contradicted it.[4] These three contributions, representing knowledge, progress, and historical justification, remain at the heart of the archaeological project in modern Israel.

YH: This is all very interesting, for many reasons. First, because of the implied link with colonialism. You said that, well before nationalist ideology in Israel became a cultural and political force, the antiquities of Palestine were of interest to Western travelers, antiquarians, and scholars, primarily because of the Biblical legacy and the idea of the "Holy Land." The sense of colonial entanglement actually unites the two cases. Something that has not been widely discussed among scholars of Greece is the fact that Greek nationhood developed at the intersection of colonialism and nationalism. In fact, in my work I follow the scholars who consider nationalism as a derivative discourse and as imaginary, as something that emerged within the colonial frame of thinking and practice, despite its anticolonial efficacy and expediency in certain contexts.[5] Western Hellenism was the form that colonization took in the case of Greece, at first a colonization of the ideal, and the vehicle that allowed the incorporation of that land and its people into the Western sphere of influence. Western Hellenism can be defined as the construction of a certain version of Hellas (which had only a tenuous connection to the social realities of Ancient Greece, as an eastern Mediterranean phenomenon) and its designation as the originary moment of Western civilization. So in that sense, Western interest was present in both cases, and the process of colonization constitutes the first common thread of the two national projects and nation-states.

The other points of interest for me in your opening remarks are the notion of visibility, and the Western reactions to the modern state of the land, the contrast between past and present, the sense of "decay" in George Adam Smith's passage. You're saying that Greek monuments were visible, whereas the ones in Palestine were not. I agree, and that provides an interesting contrast for us to think through. On the other hand, the sense of disappointment we see in the passage above was also experienced in the Western encounter with the monumental landscape of Greece. There are many examples of Western travelers from the 17th to the 19th century who were disappointed at the state of the land called Greece. They were disappointed for two reasons. One was the ruinous state of the ancient Hellas – the few remnants that testified to the Glory that *was* Greece. "Athens ... a city now reduced to near the lowest ebb of fortune," says the English traveler George Wheler, describing his impression of the city that he visited in the late 17th century.[6]

The ruination and decay they experienced, in other words the clash between dream and material reality, was only one reason for the disappointment. The other reasons were the material "intrusions" of intervening periods, the accretions of contemporary life, the reuses of ancient buildings and architecture, and the remodeling of ancient temples as mosques or other places of worship. Here too, as in the case of Jerusalem, one had to imagine antiquity. But there was help at hand: The ancients had provided guidebooks, or so it was thought, with Pausanias as perhaps the most prominent.[7] These Western travelers and scholars were often seeing ancient ruins through the eyes of Pausanias, not theirs, or rather through their own interpretations of ancient authors. Their accounts were often the retracing and mostly the illustration of these early journeys and these early texts. For example, while George Wheler, in 1675, could not ignore that the Parthenon was a mosque at the time of his visit, his drawing of it is an imagined rendering of the temple in classical times (Fig. 2.1), not a realistic depiction, although in other drawings he could not ignore the minaret and others, especially in the 18th century, would record the postclassical buildings. Interestingly, more or less at the same time (in 1667), the Ottoman traveler Evliya Çelebi would visit the site, would be awestruck by it, would connect the Parthenon to King Solomon, and would describe it as the most attractive mosque in the world.[8]

FIGURE 2.1. The Parthenon as drawn by George Wheler (Wheler 1682).

Finally, there was disappointment because, in the Western visitors' views, the living people of the land, with a few exceptions, had little knowledge and appreciation of ancient Hellas and its glory. They were often speaking different languages, and to some travelers they were barbarians who could not appreciate the grandeur and the value of ancient Greece. In doing so, most Westerners failed to recognize and understand the local modes of relating to ruins, and failed to appreciate their distinctive, indigenous archaeology, which we will have the chance to discuss later.

So, there was disappointment in both cases, it seems, although expressed in different ways. At the same time, the end of the 17th century marked the Western "rediscovery" of Greece or rather the construction of a new country out of the ancient Hellas. The material remnants of ancient Hellas were the topographic landmarks of this new territory. Athens was now emerging as a city on a par with, if not more important than, Rome, Constantinople, and Jerusalem. Despite the feelings of disappointment thus, there were enough visible material remnants to justify a positive evaluation. Western Hellenism was fast becoming a major ideological force, as Europe was constructing itself as a center of civilization in opposition to the savages in the colonies or colonies to be, and with ancient Greeks as its ancestors.[9]

In both contexts it is important to understand that in the archaeologization of the land, in the construction of its imagined and imaginary topos, living, contemporary people constituted a problem that needed to be resolved, and the attempt to find solutions took on different forms. One was to ignore them, to erase them from view, to leave them out of the picture, literally, as you were drawing your picturesque landscape, shaped by ruins and absence. So, the quotation you cited above about Jerusalem becoming alive at night is very interesting because it speaks to that sense of erasure, through an act of imagination that can be activated with the help of darkness. You could get transported "back to the past," you could go into a reverie, ignoring material reality on the ground and, of course, the people who were there at the time. Wishing people away, wishing that contemporary people disappeared is a trope you see being expressed iconographically in the case of Greece.

Another solution was to treat contemporary people as features of the landscape, remnants themselves of another time, not active social beings engaging with the world around them. The picture is diverse, of course, but most Western travelers and antiquarians who would produce engravings or other representations of monuments would very rarely depict contemporary signs of life. Empty landscapes filled with ruins was the norm, and when humans were present, they would be monumentalized themselves to provide additional folkloristic and picturesque value: A shepherd with sheep next to a standing or fallen classical column; a woman in an exotic costume; absence or museification. By contrast, Eastern narratives such as the one by Evliya Çelebi were incorporating human presence as well as local stories and interpretations of antiquities, attributing to them authority

The Colonial Origins of National Archaeologies

and value, in a multisensorial, syncretic mélange of paganism and monotheism, mythology, and empirical reality.[10] In another, recently discovered, early 18th-century account, the only surviving Ottoman history of Athens by one Mahmud Efendi who was a local Muslim scholar, Athens as "a city of sages" is presented as an Ottoman heritage too. In that account, the Parthenon is described as the magnificent temple built by Pericles because the Temple at Jerusalem was too far for the pilgrims of Athens to visit.[11] These accounts remind us that there is also an Eastern scholarly antiquarianism (as far back as the 8th–10th century Arabic reception of classical antiquity and the associated translation movement) that has been overshadowed by Western colonization and Eurocentrism.

RG: The "solutions" you mentioned to the presence of living inhabitants – somehow looking past them as if they weren't there – were certainly shared by Western observers across the Mediterranean. How would you characterize their political implications?

YH: The monumentalization of the territory, its construction as dreamed, imaginary topos not as material and social reality entering modernity; in other words, the allochronization of the region and its people as a place of another time, a chrono-political gesture and effect that lasts to the present day.[12] Or the construction of a *terra nullius*, a land empty of people, and thus fair game for conquest and colonization. Or the erasure of any local contemporary, living competitors who would claim the heritage of Hellas, constructed as a quintessential Western symbolic capital. These tropes will coexist and shape the future of the land and its people for the centuries to come.

There are of course variations to this picture, chronologically as well as by case, and by specific groups and individuals. For example, and to come back to notions of visibility and the politics of the gaze, it has been suggested that early travelers were guided primarily by a literary gaze, given their reliance on the ancient texts and their imaginary way of approaching ruins.[13] Later ones, especially the proto-scientific antiquarians, would be guided by an archaeological gaze, wanting to produce a more technically accurate account of monuments. They would also carry out excavations (or other forms of extracting and recording antiquities) that would employ local people, and they would often clash with them when Western antiquarians would attempt to pillage and appropriate antiquities. In these cases, the local stakes in the material heritage of Hellas could no longer be ignored and erased, and local people who resisted would be demonized instead as ignorant or greedy.[14]

RG: Where would you place the Greek nationalists of the same time, and what is their relationship to this discourse on the part of the West? Did they try to adopt the colonial point of view, at least a political strategy?

YH: Well, Greek nationalism is the work of many diverse groups and individuals, and it was shaped by several ideological traditions as well as socioeconomic and political developments. Depending on their specific geographical and social and political grounding, these groups would have received different influences and would develop a different sense of what nationhood is. You have the emergence of new social and economic strata, highly mobile Balkan merchants and eastern Mediterranean shipowners who could no longer operate within the structures of the Ottoman Empire – the economy of which, at least in its earlier centuries, was rooted in land. They would often use a form of Greek as the lingua franca in their transactions. You also had many scholars, and many military people and administrators, serving different political regimes, from the Sultan in Constantinople to the Russian Empire. Many of them would combine different roles, such as the merchant and the intellectual, or the scholar and the administrator. Several of them were working in the centers of Western Hellenism, so they would come into contact with the texts of ancient Greece and its mythologization and valorization by Western elites that they would then import into Greece. They would also support schools, translate ancient texts, propose the Hellenization of personal names as well as toponyms, even the names of ships. They would found printing houses in places like Venice and Vienna to print books from ancient texts to Enlightenment treatises, reminding us of Anderson's emphasis on typography in the nationalization process.[15] In other words, they would promote Hellenism as a key symbolic resource, as the heritage that needed to be rediscovered and reclaimed by the Orthodox Christians who were now called Hellenes.

Among other things, they would engage in the formation of a number of secret societies, founded mostly in cities such as Odessa, Vienna and Paris, and even Athens, promoting the national cause and at the same time advancing learning about ancient Hellenic heritage.[16] The most famous secret society with directly political–national aims was the Society of Friends (*Filiki Etaireia*), which was founded in Odessa, in 1814. It soon became the vehicle for the alliance between mobile Greek-speaking merchants and intellectuals and disenfranchised local elites who were left out of the increasingly monetized economy.[17] The one more directly linked to antiquity was the Society for the Friends of the Arts (*Filomousos Etaireia*) which was founded in Athens in 1813, with a sister organization being founded in Vienna. It included Western antiquarians in its membership and promoted a new modernist discourse on ancient things that advocated their separation from the web of the daily life and their valorization as national and aesthetic values belonging in a museum (or a private collection – some of its members were known for pillaging antiquities). In effect, it acted as a proto-archaeological service until new official state structures were established.[18]

So, a new economic reality, in some senses the emergence of new forces of capital based on trade and maritime activity, converged with the discovery of the ideals of Western Hellenism. Many of the people who would become national intellectuals were also serving the Ottoman administration, because of their linguistic skills, their education, and their ability to communicate with different populations and bridge different worlds. Some others were working in the Balkans; they were coming into contact with the Russian world and the Russian elites and they were implicated in the tensions between Russia and the Ottoman Empire. And they saw Russia as a potential major ally in liberating Greece from the Ottoman Empire. All these diverse groups of people converged on the idea of resurrection, the idea of rebirth, the rebirth of Hellas. According to this notion, Hellas was "enslaved" by the Ottomans, the latest in a long line of conquerors and oppressors, starting with the Ancient Macedonians. The nation that Hellas embodied was sleeping or had died but it could and must be resurrected. You could see here the emergence of a political theology that will shape Greek nationalism for the centuries to come.

The Greek War of Independence that followed was a global, transnational affair and it was fought on political, diplomatic, cultural, economic and military grounds. But it was also partly a religious war;[19] it was fought by the Christians revolting against the infidels, the Muslims, although the Orthodox Patriarchate (and some of its prominent scholars) based in Istanbul, at the seat of the Ottoman Empire, was officially against it.[20] As a pan-European and international event, it was war fought for Christianity. As Kotsonis has noted, the majority of non-prominent westerners who fought in the War were "Christians who fought for a clearly Christian Europe and an Orthodox Christian Greece, which in reality meant, non-Muslim."[21] Eventually, the High Porte in Istanbul also conceived of this as an all-out battle between Islam and Christianity and attempted to mount a counter-crusade.[22] As far as the Greek-speaking national intellectuals were concerned, it was also a matter of destiny and, and for some of them, and many more ordinary people, a matter of divine providence, not a matter of history: Pre-modern ideas merged with modernist concepts of liberation.[23]

We will explore the implications of this later on, but for the moment, I will only note that the national intellectuals adopted the monumentalization and archaeologization of the country produced by the Western elites, but they differed from many of them in extending political agency to the Christian populations of the land, whom they proclaimed as descendants of ancient Greeks. They believed that Hellas could be reborn, resurrected as a new political reality. In other words, they refused to see Hellenism as simply a legacy and a heritage owned and managed primarily by the West. In so doing they set the stage for the shaping of an indigenous form of Hellenism, juxtaposed to Western Hellenism.[24]

RG: Well, as we have said, the developments in Greece and Palestine are not synchronous, nor were the majority Muslim inhabitants of Palestine ever offered European support on a path to national liberation. Yet there are parallels to what was brewing in Palestine in the 19th century, not only because the fate of the country, though still under Ottoman rule, was being discussed in the Western capitals, but also because the self-fashioning of Jewish national aspirations was based on European models (albeit on the failure of those models to accommodate Jews) and on the need for Jews to realize those aspirations in a land of their own, with European support. There was some chatter in Britain and Germany – mainly among millennialists (some of whom had considerable political clout) – that the Jews could revitalize Palestine: They could bring their capital, their entrepreneurial abilities, their energy, and regenerate this decrepit part of the Ottoman East.[25] While these ideas didn't get much traction in Jewish circles, radical thinkers like Moses Hess were talking about Jewish national regeneration in secular terms, clearly inspired by the success of national struggles in Italy and Greece.[26] As for the 19th-century population of Palestine itself, there was a mix similar to what you described earlier of merchants, bureaucrats, and intellectuals of various ethnicities and religions in the increasingly cosmopolitan Ottoman cities like Jaffa and Jerusalem, but it was far less developed and self-conscious as a political class. Most of the inhabitants of Palestine were still Muslim farmers, and it is these villagers who were objectified by the Western touristic and archaeological gaze. It tended to see them as a residual population with no historical horizon, people who were virtually frozen in time and who could – when not seen as downright savages – at best offer an illustration of life in the Holy Land during biblical times.

YH: This is very interesting. When I was working on 19th century photographic renderings of monuments in Greece, I had examined the work of various commercial photographers such as the Beirut-based, French, Félix Bonfils who was active in the Middle East, Egypt and Greece, in the 1860s and 1870s.[27] It was instructive to compare the photographic canon and the gaze embodied in such works, depending on the place in which he was working. His photos of Greek monuments and sites, especially of Athens, were monumentalizing (the result of the combination of the literary and the archaeological gaze), and mostly empty of people. He was choosing the time of day to photograph these monuments when there would be minimal human presence, and he would even move the camera in such an angle as to not include buildings such as modern churches or other contemporary works. This was the late 19th century, when Athens was already a buzzing capital, but you wouldn't get that sense from his photos. In contrast to that, if you see his photos of various Middle Eastern cities including Jerusalem and Beirut, you'll see much human presence and the buzz of urban life. The scene of the bazaar, for example, was for him, central. His Greek photos, especially from Athens, were monumental and archaeological, his Middle East ones were folkloristic and ethnographic. Both sets of photos would be sold in albums entitled *Souvenirs of the Orient*. As a commercial photographer, he was responding to the demands of Western markets, and their prior perceptions and stereotypes of the various localities of the eastern Mediterranean.[28]

RG: And while you had these living ethnographic communities, so to speak, there was also a sense that they were somehow extraneous, that they were impostors, ignorant of the value of the place that they lived in and of its history, and that they should be moved aside to allow others to truly appreciate the land. These conflicting visions alternate: The same people will be one thing at night and another the next day. George Adam Smith brings that out clearly when he says, first, "wait for the night," when the city disappears and then you can really feel the city beneath the city; but then, in early morning, when people are just going about their business, only half awake, not yet conscious of what they're doing, they – the living people – will help you understand "the humblest and most permanent habits" of life, as it has always been lived, since time immemorial, in this place. The scholars had that ambivalent attitude to the local people; they were attracted and repelled at the same time. As for the Ottoman Turks – their presence was an imposition that obscured the true nature of the land and prevented it from achieving its destiny; they were to be outwitted, manipulated, and eventually replaced.[29]

YH: So, I guess it's fair to say that, in both projects, there was a strong orientalist foundation. This is clear in the many invocations of the Orient by Western travelers who came to Greece, as well as by the group of people who would be called *Philhellenes*, a highly problematic label and at the same time a troubling phenomenon that describes a very diverse group of social actors.[30] Many of them traveled to Greece in the early 19th century and some even took part in the War of Independence, siding with the Christians, now very often seen and portrayed as the descendants of ancient Greek warriors. Writing from that point of view of the Westerner who is aligned with people who are now called Hellenes and who were now rediscovering their destiny fighting against the Oriental despot, an analogical connection was made that was then adopted also by Greek national intellectuals, a connection between ancient Persians and Ottomans.[31] Ottoman Muslims were the new "Oriental Other," not only of Greece but of the West as a whole. This was a monumentalized and archaeologized war, in a monumentalized and archaeologized country. And the battles were the same: Oriental barbarian invaders versus Western/Christian/civilized Hellenes/Europeans.

To return to the issue of new forms of capital and proto-capitalist economy, the Ottomans were seen as the despots who would not allow free enterprise to develop. Furthermore, Western orientalist travelers and scholars would establish a dichotomy between verticality and horizontality not only as bodily postures but also as metaphors for activity and enterprise on the one hand, and indolence and passivity on the other. Chateaubriand, the French orientalist and Philhellene would draw such a distinction: The mobile energetic Frenchman versus the immobile Turk sitting or reclining on sofas.[32]

RG: The divan, right?

YH: Exactly. So, orientalism here meets the spirit of capitalism as a Western ideal of vitality, mobility, and enterprise.

While we're on the theme of origins, we may want to take a closer look at the processes and the events that led to the formation of the two states, and how these formative years shaped archaeology. In the case of Greece, it is worth pointing out that the formation of the modern state, starting with the 1830s, was a project that was shared between many different European powers, or Great Powers, as they were called then. It wasn't just that the state of Greece was forming itself, it was that these European powers and their elites, mostly Britain, France, and Russia (but also German elites and royal houses) were coming together to form a new state. There were even competing Greek political parties, named the French, the British, and the Russian party, siding with the policies of the respective powers. As a result, the key intellectuals and administrators who shaped modernist archaeology in Greece were coming from different European countries, and mostly from Bavaria or other German territories, as the first monarch of the country, King Otto, was from Bavaria, the son of the king of Bavaria. Munich, of course, was already the center of German neo-classicism, and important archaeologists and architects who were instrumental in the neo-classical shaping of that city and the movement of Greek Revival became Otto's entourage, and started shaping the archaeological structures of the new country.[33] So, the first director of antiquities, the first professor of archaeology, the compiler of the first archaeological law, and the architect who undertook the project of remodeling the Athenian Acropolis into the most important, national archaeological site of the country (Leo von Klenze), all came from Bavaria and other German lands. Their influence and impact in the construction of the institutions of archaeology have been fundamental. In fact, you can see their influence all the way to the present day. At the same time, you could see the tensions and the clashes with other intellectuals and scholars who were not part of the entourage of Otto, and who were educated in different environments, some of them in communication with what I have called indigenous archaeology in Greece. The first native Greek to be employed in the archaeological service, and a fighter in the War of Independence, Kyriakos Pittakis, is a case in point.[34]

But this was not just a process of shaping archaeology as an institution; it was rather a process of shaping Athens as the capital city, selected because of its classical legacy and symbolic weight, a capital that became an "appendix to the Acropolis," a city denying and mostly erasing its own Ottoman history, a "city foreign to itself."[35] It was also a process of establishing a new, archaeologized but still modern country, a "model kingdom" shaped by European modernity. Neo-classicism, not just in architecture and urban planning but also in remaking archaeological sites and shaping culture in general, became the colonial technology which was transplanted from Munich, Berlin, and Paris,[36] a technology that merged monumentalization with capitalist modernization.

One could claim, however, that the state in its current form was shaped only in the first decades of the 20th century, following the defeat in the Greco-Turkish war, the collapse of the Great Idea of expanding the nation-state and making Constantinople the capital of modern Hellenism, and of course the influx of Greek-speaking,

Christian refugees. Their resettlement, especially in the north which had become part of the Greek state recently (in 1913), would contribute to the project of Hellenization and national homogenization of the whole country. These processes went hand in hand with the continuous archaeologization of the country, now especially the new lands of the north but also major islands such as Crete. This archaeologization was expressed through unearthing ancient classical ruins, renaming the land using ancient Greek toponyms,[37] and investing it with ancient Greek mythological connections and associations. Ancient Macedonians were transformed, in the Greek national narrative, from archenemies of ancient Greece and of Hellenism to some of its most celebrated figures, especially Philip II and, of course, Alexander the Great. This process was linked to the reshaping of the national historical narrative, which started in the middle of the 19th century and aimed to bridge the historical gap from the Golden Age of ancient Hellas to the contemporary Greek nation. Certain historical episodes needed to be recast and restituted, to establish a temporality of continuity; ancient Macedonians but also Byzantium (now cast as Byzantine Hellenism, to complement Ancient Hellenism and modern Hellenism in a tripartite scheme) are cases in point. Byzantium in particular was recast as a Greek, or rather Helleno-Christian Empire, a convenient scheme which would provide support, along with the Alexandrian legacy, to the Greek imperial and colonial aspirations, especially in Anatolia, in the early 20th century.

Manolis Andronikos's widely publicized and celebrated excavations at Vergina in the late 1970s completed this transformation, and managed to restitute the north of the country but also the 4th century BCE as crucial geographical and chronological topoi of the Hellenic national imagination. Now the so-called Vergina star, a decorative motif widely seen in Ancient Macedonia, has become almost a national symbol and is often seen celebrated widely. The perceived national threat from the north linked to the long dispute with the Republic of North Macedonia, which ended only in 2019, contributed to this reshaping of the national narrative. The charisma and the public profile of Andronikos, whom I have called the shaman of the nation, a mediator between the dead and the living,[38] were also instrumental.

The latest chapter in this saga has been played out since 2013 at the excavation in Amphipolis, also in Greek Macedonia, an excavation which is, however, fascinating for many other reasons, including its investment with an economy of hope, an economy of the occult, especially for a nation struggling with a huge financial crisis. Early on in the excavation process, various scenarios circulated by some archaeologists – but also by the media, both the established and new social media – insinuated that the tomb could be a famous Macedonian royal, perhaps even Alexander the Great or a member of his family. The ruling politicians embraced such scenarios, investing politically in them and fueling further the huge public excitement: Will the "secrets of Amphipolis," the unearthing of the body of a glorious personage and his riches, bring about salvation?[39] To return to my main point, the national making and remaking of the country through its archaeologization is an on-going process, not an old and nearly forgotten story.[40]

Now, what's the situation in Israel vis-à-vis the various archaeological institutions, and how did the dominant Western national ideologies shape the archaeological realities?

RG: I think it took a tortuous track. To begin with, archaeology was subservient to British and other European colonial and imperial interests in Palestine. Eventually the British become the main actors; on the one hand, the main protectors of the Jews in Palestine, and on the other hand the European power most invested in systematic study of the land. They were already counting it as part of their future empire in the second half of the 19th century. Archaeology was somehow an intimate need, part of their own conception of their role in the world.[41] And while Christian restorationists did foresee a space or a special role for Jews within the British sphere of influence, they did not make a specific connection to archaeology at all (not even Charles Warren, one of the first archaeologists in Palestine, who envisioned the revitalization of the land by the settlement of Jewish farmers from North Africa).[42] The connection to archaeology was not immediately obvious, except insofar as archaeology was part of the project of acquiring the land through studying it, mapping it and quantifying it, as I mentioned earlier.

The Colonial Origins of National Archaeologies

Things took a dramatic turn after the Balfour declaration of 1917 and Allenby's conquest of Palestine. The Zionists now had a territorial foothold and the prospect of statehood. Again, it is difficult to say that archaeology was central to Jewish state-building, except as a corollary to the British project of modernization. But when the British mandate began in the early 1920s, archaeology was a central plank in their platform of making Palestine modern and giving science a prominent role in its administration. Officially, the mandate was supposed to give the British time to mentor the Jews, and later the Palestinian Arabs (in response to their sustained resistance to the Balfour declaration) into nationhood. Part of that mentoring would have been defining antiquities as a *corpus separatum*; something that has to be both rationalized and sanctified, protected, fenced off, relieved of the overburden of modernity.[43] But this was very much a British bureaucratic project (one that, by the way, was built on antiquities laws that were already put in place, under Western pressure, by the Ottomans).[44] Archaeology was a part of modernization, but it wasn't closely connected to the Jewish national project.[45] In fact, there was an ambivalent attitude to archaeology in the leading labor-Zionist wing of the Zionist movement, which was much more interested in the future than in a past that weighed down on the national movement. Yes, there was a vision of recovering ancient grandeur, connecting the modern and ancient national movements by evoking the ancient Hasmonaean state or conjuring up the times of the great rebellions against the Romans. But this vision relied more on selective historical memory and geography (with the histories of Josephus as the filter through which the countryside was to be viewed) and on the appropriation of the landscape through intimate knowledge of it, than on physical archaeological remains. This was perhaps because of what I said before: There weren't enough monuments to hang your hat on. There wasn't an Acropolis that you could point to and say, "This is us when we were something." In fact, most of the outstanding monuments and ruins were emphatically *not* Jewish – Crusader fortresses, Ottoman city walls, churches, monasteries and large tells that testified to a history that began before Joshua's conquest and ended well after the Jewish dispersal.

Archaeology was thus not a prominent part of the national platform until the state was established. But the moment the state was created, the moment there was a territory with more or less fixed borders, then all the trappings of a national archaeology came into view.[46] It instantly became Israel's "national pastime."[47] It is then that you begin to see the "filling in" of the national borders with relevant *antiquities*, establishing a congruence between current and former Jewish presence in a manner that parallels what you have described for early 20th-century Greece. This takes several forms. My late colleague Michael Feige has described the annual meetings of the Israel Exploration Society, held each year at a different location on one of Israel's frontiers.[48] These meetings were designed as a pilgrimage of the learned elites to towns newly populated with immigrants, with the intent of establishing or confirming the continuity of Jewish presence at each of these sites. Israel's first celebrity archaeologist, Yigael Yadin – who, like Andronikos, was perceived as possessed of an uncanny ability to communicate with the leading figures of Israel's past[49] – also excavated at the extremities of the state, at Hazor, where he reaffirmed the biblical narratives of Joshua's conquest and territorial control of the northern reaches of the Jordan valley, and in the Judean Desert caves and Masada, where he was able to confirm the almost stone-by-stone veracity of Josephus' chronicle of the siege of Masada and conjure up an intimate communication with the Jewish rebels of 135 CE (Fig. 2.2). Each of Israel's wars of expansion was accompanied, sometimes within days, by archaeological reconnaissance, as were its settlement projects in the West Bank.[50] Here too, it is an ongoing project.

Summing up the trajectory of archaeology in the national project, I see it as uneven and sometimes indirect: The colonial and mandate years provided a rational framework for managing antiquities in an ideological way, but it wasn't a high priority for the Jewish community. As soon as the state came into existence, something snapped into place; archaeology was quickly linked to the creation of the national mythology and the imagined unity of the Jewish people. Archaeology gave them something to latch onto, something material and physical: Places to be in and landscapes populated with

The Colonial Origins of National Archaeologies

FIGURE 2.2. Yigael Yadin and Israel's first prime minister, David Ben-Gurion, peer into a storage pithos from Canaanite Hazor, presumed to have been destroyed by the first Israelite settlers c. 1200 BCE. Photo, Moshe Pridan, Government Press Office.

buildings, agricultural installations, water conduits and much more, in which to evoke this glorious past.

YH: I see parallel developments with regards to colonization as modernization: I referred to Bavarians and other western Europeans. You referred to the British. In Greece, modernization and nationalization went hand in hand. Very often, modernization also meant commodification. Antiquities were transformed into national landmarks and sacred locales, but this did not prevent them from being marketed as commercialized tourist sites at the same time, symbolic capital that can be converted into financial capital. The moment that the Athenian Acropolis changed status – and from a fortress it became an organized archaeological site thanks to the efforts of Leo von Klenze – that is 1834, was also the moment when an entrance fee was introduced.[51] But I think we should stay a little longer on these early years. I recall you mentioning that under the British Mandate there were special provisions for archaeology. Could you remind us what these were?

RG: Those were the articles of the Mandate, which have formed the basis for all subsequent legislation.[52] Article 21 is by far the longest and most comprehensive of the twenty-eight articles in the 1922 Mandate, with a specific requirement to enact a Law of Antiquities and detailed provisions for the content of that law, which would ensure the protection of antiquities and regulate their excavation and management. Billie Melman, who has delved deeply into the workings of the interwar mandatory bureaucracies, talks about the centrality of antiquities legislation to the mandatory concept of "mentorship."[53] I have also spent some time in the archives trying to get to the root of the detailed effort expended on Article 21, but many questions remain. As I see it, the mandatory power assumed stewardship of both the antiquities and of the "timeless" people living among them. Both had to be coaxed into a productive relationship with modernity and with the modern economy.

YH: This is very telling in terms of Britain's own colonial archaeological aspirations, their desire to continue having a serious say on matters of archaeology. So whatever else was going to happen in the area, archaeology was something over which they would exercise control.

RG: And yet they wanted archaeology in Palestine to be open to all the members of the League of Nations. This was going to be a place that would welcome scientists from all over the world to come and do their work.

YH: Now that's very interesting in terms of our comparison, because in Greece a key feature throughout the 19th and 20th centuries, I would say all the way to the present, is competition among Western powers over archaeology, despite opportunistic alliances. This is competition between the different nation-states which shaped the fortunes of Greece. So major sites in Greece, major classical sites mostly, but also Late Bronze Age ("Minoan" or "Mycenaean") sites became the apples of discord, the bones of contention among the Great Powers, which were also major, global archaeological powers. Who is going to excavate which site? Who is going to secure the long term, almost eternal claims over certain, coveted celebrated locales? Which foreign archaeological school? The British? The French? The Germans? The Italians? The Americans? Greek archaeological bodies, especially the semi-private Athens Archaeological Society, would try to compete too, but they were often outbid. Sites such as Delphi, Olympia in the 19th century, Knossos at the turn of the century or the Athenian Agora in the early-mid-20th century became major flash points. Covert political and diplomatic maneuvering, often at the highest government levels, would at times tip the balance.[54] So, what you're saying in relation to Palestine is that these Mandate provisions were trying, in many ways, to share that resource, trying to guarantee that it would be accessible to all western European powers.

RG: So that they could compete! But I suspect that they also understood that the British public would not support large excavations on its dime; they almost certainly hoped to get Americans, and American money, involved. Perhaps I should mention that the 1928 Antiquities Law provided for a division of finds between the excavator and the Government of Palestine: Up to one half of the finds could be exported, and many were distributed across the globe. The revered ancestor of stratigraphic archaeology, Flinders Petrie, sold items from his Palestinian collection during his lifetime, and as late as 1990 the Institute of Archaeology at UCL considered selling part of it to the British Museum.⁵⁵ This was quite an incentive for foreign stakeholders.

YH: Right, exactly. But I would imagine that these provisions took into account the long history of competition and clashes over antiquities in the Mediterranean and the Middle East, and perhaps places like Greece would have been in the minds of the people who drafted them. So, getting back to your description of a progressive incorporation of archaeology by the national imagination, if we were to think in terms of the Golden Ages of different nation states, if we were to accept that every nation "chooses" its own Golden Age, and Greece having the classical era, broadly defined, as its own Golden Age, would you say that there is a Golden Age for Israeli nationalism in the 20th century?

RG: In the pre-state phase, the Hasmonaean Kingdom was generally seen as the Golden Age. That has shifted as nowadays people talk about King David and ancient (biblical) Israel, but I should think that, in times of early nationalism, they were looking at well-documented eras described by Roman historians, especially Josephus, and at the state that they could identify as a precursor of Israel: the Hasmonean Kingdom.

YH: And the associations with sacrifices and resistance to the Romans?

RG: Well, that's a celebrated heroic failure. But as a successful precursor state, they were looking to an entity that was warlike, that had expanding borders, that was independent, that fought off great powers – first the Hellenistic empires, and then the Romans – and that has palpable remains. As so few Hasmonean sites had been excavated, those palpable remains would most likely have been coins minted by Hellenistic and Roman-era rulers. Here one could actually see and touch these symbols of independence, and in due course these coins became models for the first Israeli coins and postage stamps, which all carry motifs taken from the Hasmonean Kingdom, the last independent Kingdom, or from the great rebellions – the Jewish war of 66–70 CE, or the Bar Kokhba rebellion of 132–135 CE.⁵⁶ But what is interesting is that the rebellions were traumatically unsuccessful and caused tremendous suffering, dispersal, and death, and nonetheless they were glorified; especially the Bar

Kokhba rebellion, for those three or four years of independence, of minting coins, of fierce resistance, of armed struggle.[57] So, I would say that the first archaeological connection, the first way of connecting with the past during the state-building years, would have been through those episodes – one of successful regeneration and the others of heroic defeat – and of course that characterizes the early years of the Israeli state as well.

YH: You also said that there was no Acropolis in Israel, no equivalent to the Athenian Acropolis. Would you not say then that the iconic site, the fortress of Masada, became, at some stage, the Acropolis for Israel?

RG: And then in what way is it the Acropolis?

YH: I was thinking in terms of its symbolic significance, its presence in contemporary, national iconography, and its sacralization. The fact, for example, that the military held swearing-in ceremonies there or the huge legacy and impact of Yadin's excavations; finally, the national–mythological associations with death as a sacrificial choice in the prospect of defeat and subjugation. What do you think?

RG: Yes, that's something to consider, because you might think of "Athens and the Acropolis" being equivalent to "Jerusalem and the Temple Mount." But Jerusalem and the Temple Mount were not a Zionist focus of interest at all. Nowadays they seem to be the very heart of both the national imagination and the conflict with the Palestinians, but in the formative years, the Temple Mount was out of bounds, and Jerusalem itself was largely the city of the "Old Settlement," the non-Zionist ultra-Orthodox Jews. It wasn't a bastion of the modern state-in-the-making, whose metropolis was Tel Aviv. Tel Aviv has no antiquities to speak of, so maybe Masada functioned – at least in the early years of the state – as that focus of symbolism that is free of the baggage of intervening centuries and replaces ritual animal sacrifices (which you don't really want to play up in any case) with self-sacrifice (a death wish, if you will). It has that halo around it, of stirring the nation's soul. But if it is to be seen as a "displaced" Acropolis, it is a rather dark one, as if the moment of national regeneration and rebirth is inextricable from that of catastrophic failure and death. As if only the willingness to destroy everything can summon forth the power to create. After the two world wars, the

Shoah, and the events of 1948, history presented itself as a series of zero-sum conflicts ending in the vindication of the strong and the annihilation of the weak; mid-20th-century archaeology confirmed this perception by its fascination with invasions and destruction.

YH. What's the position of classical archaeology, broadly defined, in Israel? Is there a thriving field? I know there are classicists and a strong literary tradition but how about classical archaeology itself, Greek and Roman classical archaeology?

RG: It started out as the core of Jewish archaeology, partly because of the strong central European influence on the Jewish academy, but mainly because archaeology was conceived as a historical discipline, and there's an enormous body of literary and historical information on the classical period in general and on Jewish life and history in particular. Biblical history and archaeology were meager by comparison. If you wished to establish a national archaeology, you would do well to begin with the periods of Jewish independence and rebellion, so richly documented by Flavius Josephus, by traditional Jewish sources, and, from the mid-20th century, by troves of ancient documents and scrolls. In practice, however, most of the classical remains excavated in Palestine were of the Late Roman and Byzantine periods, including many, many churches and synagogues. The period when Palestine was most densely occupied until modern times was the Byzantine period, the 5th and 6th centuries CE. A discourse, therefore, sprang up around the Byzantine period as one that proves that Palestine – and particularly the Negev desert – can be made to flourish. If the desert could be settled, then Palestine could support many millions of inhabitants. The classical scholar and archaeologist Michael Avi-Yonah was specifically recruited to write a memorandum for the commissions that discussed the partition of Palestine, proving that Palestine could support millions of people and thus support large-scale Jewish immigration.[58] In recent years I sense a decline of interest in that period, as biblical periods have become much more prominent both in academia and in the public view. I believe this shift is related to the current wave of heightened nationalism; an ethnocentric-religious nationalism that has taken the hill-regions of Palestine and the Temple Mount itself, avoided by the early Zionists, and has made them the focus both of desire and of a

The Colonial Origins of National Archaeologies

willingness to provoke deadly conflict. This has fused seamlessly with the evangelical Christian focus on biblical history and end days – seemingly bringing us full circle back to the 19th century. The new national mythology – that which privileges King David and the Israelite kingdoms and the Temple Mount – is reflected in an intense archaeological discourse, whereas the previous affinity to the Hasmonaeans and Bar Kokhba has receded. That's a shift that's related to current politics.[59]

YH: So you could see a direct mirroring effect here between the broader political scene, and the archaeological predicament. In that scheme of things, what's the role of earlier periods such as early prehistory, given the key role of the region in the global discourses on origins, especially the origins of agriculture? Because if we were to compare, for a moment, Israel not with Greece but with Turkey, we can recall how in that country the early history and archaeology of farming was central in Turkish, Kemalist nationalism that imagined the country as a land of origins and "firsts," with an at least 10,000-year-old history.[60] Are these periods and themes completely separate from the national archaeological discourse in Israel?

RG: Prehistorians would like to think so, as they have always positioned themselves above the fray, denying the value-laden nature of their science; moreover – perhaps out of deference to Jewish orthodoxy – the major discoveries of Paleolithic and Neolithic eras have not been appropriated by the state machine. But between prehistory and the Israelite kingdoms there lies a rich archive of "Ancient Near Eastern" mythology and art that was mined by individuals and small ideological groups to conjure up an autochthonous, pre-Israelite (and hence pagan) "Canaanite" or "Hebrew" cultural expanse.[61] In its most rarified form, as expressed by a small group of artists, writers, and historians in the mid-20th century, this was a radical nationalist movement, intent on separating the nation both from traditional Judaism and from the Arab world by positing a continuity of modern Hebrew-speaking settlers with a pre-Semitic Canaanism that could be shared with other minority groups in the region, such as self-identifying Lebanese "Phoenicians." More widely shared in the first half of the 20th century was a concept of "Hebrewness" that, among other things, assigned a primordial, Nietszchean

FIGURE 2.3. *Gehazi* (1940s), a now-lost sculpture by Yechiel Shemi (1922–2003), created in a Near Eastern idiom that characterized the "Canaanite" movement in mid-20th-century Israel.

vitality to Eastern pagan religion and culture (Fig. 2.3).[62] This version of regenerated indigeneity, divorced from any sense of traditional Judaism, is prominent, for example, in Moshe Dayan's patriotic passion for antiquities, which led him to use his military and political authority to amass a huge private collection that evoked, for him, what the writer Amos Elon has called "a pagan Bible of wild barbaric tribes, sweeping out of the desert to conquer the land of Canaan."[63]

YH: Since you have brought up paganism, I thought we might engage with a study that we have both read by Leoussi and Aberbach, structured around Hellenism and Judaism as concepts with long pedigrees.[64] Starting from ancient, Hellenistic times or earlier, the

The Colonial Origins of National Archaeologies

FIGURE 2.4. Upper register of the "elephant mosaic" from the Huqoq synagogue, 5th–6th centuries CE. Reproduced with permission of Jodi Magness; photo, Jim Haberman.

authors suggest that the two forces, and I guess the social agents who were actually carriers and propagators of these two forces, were ambivalent toward each other, or they were seeing themselves, at certain points as competitors. And yet, in the thinking of many modern, Western intellectuals they eventually became reconciled, they became synthesized in some way. What are your views on this?

RG: Well, they are alluding to a long and complex history of entanglement and mutual aversion, usually expressed in the form of the Jerusalem/Athens dyad.[65] Do you remember the image I used to advertise our course (Fig. 2.4)? It was of the mosaic floor from the 5th-century Huqoq synagogue in Galilee, which has a unique scene of an encounter between what seems to be a Greek or Roman general, with soldiers behind him, and a Jewish priest or religious figure, accompanied by a group of sword-bearing men (warrior-priests?). It has been said to represent an apocryphal meeting between Alexander the Great and the High Priest in Jerusalem, when the Greeks first conquered Palestine, but in the context of Byzantine Palestine it must have resonated with contemporary concerns. It's a striking figurative scene, in a surprising context, that seems to reproduce the tension of the Jewish–Greek (and by implication, the

Jewish–Byzantine) encounter.[66] So, this entanglement has been there, spawning a huge body of scholarship about what Judaism was in those first centuries of our era, about its interaction with the Greek-speaking pagan and Christian worlds, and about the way the Jewish–Greek antinomy has played out over the centuries (possibly including our own dialog!).

Leoussi and Aberbach take this all the way down to the 19th century, showing that the awakening of modernism and nationalist thought among the Jews also meant a resurrecting of the Jewish body; one that is no longer the feeble Jewish body of the ghetto, of the Yeshivot (religious academies), of the synagogues. The virile, masculine body is no longer denied, but affirmed, on the basis of a Romantic vision of beauty and the philhellenic appreciation of classical sculpture.[67] They mention the phrase "let the chief beauty of Japheth be in the tents of Shem," – from a 3rd-century CE homily on the Biblical text (Gen. 9:27) referring to the translation of the Jewish Bible into Greek. This homily was reinterpreted by later Jewish writers as a reference to beauty in general (Japheth [*yefet*], the name of the mythical progenitor of the Greeks, was associated with beauty, due to its similarity to *yafeh*, "beautiful"), implying a possible reconciliation of Judaism with a pagan aesthetic. This move toward secularization, alongside expectations for political/legal emancipation and equality in western Europe, preceded Zionism and is considered part of its groundwork, but if we stick to the perception of the Jewish or Hebrew body and its regeneration, the relation to the Hellenic ideal is not straightforward, not only because of the long history of its disparagement among Jews, but also because Semitic antecedents – Canaanite or Phoenician – were also part of the discussion of Hebrew regeneration, right up to the middle of the 20th century.[68]

YH: One of the things I actually found enlightening in this article is the emphasis on the body, and one of the authors, Athena Leoussi, has written extensively about the cult of the body in recent European thought, and the links to the Hellenic ideas of the body.[69] And I found it interesting because it can shape some of our discussions here, including in relation to notions of purification which we will be exploring later on. A key attitude that they're investigating is the one which articulates the body as beauty, but also as sinful, the body as something that is polluting and polluted. And then, of course, the other interesting thing in the article is the links they trace between such attitudes and certain trends within recent, 19th- and 20th-century CE thought, when racism becomes a major force in European thinking, and leading all the way up to the fascist and Nazi regimes in the 20th century. As we know, such regimes were drawing on Hellenism in many ways. They were drawing on the ideas of the body, foregrounding a cult of the body which became the fascist body of perfection, regimentation, and war.[70]

An interesting detail in this study is their discussion of athleticism and sport as one way in which the Jewish body was thought to become a powerful body. The authors mention certain examples such as the formation of the first athletic association among Jewish communities, which happened in Istanbul, in 1895. That's a very interesting year, because that's one year before the modern Olympics, which took place in Athens in 1896. We know that modern Olympics were part and parcel of the promotion of the ideas of Hellenism, but also the ideas of race.[71] We know that the third modern Olympics, held in Saint Louis, USA in 1904, became a celebration not only of American Imperialism but also of racism and white supremacy.[72] We know how keen the Third Reich was on Olympics. We know how Hitler showed a keen interest in the German excavations of Olympia, drawing on the cult of the strong, athletic body. We know that the elite academies, schools and gymnasia in Nazi Germany were drawing on classical education, especially the legacy of Sparta, promoting at the same time athleticism and the cult of the body, in their attempt to construct a new German or rather Aryan body, and the new German self.[73] Ancient Olympics, and the modern Olympics movement meet the biopolitics of race, and the thanatopolitics that shaped the racialized national order and imagination, especially in the 20th century. Were the late-19th-century diasporic Jewish communities caught up in the early biopolitical imaginings around the strong body, crucial for the religious-political community?

RG: They certainly were. The need to be reborn as a complete person was a significant feature of European 19th-century nationalism, so it is not surprising that it was adopted by Jews, especially in view of the antisemitic stereotypes current at the time. Also, the gymnasia were pivotal in the emancipation and secularization of the Jews in Europe, and then as part of the Zionist educational project in Europe and in Palestine, while the Spartan concept is often linked to Jewish pioneering and survival in hostile surroundings. There's a whole world of associations there. This is part of what Daniel Boyarin calls (after Homi Bhabha) "colonial mimicry," and in his fascinating study of the "muscle-Jew," Todd Presner shows how Zionist concern with the Jewish masculine body resonated with broader, fin de siècle anxieties over "degeneration."[74]

The rise of gymnastic associations in 19th-century Germany, followed by England and France, must have absorbed concepts of

FIGURE 2.5. Moses Lilien's masthead for the journal *Altneuland* (1904).

The Colonial Origins of National Archaeologies

the ideal body from philhellenism, and Jews (who were barred from most of these organizations) followed suit (the connection you noted between the first German–Jewish gymnastic association in Constantinople in 1895 and the 1896 Olympic games seems obvious). But Presner shows that while Zionist artists like Moses Lilien grafted the classical sculptured body onto ancient Jewish heroes like the Maccabees, Bar Kokhba, and even the ancient Israelite spies to Canaan, they added – as in the canonical tableau of the two figures carrying a huge bunch of grapes (Fig. 2.5) – components of fertility and homoeroticism that go beyond classicism to address late 19th-century concerns with vitality and regeneration, not so much of the individual, but of the nation and of the soil. Boyarin goes even further, stating that – at least in Theodore Herzl's vision of *Altneuland*, the ideal Jewish state – it was "whiteness" that the Zionists were striving for. But these are matters that we want to talk about later, when we get to race and indigeneity.[75]

Notes

1 Hamilakis 2007.
2 Díaz-Andreu 2007; McGeough 2015; Silberman 1982.
3 Smith 1907: 25.
4 Hilprecht 1896.
5 Cf. Chatterjee 1986.
6 Even Theodor Herzl, who is considered "the father of political Zionism," expressed such a disappointment when he visited Greece in 1898 and was photographed on the Acropolis, on his way to Palestine (Fleming 2010); for the photo, see cover illustration.
7 Yakovaki 2006: 271.
8 Fowden 2019.
9 See Yakovaki 2006 for the most comprehensive and important discussion on this process.
10 See studies in Georgopoulou and Thanasakis 2019, especially by Fowden.
11 Fowden 2019; Tunali 2019.
12 Cf. Fabian 1983.
13 Kaplan 2010.
14 Cf. Hamilakis 2011b.
15 Anderson 1991.
16 Cf. Papanikolopoulos 2021: 87.
17 Papanikolopoulos 2021: 47.

18 Hamilakis 2007: 79–81; Velianitis 1993.
19 Cf. Karakatsoulis 2016: 65; Kotsonis 2020: 28–29; Koulouri 2020: 48–49.
20 As it was an Ottoman institution aimed at keeping the peace among Orthodox Christians and guaranteeing their acquiescence in exchange of certain privileges, the Patriarchate declared the insurrection as sinful; see Anagnostopoulou 2021 and Matalas 2002.
21 Kotsonis 2020: 28.
22 Kolovos et al. 2021: 99; Moiras 2020: 144; at the same time, the Porte realized the hugely important symbolic role that the ancient Hellas played in the insurrection, and in fact, when it eventually recognized the new political entity that emerged, it called it *Yunanistan* and its citizens *Yunan*, name that it had previously reserved for ancient Greeks; the rest of the Orthodox Christians would continue to be called by the Ottomans *Rum*, a name that previously included the people who were now called *Yunan* (Moiras 2020: 166).
23 Cf. Theotokas 1992, 2021.
24 Hamilakis 2007.
25 Bar-Yosef 2003; Crome 2018.
26 Avineri 1985.
27 Hamilakis 2001; Szegedy-Maszak 2001.
28 On Greece and photography in relation to this and more broadly, see Carabott et al. 2015.
29 Conder 1878; Warren 1875.
30 Cf. Gourgouris 1996; Karakatsoulis 2016; see also for rich but more conventional accounts, Hering 1994; St Clair 2008; and an interesting historiographic overview Tolias 2016.
31 Cf. Koulouri 2020: 48.
32 Dobie 2001: 124.
33 Petrakos 2013: 85–104.
34 Petrakos 2013: 103.
35 Tsiomis 2021: 212 and *passim*.
36 Ibid. 264.
37 Cf. Kyramargiou et al. 2020, esp. 208, 224–228.
38 Hamilakis 2007.
39 Hamilakis 2016; on other treatments of the Amphipolis saga see Fouseki and Dragouni 2017; Plantzos 2016; Vournelis 2016.
40 For various 20th century studies on archaeology and national imagination see also Damaskos and Plantzos 2008, and on challenges and contestations "from below," Solomon 2021.
41 Bar-Yosef 2005.
42 Warren 1875.
43 Abu El-Haj 2002.
44 Kersel 2010.

45 Shavit 1997b.
46 Kletter 2006.
47 Elon 1971.
48 Feige 2001.
49 Silberman 1993.
50 Feige 2007.
51 Petrakos 2013: 94.
52 League of Nations 1922.
53 Melman 2020: 36.
54 See Bohotis 2015; Hamilakis 2013a; Kalpaxis 1990, 1993; Sakka 2008, for examples.
55 Ucko 1998: 367.
56 Zahavi 2009.
57 Zerubavel 1995; Ohana 2017.
58 Vaad Leumi 1947.
59 Gorenberg 2002; Hummel 2019.
60 For critical studies see, for example, Gur 2010.
61 Shavit 1987.
62 Zalmona and Manor-Friedman 1998.
63 Elon 1979.
64 Leoussi and Aberbach 2002; the classic study on the links between Hellenism and Judaism in modern European, especially literary and cultural, thought is Lambropoulos 1993.
65 Shavit 1997a.
66 Magness et al. 2018.
67 Presner 2007.
68 Schulte 2013.
69 E.g. Leoussi 1998.
70 Cf. Chapoutot 2016; Mosse 1995.
71 Yalouri 2004; on the political dimensions and meanings of contemporary Olympics, especially the Athens 2004 ones, see Hamilakis 2007: 1–5, and Plantzos 2016.
72 Cf. Brownell 2008.
73 Cf. Roche 2013.
74 Boyarin 1997; Nordau 1898; Presner 2007; Tosh 2005.
75 Boyarin 1997; also Stähler 2013.

CHAPTER 3

Archaeology in the Crypto-Colony

We discuss the important – but rarely scrutinized – role of archaeology in the constitution of Greece and Israel as contemporary crypto-colonized states, defined by Herzfeld as countries with a strong national sentiment that serve as buffer zones and whose political independence is accompanied by massive economic dependency. We elaborate on what this crypto-colonizing process mean for the two societies.

YH: In the last chapter, we touched briefly upon the intersection of colonialism and nationalism in the foundation of the state of Greece. Greece is not considered by many scholars as a country and a phenomenon that should be discussed within the frame of colonialism, despite the few exceptions.[1] Things have changed recently in this respect, and an event that reignited the discussion was the financial (and the broader social and political) crisis of the 2010s. There is now more debate in the public arena and in scholarly venues on colonization as a process, on financial colonialism by institutions in western European countries such as Germany, and on the creation of long-term dependence through financial debt. Unfortunately, this discussion is often conducted within a nationalist, generalizing frame of understanding, lacking nuance and historical depth, and mostly avoiding any connection with decolonial movements in other parts of the world. Nevertheless, the contingency brought about by the financial crisis provided an opportunity to revisit these matters.[2] An additional factor that promoted such a

Archaeology in the Crypto-Colony

discussion is a recent, and increasing, interest among scholars of Greece in post-colonial and decolonial theory, often spearheaded by researchers living abroad. And finally, there is a growing interest in parts of the country that used to be subjected to colonial rule proper, such as the Ionian Islands, which were under the French in the late 18th century, and under the British between 1815 and 1864,[3] and the Dodecanese, which, after the Ottoman period, became Italian colonies, until 1947.[4]

A key article in this discussion, especially because of its direct relevance to Greece, has been the one by the anthropologist Michael Herzfeld where he launches the idea of Greece as a crypto-colony.[5] Here is how he defines crypto-colonialism:

> ... the curious alchemy whereby certain countries, buffer zones between the colonized lands and those as yet untamed, were compelled to acquire their political independence at the expense of massive economic dependence, this relationship being articulated in the iconic guise of aggressively national culture fashioned to suit foreign models.[6]

There are some important points in this passage to which I will return in a minute, but what I want to say, for a start, is that in the Greek case the idea of the crypto-colony is increasingly seen as pertinent and productive because it provides a way of thinking about issues of colonization and at the same time points to the intentionally cryptic, or rather masked, character of such a relationship.[7] It explains, in other words, why the colonial character of the national project has not been discussed as such; why there is such a resistance to discussing it. So, the notion of intentional hiding, of masking that relationship of dependence, was and is central to the constitution of the crypto-colony. The Greek elites who spearheaded the national project wanted to mask their subservient relationship to the Western elites and to various Western powers in general. Furthermore, the Europeanization and westernization of the country, and the subsequent tropes of orientalism, the adoption of Western cultural and geopolitical regimes and hierarchies of value[8] meant that very few people wanted to associate themselves with countries that were considered colonized by European powers, countries in Africa or in

South Asia. And yet, the colonial relationships of dependence were there in plain sight from the very beginning, more broadly and in relation to archaeology, as we discussed in the previous chapter.

RG: Would you characterize the condition of being a crypto-colony as an essential attribute of the Greek state, a permanent feature of its existence?

YH: Generally, I am not that keen on the concept of the crypto-colony if that defines a type of country in a static, morphological and typological manner. I would rather deploy the concept more as a process, as the on-going dynamic of crypto-colonizing (and being crypto-colonized), which is tightly entangled and interwoven with the on-going nationalizing process. I believe that this was also Herzfeld's original intention. A key feature of this crypto-colonizing process is that of buffering, as we can see from the definition above. I see Greece being constituted as a buffer zone for the Christian, "civilized" West, a process that was, at least implicitly, initiated in the early 19th century, even before the foundation of the Greek state, during the War of Independence. For example, take the writings of Romantic Philhellenes, or "romantic imperialists" according to others,[9] who were partaking in an orientalist discourse on the nature and character of the emerging Western empires, as old ones such as the Ottoman were in retreat. They would also often write from the point of view of the defender of the Western colonial order and see Greeks in that intermediate position, neither oriental "slaves" nor Western citizens like them but as subjects akin to colonized people in need of supervision. For example, the most famous of them all and a still venerated figure in Greece, Byron, the radical aristocrat, romantic nationalist, self-conscious (often self-ironic) orientalist, and pioneer of the classical ideal, would write in 1812:

> The Greeks will never be independent; they will never be sovereigns as heretofore, and God forbid they ever should! but they may be subjects without being slaves. Our colonies are not independent, but they are free and industrious, and such may Greece be hereafter. At present, like the Catholics of Ireland and the Jews throughout the world, and other such cudgelled and heterodox people, they suffer all the moral and physical ills that can afflict humanity.[10]

Archaeology in the Crypto-Colony

This passage speaks to our comparison in this book in interesting ways. As Franklin notes,

> ... we can see that proto-Zionism can be compared to Philhellenism as an apparently Utopian ideal, which sometimes proved useful to European powers scheming to dismember the Ottoman empire ... Byron habitually connected the Greeks and the Jews in his mind as the scapegoats of the world ... He was perfectly aware of treating Philhellenism and proto-Zionism as symbolic nationalist causes, having no pretensions to seem a democrat, or even free of racial prejudice.[11]

Neither racially nor geopolitically were modern Greeks to be admitted to the western European family as full members but as a dependent entity, an entity in-between. Here is what Byron would say in 1823 in Cephalonia, just before he crossed to mainland Greece to join the fight and, one year later, die for the cause:

> I love the cause of liberty, which is that of the Greek nation, although I despise the present race of Greeks, even while I pity them ... I am nearly reconciled to St. Paul, for he says, there is no difference between the Jews and the Greeks, and I am exactly of the same opinion, for the character of both is equally vile.[12]

The aristocrat Byron here despises the people on the ground but champions the ideal of Greece as an eternal nation. He also adopts, out of idealism as well as pity, the *cause* of two imaginary "chosen peoples," becoming thus a prophet of nationalism.[13] And as Beaton has noted, Byron would echo the view that a new independent Greece "would succeed to the mantle of Turkey ... as a bulwark against Russia for the powers of the West"[14] – a buffering role, in other words.

RG: It sounds like Byron – who was probably the favorite British Romantic poet among Jewish intellectuals in the 19th and early 20th centuries, both for his engagement with Jewish themes and for his belief in national redemption[15] – is echoing a fairly conventional, if bigoted, trope: the Greeks cannot live up to their past, while the Jews fail to escape theirs, and as long as that is the case, they will remain "equally vile." But you are suggesting that even for these champions of liberty, Greek (and, theoretically, Jewish) national redemption had to be realized under the aegis of Europe.

YH: Even a seemingly radical, anti-tyrannical figure with atheist credentials such as Percy Bysshe Shelley, a close associate of Byron, in his lyrical poem, *Hellas*, could not escape producing the imagined topos of Greece as a freed land that should be part of the Christian West and perhaps under the sphere of a friendly power such as Britain. This is a minor work in his oeuvre, but an extremely important one for our discussion and for the study of modern, Western Hellenism. This was the work that introduced the phrase "We are all Greeks," although his ambivalence about Hellenism seen in the rest of the passage is rarely remembered.[16]

Hellas was inspired by Aeschylus' *Persians* and published in 1822 to fund the Greek War of Independence. The *Persians* deals with the defeat of Xerxes at Salamis, and it is narrated from the point of view of the defeated. Through the selection of this play at that specific moment, Shelley portrays contemporary fighters against the Ottomans as descendants of ancient Greeks, and evokes the ancient Persian wars as an analogue of and a precursor to the Greek War of Independence, helping thus to produce Orientalist fantasies and stereotypes. At the same time, he projects, in the preface of the poem, a sense that what is at stake is not just the liberation of these people from the Ottomans but something far more important: the future of "free" Christian, western Europe. In this frame of thinking, Greece was seen already as the frontier in the battle against Islam. "The wise and generous policy of England," he would write "would have consisted in establishing the independence of Greece and in maintaining it both against Russia and the Turk."[17] Shelley was worried that (as the poem itself notes) "The bought Briton sends The Keys of Ocean to the Islamite,"[18] while wondering at the same time of the meaning of such victory.[19] Shelley was constructing, through his writing and thinking, a borderland between east and west, between Christianity and Islam,[20] anticipating thus the crypto-colonial geopolitics of buffering of the later years. Greece was squarely situated in such a borderland. And he seemed to be doing so while at the same time aware of the limits of imperial politics and of warfare as one of its main modalities, dreaming perhaps of an unrealized, emancipatory future.[21] Shelley was not the only one to express such views and concerns. He was part of a group of authors and writers who helped prepare the ground for what was to follow, as such imaginaries gained geopolitical potency in the following decades and centuries.

As we already mentioned, the image of the 19th-century fighters as the new Leonidases fighting against the new Persians, the Turks, to defend Europe and the European civilization as a whole, can be also found in many Greek writings of the time, including in the initial declarations of the uprising against the Ottomans.[22] Moreover, even today we see popular books describing, for example, the 480 BCE Battle of Salamis against Xerxes' army, as the "naval encounter that saved Greece-and Western civilization."[23]

Beyond its conception as a buffer area, the crypto-colonized character of the country can be also seen in the various paternalistic plans by philosophers and social reformers such as Jeremy Bentham and Saint-Simon who saw the country as an ideal place for social experiments of good governance,[24] ideas that were propagated or rather enforced upon people on the ground by some Philhellenes. So, the British Colonel Stanhope who had been to South America and to India, upon arriving in Greece in 1823 strove to set up a printing press to publish Bentham's writings and Byron's letters. The colonial experience of India seemed to have been his model. "In all things connected with Greece, consult those Anglo-Indians who understand the character of Asiatic nations. It is thus that I find myself quite at home in Greece," he would write,[25] and elsewhere, "[M]y room is full of natives from morning to night, and the object of every word I utter is to impress upon their minds the advantages of liberty, education, the pure administration of justice, etc."[26] And we saw in the previous chapter how such crypto-colonization shaped both archaeology and the country in the 19th century. After all, the technologies of crypto-colonial governmentality in operation in mainland Greece had been already developed, in more overt ways, in places such as the Ionian Islands since the 18th century.[27]

RG: But did these antiquated notions persist into the modern nation-state era?

YH: The notion of Greece as a crypto-colonized buffer zone for the West survived into the 20th and even 21st century. Take, for example, the Greek Civil War (conventionally, 1946–1949), in many ways the first episode of the Cold War, globally. Following WWII,

Greece was seen by the Western Allies as a country that needed to remain a Western liberal democracy, to act as a barrier, otherwise communism was going to spread like a contagious disease and dominate southern and western Europe. In this effort, they encouraged or directly supported the deployment of not only military means and strategies of detention and persecution but also a huge ideological and propagandistic armory, including the unique "civic re-education" camp of Makronisos that became known as "The New Parthenon."[28] This was the time when the battle against communism utilized the usual platitudes about Greece as the cradle of democracy, now helping defend democracy against communists.

Interestingly, the first episode of the civil war was the so-called "Battle of Athens," in December 1944 (also known as *Dekemvriana*, or The December Events). This was a bloody confrontation between communists and other left-wing people (organized by ELAS, the National Liberation Army that played a central role in fighting the occupying Nazi forces) and nationalist government forces that were supported, crucially, by significant British troops. The British had fought alongside these left-wing guerillas against the Nazi occupation army, and they were celebrated by Greek people as liberators. Now, only a couple of months after the departure of the Nazi forces, these British forces had been instructed by Churchill himself to act as if they were facing a local rebellion in an occupied country.[29]

RG: So there is a significant pivot here from the Ottoman "East" of the 19th century to the new mid-20th century threat: the Soviet "East." The interventions of the West track closely with contingent Western interests; this is one of the markers of crypto-colonialism that can apply to Israel as well. It seems as if the very existence of the crypto-colonized nation is contingent on imperial "geopolitics" and national identity is constantly measured against an external yardstick. Kissinger famously said of Israel that it has no foreign policy, only a domestic one; but this cuts both ways – the "foreign" is internalized domestically, and we are constantly agonizing over how we are perceived abroad, and if we live up to foreign expectations.

YH: Exactly. "What foreigners would say" (*Ti tha poun i xeni*) is a constant anxiety in Greece too, the hallmark of a crypto-colonized as well as self-colonized society, experiencing what W. E. B. Du Bois has called "double consciousness": seeing oneself through the eyes of the other.[30]

In the geopolitics of buffering and crypto-colonization, antiquities and the glorious ruins were again central. In that December battle, the Acropolis, due to its hilltop location and fortified nature became an important battleground, and suffered serious damage. Despite a pact between the warring parties to respect the monument, British forces set up camp on the Acropolis and established launching pads in the Propylaia, in the Erechtheion, even in the Parthenon, attacking the left-wing forces on the opposite hill and the surrounding neighborhoods (Fig. 3.1). The reports submitted by the archaeologist Georgios Bakalakis and the chief guard of the Acropolis, Dimitrios Diamantis, in January 1945, following their inspection of the site, are astonishing historical documents. They outline not only the extensive militarization of the site but also the complete disregard or rather total contempt shown by the British military toward the monument: ancient architectural parts were deliberately destroyed to build barricades, a surviving prehistoric wall was dismantled to secure a launching pad, the safe of the museum where antiquities were hidden by archaeologists was broken into, small finds were looted, books were destroyed or burnt as cooking fuel. ". . . They had installed a launching pad in the NW corner of the wing [of the Parthenon] and they placed other machine guns in the windows of the bell-tower/minaret," Bakalakis would note, and in the postscript of his detailed report he would emphasize his disgust at the defilement of the most sacred monument of the nation: "PS. 6.1.44. The British soldiers who are still inside the museum carry out many ugly things, especially with women, at night."[31] Even the presence among the troops of the classical archaeologist, J. M. Cook, who was then serving with the British in Athens and who was to become, two years later, director of the British School at Athens, did not seem to have had any impact in protecting the monument.

The shelling of the hills and neighborhoods opposite the Acropolis was relentless. The left-wing forces denounced the British "barbarity" of militarizing the site and it seems that they were reluctant to shoot back, fearing that they would destroy the monument. This was

FIGURE 3.1. British troops on the Acropolis, during the battle of December 1944. Photo, Dmitri Kessel (Kessel 1994); reproduced courtesy of Petros Gaitanos and Ammos publishers.

disputed by nationalist sources, and some shelling must have occurred, given the damage that archaeologists later encountered.[32] Respect for the Acropolis and its national sacred and symbolic role, however, must have been felt strongly among the left-wing forces, and initial thoughts to fortify the Acropolis were rejected by them as sacrilege. Such attitudes must have prevented further, extensive damage, and even conservative commentators laid blame on the

British forces for the militarization of the monument.[33] My point is different, however: The cynical move on the part of the British to militarize the Acropolis shows that, as is often the case, the Western pronouncements on the role of Greece and its classical heritage as the progenitor to what is called Western Civilization, is exposed as empty rhetoric in the face of contemporary political (and military) expediency. As for the Greek communists, their adoption of the idea of the sacred classical heritage betrays the power of the overarching national-colonial narrative. It is not the first time that even the internal national "others" operate within the same ideological universe, especially in the absence of an alternative discourse on monuments and material heritage;[34] in this case, however, one could argue that their reaction was also due to the sense of embodied familiarity with the monument, and their affective connection with it as a constant presence in the landscape of the city.[35]

Incidentally, and pertinently for our comparative discussion here, the historian Mark Mazower has brought to our attention the fact that a key figure in the organization of the policing apparatus of the Greek state immediately after this battle was the British Charles Wickham, a veteran of the Second Boer War, a fighter with the White movement against the Bolsheviks in Russia, and the founder and the first inspector of the Royal Ulster Constabulary in Northern Ireland, in 1919.[36] He arrived in Greece in 1945 and stayed until 1952. In addition to advising the nationalist, anti-communist state in Greece, a state that was busy founding various detention camps for dissidents, including the "New Parthenon" of Makronisos, he was also asked to investigate the Palestine Police force. The point here is not the mechanisms of policing in Greece but the threads that connect a global imperial, colonial, and in the case of Greece, crypto-colonial order.

Indeed, such a crypto-colonial relationship, in this case between Britain and Greece, was made at times explicit, at least in discussions among British politicians who were very keen to avoid a left-wing government in Greece, and what they saw as a possible outcome: the incorporation of the country within the Soviet zone of influence.[37] British "overseers" were installed in most government departments at the time, and Ambassador Leeper would even suggest, in 1946, that

Greece should become a member of the British Commonwealth, to which his superiors would respond that:

> ... colonial treatment whether by us or some trusteeship group is the only method of nursing Greece towards solvency and political stability ... Greece is a backward, extravagant and irresponsible country whose vanities are made greater and whose difficulties are therefore accentuated because for both us and the USSR Greece has strategic importance.[38]

RG: That attitude of course continues into this century ...

YH: It does. The latest episode in the process of constituting Greece as a crypto-colonial buffer zone for the West is the so-called migration crisis of 2015–2016.[39] Here, Greece (and, to some extent, Turkey too), was asked by the West, in this case by the European Union, to stop the "new waves" of "invaders" from the East (in truth, from the Global South). On the occasion of the official, state-sponsored celebrations of the 2500 anniversary of the Battle of Salamis (a commemorative event that is absurd in itself), Greek politicians would make a direct connection between the Persians in 480 BCE and the new oriental invaders, meaning migrants and border crossers, today.[40] Here is the Greek Prime Minister, announcing the celebrations for the battle:

> [T]he Battle of Salamis ... paved the way for the liberation of territories under Persian rule ... [and] thus created the image, for the first time, of a nation, with Greece as its homeland, but with horizons throughout the world ... In our times, the challenges are different. Waves of refugees and migrants are now besieging countries.[41]

In this, and in other similar public statements, the target audience is not only the people of Greece but also, and perhaps primarily, the Western elites and governments, reminding them of that buffering role that Greece has been playing since 480 BCE.

RG: And this came naturally, since the West had maintained its investment in archaeology all along?

YH: As far as the institution of archaeology is concerned, one can trace the process of crypto-colonization in the first years of the foundation of the country, as we discussed in the previous chapter:

Archaeology in the Crypto-Colony

the setting up of the various administrative, educational and legal frameworks and institutions of archaeology, primarily by the Bavarians, and more broadly the establishment of relationships of dependence. The ideological crypto-colonization of the place by the ideas of Western Hellenism was, of course, older, and preceded the institutional and material colonization.

We can add here the role of foreign archaeological schools and missions that we briefly discussed in the last chapter in relation to competition. Such institutions embody the impact of the Classical legacy and its glorification, primarily by the elites (as well as certain subjugated groups at specific historical moments) in the Global North, its constitution as shared, Western symbolic capital, not just a national symbolic capital for Greece. But they also recall, materialize and sustain the colonial legacy of archaeology in Greece, as well as the crypto-colonial status of the country as a whole. Through their impressive, often neoclassical buildings as well as their rich and diverse activities, they remind the citizens of Greece, not just the archaeologists, that their state was founded partly through the intervention of the "Great Powers." This began a relationship of dependence that has been in operation ever since; a very complicated one, and not one between a foreign colonizer and the local colonized.

Such institutions operated from the beginning, as we already noted, in a fiercely competitive manner, mirroring the global competition of the respective imperial powers. The "concessions" given to them by the Greek government to dig certain key sites, mostly in the 19th and the early 20th century, established a regime of *de facto* "ownership." These "concessions" were entangled with matters of economic and directly political nature, such as diplomatic favors, financial loans to the country, or various commercial deals, often in violation of the state legislation over antiquities.[42] These are cases, in other words, where the symbolic capital of antiquity was exchanged for political or economic capital, although within the crypto-colonial framework these exchanges had to be masked and misrecognized as such. The state archaeologists' exclusive right of access to the materiality of the past, combined with their shortage of the necessary resources to manage, protect, and study it, led to various negotiations, deals, and arrangements with the foreign schools, entangling tightly these two components of the assemblage of archaeology in Greece.

RG: I'm glad you brought this up. "Concession," according to the OED, acquired two connotations in the 19th century, a territorial one, as a place ceded to a foreign power, and an economic one, as a resource that can be exploited; this double meaning has had a very long life in archaeology. Originally part of the regime of "capitulations" imposed on the Ottomans by European powers, the modern-day excavation license still confers broad powers on its holders – who nonetheless have been complaining about the erosion of their rights for at least 150 years! You can still find archaeological real estate (dig houses), rural villages that function as "company towns," and "expeditions" that take on attributes of heterotopias, with their inmates subjected to rules of time, space, behavior, and hierarchy (including gender hierarchies) that are at odds with those of the host countries or, indeed, with the rules back home. John Tosh has written of empire that it "promised escape from custom and convention" (at least for men) and was "synonymous with adventure."[43] Many archaeological digs, especially those mounted by wealthy metropolitan institutions, carry on in this tradition and even exploit it to market themselves as a symbol of a certain type of social distinction, for those who can afford it.

At another level – and going back to what you have described as Western paternalism and orientalism – local archaeologists (Greek, Israeli, or otherwise) are often seen as unable to transcend their locality, their passionate attachments, or their patriotism, to become rational and objective observers. They require external monitoring and validation.

YH: Absolutely, but for many archaeologists in Greece, these schools provide access to international networks through their journals, and conferences. This entangled relationship has its benefits for all concerned, but it also encourages conformity and acquiescence rather than critique and debate. That's why to see the foreign schools today simply as forces of archaeological colonization is misguided. Their facilities, their impressive libraries and labs, unmatched by any Greek institution, sustain the work of many archaeologists in Greece, foreign and local, and their activities, most of the time, are regulated by the Greek archaeological law and service. Yet, that very same legal and institutional framework gives them immense authority to filter the work of archaeologists from their respective countries in Greece, to control who can do work in Greece and who not, and what kind of archaeology can be done. Partly because the management caste of these schools tend to be conservative and partly because this caste, for obvious reasons, does not want to offend the Greek archaeological establishment, rarely are critical, decolonial archaeologists of these countries encouraged or allowed to work in Greece, leading to a continuous reproduction not only of the crypto-colonial regime but also of the archaeological theoretical orthodoxy. It is often assumed that nationalist archaeology in Greece is produced just by Greek archaeologists, yet it is not uncommon to see extremely conservative, nationalist narratives and practices perpetuated by archaeologists of these foreign schools as part of this crypto-colonial relationship, despite the recent improvements and the occasional critical voices.[44] In other words, this is a complex network or assemblage of heterogeneous actors that coheres and co-constitutes the crypto-colonial regime of archaeology in Greece. The ongoing crypto-colonization of the country is due to many and diverse actors and processes, local and non-local, and the crypto-colonized would at times forge alliances with the crypto-colonizers to engage in their own colonial projects.

In the *Nation and its Ruins* I spoke about the process of partial emancipation of Greek nationalism from the middle of the 19th century onward, a process of transforming Western Hellenism into a form of Indigenous Hellenism incorporating the Byzantine heritage, a distinctive form of Hellenism.[45] This did not, of course, undermine the crypto-colonial regime under which the country operated. It simply offered a home-made recasting of it, which allowed the nation to reconcile various tensions and to synthesize seemingly contradictory facets such as Orthodox Christianity and classical, pagan heritage.

At the level of structures and institutions, recent archaeological laws, though not radically different from earlier ones going back to the first one devised by the Bavarians, imposed limits and established regulations on the archaeological activity of foreign archaeological entities. But the effects of that early colonizing process are still present. Take Crete, for example. The zones of archaeological influence there were established in the period of the fifteen years when the island was semi-autonomous (1898–1913), nominally still under the Ottoman Empire but in fact under the military occupation of foreign powers, namely Britain, Italy, France, and Russia. The first three managed to establish zones of archaeological activity and influence, in alliance with Cretan intellectuals who desired unification with Greece and saw archaeology as a key way of achieving it. These zones of archaeological activity and influence are still, more or less, present, and mirror, to some extent, the British, the Italian, and the French sectors of the period of the military occupation.[46] This is just one example; there are others where the direct effects of the crypto-colonizing process can be seen archaeologically, as well as economically, and geopolitically. And at the broader, ideological level, the crypto-colonizing relationship is still intact.

RG: And how would you define the role of the American embassy vis-à-vis archaeology?

YH: Today? Again, it seems that the role and influence of the USA in Greek archaeology followed in some way its increasing economic, diplomatic, and political influence upon Greece, especially in the 20th century, mirroring at the same time the decline and the problems, financial and other, of western European powers. There were, of course, American archaeologists working in Greece even in the 19th century, especially since the foundation of the American School of Classical Studies in Athens, in 1881. Its first major site, and one where it is still active, Corinth, is seen even today, as an "American" dig. Excavations there started in 1896. But it was with the start of the excavations at the Athenian Agora, in the 1930s, that American archaeology became a major and increasingly powerful presence in Greece. Until then, American archaeologists felt that they were left out in some way, seeing the French securing the right to Delphi, the Germans to Olympia, the British to Knossos, and so on. The Agora was a site to rival such localities. The negotiations lasted for almost a decade. I have discussed this process at length elsewhere[47] but the American success to gain the permit to excavate was due to the confluence of many processes. These included the favorable (for the USA) political situation in Greece, the dire economic state of the country, especially after its defeat in the Greco-Turkish war in 1922, and the influx of around one million refugees in a country of five million people, the outmaneuvering of competitors such as the Athens Archaeological Society, and most importantly, the ability to mobilize the huge funds required, through a donation by the Rockefeller empire. Neither the British, who were interested, nor the Greeks, who desired it, were able to undertake such a project, especially since it involved the demolition of an entire neighborhood, and the displacement and compensation of thousands of people. Interestingly, it was the American School itself that published, very recently, a book reconstructing, in careful and systematic detail, the demolished neighborhood,[48] a move that can be seen both as the fulfillment of an ethical obligation especially toward the descendants, and an act of what Renato Rosaldo has called, imperialist nostalgia[49] – feeling nostalgic toward something you have helped to destroy.

American capitalism, and philanthropy as one of its key modes of being and reproduction, carried the day. A loan to the Greek state was approved by the American government at the same time, a loan that was used as a negotiating chip in the discussions over the Agora permit. All the terms of that concession, including those to do with the compensation of the local inhabitants, were very favorable for the American School, by its own admission. A project that was meant to be a collaboration project with Greek archaeologists, ended up being an exclusively American project, and the excavation became the main training ground for American classical archaeologists for decades, to the present day.[50] Even the American financial crash of 1929 did not affect the funding and the launching of this project.

In later years, especially during the Greek Civil war and its aftermath and up to the military dictatorship (1967–1974) and the early 1980s, the USA became the dominant foreign player in the country, which also contributed to the flourishing of American archaeology in Greece. This started immediately after WWII when the British decided, in 1947, to pull out of Greece, contributing to the launching of the Truman Doctrine that aimed at containing communism and Soviet influence. Greece was central in this doctrine, which was later expanded to include the rest of Europe.

So, for more than thirty years, the USA, through its powerful foreign policy institutions, became the dominant foreign political force in the country, shaping its structures, propping up its elites, and even supporting the military coup of 1967. It was only with the 1980s, when Greece joined the European Economic Community (which became the European Union), and when global geopolitics changed and American priorities shifted, that this relationship waned.

Enough about Greece, for the moment. How about Israel? Does the concept of the crypto-colony resonate among scholars, archaeologists and others, and the critical public?

RG: I should begin by saying that although the application of colonial terminology to Israel has become in many quarters a litmus test for "pro-Zionism" or "post/anti-Zionism"[51] we should still try to judge the utility of the crypto-colony concept on its merits, as a way of categorizing and interpreting actions and objective relations. These actions and relations can often be multivalent and even contradictory (for example, a group may be both colonized and colonizing), resulting in what I would term superimposed colonialisms in Palestine and Israel; formal or informal colonialism by the West, Zionist settler colonialism, and crypto-colonialism in 20th century states. Moreover, just as the ancient precursors of the national sentiments that we are both describing do not make contemporary Greece or Israel any less a product of modernity,[52] the existence of tangible Jewish antiquities in Palestine does not detract from the colonial attributes of modern Jewish settlement. It is therefore interesting to note that, while so much energy has been expended on the settler-colony debate, the idea of Israel as a crypto-colony has achieved no traction at all, as far as I know, despite the close fit between Herzfeld's definition that you cited earlier (buffer state, massive dependence, aggressive nationalism), and the reality of Israel's existence. I think this lacuna is owed to Israel's success in configuring the massive economic and political support that it has received over the decades, first as restitution and reparations (owed by Germany), then as the natural cost of a strategic partnership, based on a shared ethos, with the USA. In contrast with what you have described concerning Greece, Israel sees itself as an equal partner and judge of whether it has received sufficient compensation for serving as a buffer state and this has successfully masked and naturalized the massive impact of Western – and especially American – values and interests, to the extent that Israelis are often happy to characterize themselves, simultaneously, as proudly independent and as "the 51st state" of the USA.

Going back to the origins of this shared ethos, we already mentioned how the British, but also Americans and other Western nations, considered Palestine theirs by right. Why? What in it was theirs? The answer lies in the centrality of an unmediated reading of the Hebrew Bible to Western political thought and to concepts that later became known as "the Judeo-Christian tradition," or "Judeo-Christian values." These – in their most superficial and commonly used sense – might be defined as a modern, usually Protestant morality established on biblical foundations; a morality that justifies global dominance.[53] On that basis, the antiquities of Palestine became part of the origin story of the West itself, just as ancient Greece was. And because of the continued strong interest in the biblical past, modern Israel is still viewed as a "bastion" of Judeo-Christian values, serving both as a buffer and as an outpost. It is nominally independent but also completely dependent; the common thinking in Israel is that all the important decisions are taken in the American embassy, or in Washington. The last thing that every Prime Minister does before elections and the first thing they do after them is to place a call to Washington. So, politically, it's not difficult to accept the concept of Israel as a crypto-colony: a nominally independent state that is seen by the West – as well as by itself – as an outpost for the West. Of course, Israel is not the only Middle Eastern state covered by that definition; I would say that the Kingdom of Jordan is even closer to Herzfeld's archetypical crypto-colony because the whole system is propped up by Western aid and loans. If you were to pull the plug on this support system, it would collapse in a moment, whereas in Israel there might be a somewhat different dynamic, because of the deep entanglement between Israel, Judaism, and Western culture.

YH: How is this played out in archaeology?

RG: I suggest that archaeology has been quietly groomed by means of a constant presence of European and American sponsors and excavators throughout the 20th century. This began, as I mentioned before, during the Mandate period when Palestine was "opened up" for overseas expeditions. That's when the Oriental Institute at the University of Chicago came in, with Rockefeller's support, but there were also Harvard excavations, University of Pennsylvania excavations, privately funded British excavations, and many more associated with the American and British Schools in Jerusalem (the French had their own Mandate to work in, that of Lebanon and Syria, while the Germans lost the foothold that they had before World War I).

We have mentioned John D. Rockefeller Jr., who – even as he was funding the excavations of the Agora – underwrote the construction of the Palestine Archaeological Museum and the Chicago excavations at Megiddo, which were the largest and most powerful expedition in Palestine in the late twenties and thirties. This was a form of "soft power," wielded by the large foundations and philanthropists. As shown in several studies,[54] the values governing the way the money of those foundations was used – the Rockefeller foundation, the Carnegie foundation, the Ford foundation, and others – shored up the interests of American capital and American foreign policy. Among other things, they promoted a particular view of progress and the subsequent division of the world into developed and undeveloped nations, underwriting an anthropology that sustained that view and became embedded and normalized in the structure of Western academia to the point where we are hardly aware of it. Likewise, many of the aspirations and assumptions baked into the archaeology of Mandate Palestine and Israel are rooted in worldviews that were introduced through the "soft" influence, which is a form of conquest not by troops, but by American money. I am speaking, for example, of ideas on geographic determinism and the inexorable march of technology and civilization (from Sumer to Chicago) that are on display on the famous Oriental Institute tympanum (Fig. 3.2).[55] They are also evident in classic products of interwar American archaeology in Palestine such as Wright and Filson's *Historical Atlas to the Bible* (1945) and Albright's *The Archaeology of Palestine* (1949), where archaeology is presented as a necessary means to provide a basis for a modern reading of the Old and New Testaments and confirmation of the divine destiny of Palestine. I am also speaking of the proprietary rights that this necessity conferred on

Archaeology in the Crypto-Colony

FIGURE 3.2. The Oriental Institute tympanum, illustrating, at center, the passing of the torch of knowledge from the Orient, left, to the Occident, right; note the pyramids and minarets in the background at left; the Acropolis and skyscraper at right; and the archaeologist at far right. CC0 1.0 Universal.

archaeologists (by means of site "concessions" and excavation permits) and of the gender and racial hierarchies embedded in archaeological expeditions, which we discussed earlier. The enduring effects of American imperial values can also be discerned in the moral virtues ascribed to advanced methods and technologies used in excavation and analysis, and in the prominent role of capital in funding research and in the organization and regimentation of local labor. We will return to this when we discuss the ancient DNA "revolution" in archaeology.

The more recent iteration of this impact can be traced back to Yigael Yadin's excavations at Masada, which mark a swerve or a pivot in the way Western interest in Holy Land archaeology was manipulated (because, of course, local actors perform their own manipulations of foreign interventions). For the first decade or decade-and-a-half of statehood, after 1948, the popular myth of archaeology as the "national pastime" of the Israelis can be said to hold some water.[56] There was a large proportion of Israelis – especially the highly educated – who felt a strong connection to archaeology and formed a virtually self-sufficient supportive community. This support permitted archaeologists to carry on with their small-bore scientific program of historical and biblical confirmation that provided the political class with a basis for affirmation of the National Destiny. But this symbiosis had begun to fray because of changes within Israeli society and a gradual erosion of the patriotic fervor that accompanied the first years of the state. Yadin had to find a new way to mobilize people at a time, in the early sixties, when political disillusionment had begun to set in and local enthusiasm for archaeology declined. What he did at Masada was to market an Israeli national symbol to the international community. Following the lead of early 20th-century archaeologists such as Leonard Wooley, the excavator of Ur,[57] he went directly to British newspapers (David Astor, the editor of *The Observer*, bankrolled the Masada project in return for exclusive rights to the story) and invited the public, in England and beyond, to join the excavation.[58] This internationalized Israel's archaeology, converting it into an object of fascination across the English-speaking world.

This is a major pivot – an outsourcing of a facet of the national ethos – that I don't think has been given enough attention. He inaugurated an influx of volunteers into excavations in Israel, and since that time they have become a mainstay of our academic excavations. From the mid-sixties and for several decades, until the neoliberal revolution of the 1990s that has engendered huge developer-funded "salvage" excavations, academic archaeology was the main engine of archaeology in Israel. That engine was fueled to a great extent by the participation of volunteers from the USA and Europe, who might be categorized as supporters rather than collaborators in the academic sense. And while in the early years they were composed of individuals who came on their own, over time their recruitment became more institutionalized, with the most dependable source of volunteers being evangelical Christians. Many excavations partnered with Bible Belt colleges and seminaries in the USA and occasionally in Europe and other parts of the world. This involvement with an evangelical agenda – together with the impact of settler nationalism that I mentioned before – has pushed Israeli academic archaeology toward an increasing focus on the biblical periods, actually reviving some of the "Judeo-Christian" aspects of archaeology that had been put on the back burner after 1948. That is what attracts those volunteers; the unique thing that is on offer. Prehistory is fascinating, but it challenges creationism and can't be related to biblical stories. Even classical archaeology, usually associated with the life and times of Jesus, has lost its luster because excavations are not to be confused with pilgrimage: Christian groups will visit New Testament pilgrimage sites for the religious experience, but excavating Old Testament biblical sites offers them a path to discover the Judeo-Christian foundations *for themselves*. The impact of evangelicals has become quite remarkable in recent years within academic archaeology (mirroring its political impact in the region).[59] It is a new-old strand of crypto-colonialism identified as such because Christian sentiment was prominent in colonial ideologies and because client countries in this disguised relationship respond even to subtle political changes in the metropole; academic archaeologists in many biblical-period sites have become dependent on it; they can't imagine their projects going forward without that participation.

YH: As I mentioned earlier, I had found it difficult, especially in the past, to engage colleagues in such a discussion, especially colleagues living in Greece. One of the reasons, I think, is expediency; there is still academic and cultural capital to be made if you tie yourself to the European project and see yourself as part of the Global North and its assumed superiority. If you accept that you were colonized, and that you are still colonized in some ways, ideologically but also materially and organizationally, you become like a country in Africa or South Asia. I've seen this being played out, especially in relation to claims for the restitution of antiquities from major Western museums to Greece. There was and is resistance to ally such claims with the claims by countries in Africa, for example, because the Greek claims were presented as exceptional; for example, the Parthenon marbles are linked to a monument that, symbolically, is at the center of Western psyche and civilization, as the Greek campaign for their return argues. It's not to do with postcolonial claims and the history of colonization, the same advocates would insist. To what extent is there a similar situation in Israel?

RG: Most of my colleagues, I suspect, would also resist the characterization of being colonized. One reason Israelis won't recognize that they are being colonized is a fierce exceptionalism – like the one you noted among Greeks – that resists any inclusion in a global trend or category (*our nationalism is like no other; we are not colonized, nor are we colonizers*). Another is the typical cognitive dissonance that one so often sees in marginalized countries – again, it must be similar in Greece – in which the stamp of value, the imprimatur, is provided by the major English-language journal or university, but is also resented: You publish in *Nature* or spend your sabbatical at Brown University – that's a sign of success, of prestige – but at the same time you maintain a strong sense of self-sufficiency and pride in local expertise, deriding the foreigner who "doesn't speak the language" and "doesn't know the country." These attitudes coexist. But when push comes to shove, it is the publication in the high-profile, open-access journal that will be counted. We're still being controlled by a set of values arbitrated by the anglophone North that determines what is "important," "significant," or "prestigious."

YH: Your comments on national exceptionalism resonate very much with Greece too. I know there is a robust culture of debate and discussion both in the country and outside, especially among recent expat intellectuals from Israel. To what extent do others, outside of archaeology talk about this colonizing process as well as the role of the country as a settler colony?

RG: The recognition of Israel as a settler colony – in addition to the other colonialisms that collide in Israel and overlap with each other – has expanded its scope among some academics, but it hasn't made its way into archaeology or into the public arena. I spoke earlier about the political cachet attached to the use of colonial terminology with respect to Israel; this is a particularly sensitive issue for archaeologists (whether Israeli, or only seeking to excavate in Israel), who are heavily dependent on outside funding by donors, participants, and government bodies. Their avoidance of the issue is hardly surprising. What I find more disappointing is the lack of interest among critical intellectuals in the nuances of the deployment of archaeology under different colonial regimes. It is too easy to stuff archaeology into compartments such as "myths of the nation," "invented traditions," "selective memory," and so on, without recognizing the enduring world-making properties of archaeological praxis and the way archaeology can serve different agendas, including emancipatory and decolonial ones.

But before we move away from the crypto-colony, I wonder if the ease with which Israelis can shrug off their own dependency, in contrast to the constant Greek and European angst over "the Greek Debt," might not be attributed to the persistent perception that the modern Greeks are imperfect vessels for the defining Western values (like Democracy), whereas virtually no-one questions the historic continuity of Israel with the "Judeo-" part of Judeo-Christianity?

YH: I think you are right. As we discussed in the previous chapter, the presence of living humans in the antique land of Greece posed a problem for Western Hellenism, hence the various ambivalent and often contradictory responses, from the dismissal of these living humans as barbaric and ignorant peasants to their rendering as living fossils of ancient Hellenes, and more in between. The trope of "unworthy descendants" has been also key in various European reactions, and it is often internalized by the people of Greece, producing a constant sense of shame and inferiority; Western Hellenism has colonized not only the imagination, but also the emotions, and the affective responses. In the recent financial crisis, many western European popular responses repeated such tropes, adding that modern Greeks were not only imperfect vessels for the idea of democracy invented by their ancestors, but also for capitalism, as they were "the fraudsters in the family," as the cover of a German magazine proclaimed, masking once more the inequities of the European and global neoliberal system as well as its hypocrisy.[60]

As a concluding thought, perhaps we should not leave the impression that the crypto-colonizing processes we have traced here should lead us to consider the countries that were subjected to them as victims of some sort. Further, it should have become clear that the discussion on the crypto-colonial should not fall into the trap of nationalism or other essentialisms; instead, we should be aware of the complex constellation of diverse social actors who played key roles in these processes, a further reason that renders the crypto-colony, as a typological category, problematic. Even without the crypto-colonial effects, nationalism, as a derivative ideology and concept, shares with colonialism the main essentialist principles, and nationalism itself has set in action a colonizing process: In homogenizing the land and its people, in imposing upon a diverse range of attributes one crucial difference, that between the national self and national other, in erasing class, gender, and cultural and ethnic diversity.[61]

Nationalized or not, a crypto-colonized country can at the same time gain a colonizing and crypto-colonizing role itself. The case of Israel is obvious and extensively discussed, the case of Greece less so. Beyond the colonization of the land and its people by the ideas of Western Hellenism and nationalism in the late 18th and early 19th century, Greece itself engaged in overtly colonizing processes (conquering what it claimed to be "unredeemed fatherlands"), in which archaeology was extremely important. Take the military expansion of the kingdom of Greece in new territories such as Macedonia, Northern Epirus, and Thrace, including Eastern Thrace, in the first decades of the 20th century. The Hellenization of these ethnically and linguistically diverse lands was carried out with the significant contribution of archaeology, and the deployment of antiquity more broadly. Archaeological departments were set up as soon as these areas were conquered, excavations aimed at proving their Hellenic character were carried out, and local, indigenous toponyms were replaced by ancient Greek ones, inspired by ancient Greek literary and mythological sources[62] and classical iconography operated as a propagandistic, colonizing tool. Take the image shown in Fig. 3.3, for example: it shows a postal stamp issued in 1913,[63] depicting the Acropolis but also the island of Salamis below a cross and the phrase, *"En Touto Nika"* (*In this, conquer*). This phrase is linked to the Byzantine Emperor Constantine who, apparently, before his conversion and during a military campaign, saw a vision with a cross and this phrase in the sky. In effect, this stamp condenses the national historical-ideological scheme of Indigenous Hellenism in which ancient Hellas and Byzantium are reconciled and combined as a Helleno-Christian synthesis. It was on these symbolic-propagandic grounds that the colonizing 1912–1913 military campaigns in Macedonia and Thrace, areas ethnically and religiously diverse, were founded.

These endeavors were part of the 19th-century vision or national dream of the "Great Idea" that saw Hellenism as a concept both topographically and culturally far wider than the boundaries of modern Greek state. The Great Idea expressed the national desire

FIGURE 3.3. A Greek postage stamp, issued in 1913 to commemorate the 1912 military campaign. Tsitselikis 2021: 138; reproduced courtesy of the author and of the Laskaridis Foundation.

to reunify within the boundaries of the nation-state what were seen as Hellenic territories, based mostly on a perception of the ancient Greek topography.[64] Interestingly, this applied mostly to the territories in the north and the east (Macedonia, Thrace, Anatolia), against enemies that were seen as culturally inferior – not, say, to the territories in the West, such as Southern Italy and Sicily - the Magna Graecia of ancient Greek colonization.

The most characteristic example, where military-political and archaeological colonization worked in tandem, was the case of Asia Minor between 1919 and 1922. Following military occupation by the Greek army and the setting up of a Greek-administered sector around Smyrna, all with the support of the Great Western Powers (who divided the region into sectors-protectorates under their control), an archaeological department for the area was established; antiquities collections were organized; and several, well-funded excavations were carried out, often with the collaboration of the army and the deployment of prisoners of war.[65] Within the national discourse, such measures were (and are) seen as attempts to protect "Greek" monuments that were suffering due to the negligence of the Turkish administration, a narrative that masked this colonizing process although, at times, some military and political leaders would be explicit about the colonial nature of the campaign.[66] While the demographic composition of the area was a matter of dispute, the Greek national discourse would insist that there was no need of a census, as "Greek" antiquities in the area proved its Hellenicity beyond doubt. Needless to say, monuments of diverse cultural nature were Hellenized in this process.

Moreover, the French and the American foreign archaeological schools of Athens as well as American universities were encouraged to carry out systematic excavations on sites in Asia Minor such as Colophon and Sardis – carried out by American archaeologists – and Notion – carried out by the French in collaboration with the Ottoman Greek archaeologist, Theodor Macridy Bey (Fig. 3.4).[67] Here, the crypto-colonized state of Greece entered into an alliance with some of the colonial powers upon which it depended to expand the imagined territory of the Hellenic nation-state, becoming thus a colonizing force itself and participating at the same time in a transnational colonial project. The military occupation of the area was thus further legitimated by the foreign powers whose archaeologists were carrying out excavations, while these archaeologists and their sponsoring institutions saw an opportunity for archaeological expansion in a new area. They also benefited in working under a fluid,

FIGURE 3.4. The director of the American School of Classical Studies at Athens B. H. Hill (with the white suit) on the visit to Asia Minor to locate a suitable site for excavation (c. 1921). To the right with the dark suit is Konstantinos Kourouniotis, the archaeologist in charge of the Greek archaeological mission. The two men, together with the American archaeologist, Hetty Goldman, spent two weeks exploring various sites. American School of Classical Studies at Athens Archives, Carl W. Blegen Papers; reproduced with permission.

militarized regime that would allow them more freedom to export antiquities to their metropolitan museums (antiquities that were legally the property of the Ottoman state), something they could not do within the boundaries of Greece itself, due to the Greek archaeological law.[68] Greek archaeologists saw in this bargain an additional opportunity for ancient Greek cities to be unearthed, producing further material landmarks in the construction of the imagined topography of Hellenism, in the heterotopia of the Greek nation that was now expanding to include some of the "unredeemed fatherlands."[69]

This can be seen as a process of re-making the geo-body of the nation, to use a concept proposed by Thongchai Winichakul:[70] A concept that denotes the merging of the *topos* (the soil, the earth, the territory) with the body, the body of humans, alive and dead, and the body of the earth. The geo-body is also about the affective and emotional threads that link all these elements. Furthermore, in the *Nation and its Ruins* I suggested that this episode is another facet of a key Hellenic national desire: the nostalgia for the whole, the longing for the reunification of all the dispersed and scattered fragments of the national geo-body.[71] The soil of Anatolia held the bones of ancient Greeks that were calling for their unearthing, sometimes through dreams and visions.[72] The same soil preserved the white columns of ancient Greek temples, the marble skeletons of the Hellenic, patriarchal geo-body. They all had to be reunified through this military campaign. As in other cases, archaeological dreams and realities and the dreams and material realities of the crypto-colonized and crypto-colonizing nation were being mutually constituted. It is worth noting, however, that there were groups and movements inside the country, and even inside the national army – with most prominent being the newly formed Greek Communist party – who opposed the Greek military campaign, characterizing it as an imperial war; their impact, however, was limited.

This dream of imperial expansion, as far as Asia Minor is concerned, was short-lived. It was buried, together with the broader "Great Idea," under the ashes and the rubble of Smyrna in September 1922. Echoes of them, however, can be heard to the present day, when, for example, fringe groups and nationalist and fascist politicians champion the cause of "unredeemed fatherlands." In some cases, such echoes gain wider resonance and prominence, as happened in 2020, when the Turkish government opened Hagia Sophia in Istanbul (a monument with huge symbolic weight in certain strains of Greek national imagination) as a mosque, returning it to its prior use that had lasted from the end of the 15th century CE to 1931.

RG: This is such an interesting parallel to the Israeli praxis that I mentioned before (itself inherited from the French and British) of carrying out archaeological surveys in every conquered or even temporarily occupied territory, including parts of Egypt that were occupied briefly in 1973 and southern Lebanon in 1982 – not to mention the instant appropriation of the West Bank, Golan, and

Sinai in 1967.[73] As you said, it speaks to the essentialism of the national project and the sacralization of ethnic territories (A.D. Smith's "ethnoscapes")[74] that it entails – the literal or figurative ethnic cleansing and purification of what are often disordered, polysemic, multi-temporal landscapes.

YH: Yes, we will discuss purification and its multivalent nature at some length in the next chapter.

Notes

1. E.g. Calotychos 2004; Fleming 1999, 2000; Gourgouris 1996.
2. Efi Gazi (2020) has studied a number of early 20th-century nationalist intellectuals who developed a sort of essentialist, supra-nationalist anti-colonialism, critiquing the colonizing influence of the West, and often dreaming of an oriental, federal empire with Hellenism at its center. See particularly the thinking of Ion Dragoumis on this (2020: 262). There have been also earlier studies that have attempted to analyze Greece as a colonized country, but more often than not, they have stayed within the nationalist framework. See, for example, Tasos Lignadis's 1975 book that has been rediscovered by nationalists today. He concludes that study, focusing mostly on the loans of the new state, by saying: "The Greek statelet from the 1821 Revolution to our times lived a life which was 'legally' independent but in reality it was of the colonial or neocolonial type" (2020: 165).
3. On the Ionian Islands and their colonial entanglements see Arvanitakis 2020, and mostly Gekas 2017, where the author concludes his study of the British colonial regime stating that "the colonization of Greece begun with the Ionian Islands two hundred years ago and could be argued that it continues today with Greece as a 'debt colony'" (335–336). On the Ionian Islands as a transnational space for the emergence of nationalist ideas, see Zanou 2018.
4. Doumanis 1997.
5. Herzfeld 2002.
6. Herzfeld 2002: 900–901.
7. Papagiannopoulos (2019: 130) makes the pertinent observation that the description of Greece as a crypto-colony invests it with additional interest since the assumed ancestral home of the colonizing subject (the West) becomes at the same time the object of that subject's colonizing efforts. Of course, from the point of view of the colonizing West, this is not colonization (hence the crypto- again) but rather an act of reclaiming that ancestral home.

8 In the *Body Impolitic*, Herzfeld (2003) has explored the concept of the global hierarchy of value in relation to craftspeople in Greece, showing how the dominant, Western aesthetic norms (for the formation of which ancient classical monuments played a key role) devalue the labor and craft sensibility of ordinary people, another facet of the crypto-colonizing process.
9 Makdisi 1998.
10 Cited in Franklin 1998: 225
11 Franklin 1998: 239
12 Kennedy 1830: 246–248; cf. also Franklin 1998; Karakatsouli 2016: 295–296.
13 Cf. Beaton 2013: 189–191.
14 Ibid., 226.
15 Spector 2010.
16 van Kooy 2009: 47.
17 Shelley 1866: x.
18 Ibid., 49.
19 Kipperman 1991: 165.
20 van Kooy 2009.
21 Kipperman 1991.
22 Koulouri 2020: 48–49.
23 E.g. Strauss 2005.
24 Cf. Karakatsouli 2016: 58; Baloglou 2009.
25 Stanhope 1824: 80.
26 Stanhope 1824: 63.
27 Gekas 2017.
28 See Hamilakis 2007: 205–242.
29 Cf. Close 1995.
30 Du Bois 2007 [1903]: 8; cf. Calotychos 2004: 49-50, on Du Bois's thinking in relation to Greece.
31 Petrakos 2013: 380–396.
32 Ibid.
33 cf. Kostopoulos 2016: 166–168.
34 Cf. Hamilakis 2007 for other examples. See also the text by Yannis Zevgos (2021[1945]), an important communist intellectual and leading cadre of the Communist Party (KKE), on the Battle of Athens. He would speak of the "transformation of Greece, in essence, into a British colony" (2021: 87), declare, in a rather racist remark, that the British gathered in Athens "substantial forces, including English, Indians, and dwarfs from Uganda" (2021: 52), while at the same time prominently evoking the ancient Battle of Thermopylai (2021: 60).
35 cf. Yalouri 2001, on the meaning and social roles of the Acropolis, more broadly.

36 Mazower 1997.
37 cf. Liakos 2019: 272, 294.
38 Hector McNeil, Parliamentary Under Secretary of State for Foreign Affairs, cited by Sfikas 1994: 80.
39 Cf. Christopoulos and Spyropoulou 2019.
40 Cf. Hamilakis 2016.
41 Cited in Kambouris 2019.
42 Bohotis 2015; Hamilakis 2013a; Kalpaxis 1990, 1993; Sakka 2008, 2021.
43 Tosh 2005: 199–200.
44 See, for example, the work of Jack Davis, former director of the American School, and the volume edited by Davis and Vogeikoff-Brogan (2013) or the work of Alexandre Farnoux, former director of the French School, or the work done by the Swedish Institute at the site of Kalaureia on the island of Poros, and on which I have collaborated (cf. Hamilakis and Ifantidis 2016).
45 Hamilakis 2007: 57–124.
46 Cf. Hamilakis and Momigliano 2006; McEnroe 2002; Varouchakis 2017.
47 Hamilakis 2013; see also Sakka 2008.
48 Dumont 2020.
49 Rosaldo 1989.
50 Dyson 2006.
51 Stoler 2016; Sabbagh-Khoury 2018.
52 Smith 1997.
53 More recently, "Judeo-Christian values" have acquired an overt political quality, as they were set up in stark opposition to a global, non-Western, other (Soviet atheism, or, later, Islamic fundamentalism; see Silk 1984; Harvey 2016; Nathan and Topolski 2016).
54 E.g. Marks 1982; Krige and Rausch 2012; Parmar 2012.
55 Emberling 2010.
56 Elon 1971.
57 Melman 2020.
58 Silberman 1993; Ben-Yehuda 2007.
59 Greenberg 2021.
60 Hamilakis 2016.
61 cf. Chatterjee 1993.
62 cf. Davis 2000.
63 Tsitselikis 2021: 134–138.
64 Cf. Skopetea 1988.
65 Cf. Davis 2000; Pavli 2014.
66 Pavli 2014, 47.
67 Davis 2000, 2003, 2021.
68 Davis 2003.
69 On Hellenism as a topographic project in modern Greece, see Peckham 2001, and especially Leontis 1995.

70 Winichakul 1994: 17, and *passim*.
71 Hamilakis 2007: 243–286 and *passim*.
72 Ibid., 119–122, for an example of dream archaeology during that war.
73 Described in Greenberg and Keinan 2009.
74 Smith 1997.

CHAPTER 4

Archaeology as Purification

In this chapter, we explore the concept of purity and the processes of purification in their archaeological as well as broader national expressions. The discussion touches on aesthetic and religious conceptions of a pure, sacralized past, on the removal of living people from archaeological landscapes, and on the modernist separation of past from present, science from culture, and of the rational from the affective.

YH: So far, we have explored the origins of the two national projects, and the processes of crypto-colonization that have shaped and continue to shape not only the two archaeological apparatuses, but also the two countries more broadly. As we have already mentioned, archaeological colonization has always been accompanied by concepts of purity, which we discuss in this chapter, and by a racial logic which we discuss in the next. There is an implicit connection between these two themes, but for the sake of our analysis let's keep them separate, to start with.

Now, on the purification theme, we can recall the well-known, extensive national archaeological practices of cleansing, of the removal of layers, buildings or traces that are not seen as appropriate or fitting to the national narrative. Rather, they are seen as matter out of place, to use the definition of pollution attributed to Mary Douglas.[1] Purification can be also linked to other matters and concepts. One, which we already touched upon is to do with the human body, bodily cleanliness and pollution, associated with specific aesthetic–sensorial regimes and hierarchies which may also acquire at times ethical and moral connotations.[2] I think that's an important thread to follow because it also relates to Judeo-Christian traditions about purity and pollution, which are central for us here, not only because of the nature of our case studies, but also because of the role of Judeo-Christian ideologies in the constitution of modernity, as well as the constitution of archaeology as a distinctive apparatus of modernity.

A second thread we may wish to follow relates to the sense of purification as the removal of people from spaces colonized by archaeology and heritage practices; the cleansing of sites from living people, people who are seen as interfering with sites and monuments, who are out of place in these spaces of heritage. We could take this further and discuss archaeological purification as gentrification, a process through which the senses of purity/pollution, morality, and class merge to produce new spaces of modernity.[3]

I know that in Israel, and in debates on Israel and Palestine, there is much discussion about these matters, linked to the broader colonization project, and you yourself are personally involved in opposing processes of cleansing, purification, and gentrification. In relation to this, there is an image that has stuck in my mind: It is from a context you know very well, the neighborhood of Silwan, in Jerusalem. "Expulsion disguised as archaeology" the paper sign reads (Fig. 4.1).

So, would you like to start with some thoughts?

RG: Before I talk about the image you mentioned, from a protest tent in Silwan's al-Bustan (Garden) neighborhood, I'd like to bring in another kind of purification, clearly related to the ones you mentioned, and that is the purification required by "the modern constitution," according to Bruno Latour. In the modern mode, everything must be classified in clear-cut categories – as entirely natural or entirely cultural, as rational or irrational, as fact or as value – and our time entirely separated from what preceded it; he puts it this way: "the moderns have a peculiar propensity for understanding time that passes as if it were really abolishing the past behind it."[4]

YH: Which book is this in?

RG: In *We Have Never Been Modern*, where Latour is preoccupied with restoring the hybrids – human/non-human or, in our case,

Archaeology as Purification

FIGURE 4.1. A protest tent in Silwan's al-Bustan neighborhood. Photo courtesy of Donald Rallis.

past/present – to our view, and in his *Inquiry into Modes of Existence*, where he elaborates on his anthropology of "the Moderns."[5] In terms of archaeology, the modern determination is clear cut as to what is ancient and what is not, what has value and what does not. And this quest for categorical purity ties into the moral, physical, and ritual dimensions that you brought up, and to the modern Western need to put order into chaos, which was part of the burden of the colonizers in the East and certainly in Palestine. I also see a parallel in the archaeological method itself, because its "plan of attack," as they used to call it in the early (and not so early) days – drawing up a grid, trenching, cutting sections – is all about reducing the chaos of the archaeological site into an order that we can control. It's so embedded in archaeological thinking, these acts of purification, of creating distinctions. We talk about "contamination" of layers and "clean contexts." Just think of those semantic fields: "clean," "uncontaminated," "secure," and "ordered," and how they are all bound up in our work. You might say that Douglas's definition of pollution as "matter out of place" is redefined in archaeology as "matter out of time," and carries with it more than a vestige of concern for ritual purity.[6]

Getting back to the image from Silwan, it appears to be quite straightforward, but it in fact references several dimensions of "purity" and of archaeology's entanglement with that concept. At one level, it is a case of gentrification that could occur anywhere in the world: The makeshift houses of al-Bustan neighborhood have risen, unplanned, on the previous garden plots of Silwan village in the valley beneath the Temple Mount (Haram al-Sharif), and the municipality wishes to resort to legal sanctions and have the houses removed, restoring the valley to its previous state. Archaeology is invoked, since al-Bustan is reputed to be the site of the biblical Kings' Gardens and the municipality intends to incorporate it in the Jerusalem archaeological park, one of the city's main tourist attractions. "Cleaning up" the al-Bustan shantytown is thus presented as a question of aesthetics. At another level, however, it is an issue of expropriation and appropriation: Silwanis had been tending the garden plots of al-Bustan for centuries when, in the wake of the Oslo accords in the 1990s and the later al-Aqsa uprising in the early 2000s, dire overcrowding and the construction of barriers around Palestinian Jerusalem forced them to build new, unlicensed homes in the valley (there is no approved development plan for Silwan, and its inhabitants are rarely permitted to build, in contrast to the Jewish settlers there). Now their right to both house and land are being literally undermined by an archaeological claim: The 10th century BCE trumps the 21st century CE. Thus, not only are their homes to be demolished, but their plots are to be expropriated for the benefit of tourists and "restored" to their ancient, pre-Palestinian, state. There is yet a third dimension of purification, and that concerns the waters that flow into the valley. As the standard, sanitized, and mythologized accounts would have it, al-Bustan has always thrived on the overflow of Jerusalem's main source of spring-water, the cool clear-running spring of Gihon (also called the Waters of Siloam, Ain Silwan, and additional names). But it is in fact common knowledge that these waters are augmented by sewage disposal systems that have, since quite ancient times, deposited the wastewater of the Old City of Jerusalem in the same valley. A running joke that I heard in Silwan is that, when urban Jerusalemites used to taunt Silwani vegetable vendors for living in their sewage, the Silwanis would reply "yes, and you're eating it." This sewage line is constantly intruding – in the form of leaks, blockages, and unfulfilled plans for treatment – upon the idealized scene of the "Kings' Gardens," mixing the "ancient/natural" and "modern/corrupted" water to form a disturbing hybrid that refuses to stay within its prescribed boundaries. In this manner, al-Bustan is a porthole to an entire "poetics of pollution"[7] that has surrounded the archaeological discourse on Jerusalem since its inception.

Indeed, the project of purification began the moment archaeology began. The very first archaeologists would have been saying that they've got to get beneath the layers of Ottoman filth and ignorance to shine the light of science on the ancient remains. The moral connotations of their work would also have been unambiguous to the Western ear: Scientific work bore the same relation to ignorance as the light of day to corruption. It is therefore more than a little ironic that archaeology in Palestine, and specifically in Jerusalem, began with misdirection of the Ottoman authorities: Ostensibly conducting an "ordnance survey" of Jerusalem's water infrastructure, a party of British military engineers produced the first detailed map and survey of Jerusalem's Old City while establishing if there were any antiquities to be seen below ground.[8] It had long been assumed that centuries of conflict had wiped out ancient Jerusalem, leaving little to recover. Once the existence of "underground Jerusalem" had been established, the next stage was to imagine Jerusalem without its modern people and buildings, ridding it of its false veneer in order to understand the true soul of the "Essential City" that I mentioned earlier. The idea that the recent past – the 18th and 19th century – was not only extraneous but also unclean and morally suspect was widespread.

Once the British took over in 1917, they ramped up the modernization-as-purification narrative by doing a couple of things. The first was establishing AD 1700 as the use-by date for the definition of antiquities. Anything earlier than that – a monument, a building, a tomb – is old and has intrinsic value; anything later is new and lacks value. The second was protecting those ancient things by creating an antiquities law, which we have already seen was required by the terms of the mandate, and bringing the antiquities themselves to light, figuratively and literally, by promoting excavation; excavation that was conducted in the open, not in tunnels and half-secretively as in Ottoman times. Large expeditions, bringing in large amounts of money, employed hundreds of laborers to extract the antiquities from the soil, while underscoring the separation between the past and the present and setting off the past as something that is to be examined, analyzed, and protected (and, if necessary, appropriated by the government or museum).

By this time the British had already elaborated the idea of stewardship.[9] They were self-proclaimed, proactive stewards of this past, replacing the "Orientals," whose passive stewardship was perceived as an unintended consequence of their general inaction and decadent culture. The British administrators saw it as their task to get all the communities in Palestine on board, while realizing that they were going against the grain in terms of the local people, who see their countryside, their landscape, their villages, as a continuum, as a past that is constantly worked into the present; for them, the things and the materials of the past are legitimate materials of the present as well, and our current actions grow organically out of what we did in the past.[10] Nadia Abu El-Haj and Albert Glock discuss these matters in their work on *Archaeology and Power in British Mandate Palestine*.[11] They show how the British concept of antiquities gave Jewish scholars a leg up, allowing those who had come from Europe, or had got their education there, to become part of the academic and professional echelons of the Department of Antiquities. This effectively established a baseline for Israeli state archaeology, while leaving the Palestinians – who held a very different conception of the past – under-represented in the Mandate's archaeological administration. A divergence began, which has become very stark, in which archaeology is largely a Jewish project, and considered a threat by many Palestinians. This brings us back to what lies at the heart of the project of purification and can even be said to afflict archaeology at its very source, since it was and still is seen as a way to prioritize certain periods of history and dematerialize the rest, especially those of the contemporary era, in Palestine and across the region.

In Jerusalem, Palestinian lives, homes and places have become ephemeral, something to be seen through or peeled away. Achille Mbembe characterizes the life of those who are marginalized and repressed by liberal democracies as spectral and valueless, incompletely materialized.[12] The archaeological project in Palestine has contributed to this spectralization: Houses built upon ancient sites are candidates for demolition; their inhabitants are policed as trespassers. These are all artifacts of dematerialization, and I do connect it to the longstanding rhetoric of Ottoman and Arab Palestine as an imposition; a veil that has to be moved aside to reveal something more essential beneath it.

YH: There are lots of interesting thoughts here, and I suggest that before we move to Greece, we stay a little longer on Israel and Palestine and go into some depth on a couple of the themes you developed. I would like us to comment on one of the issues we started this chapter with, the religious feelings regarding purity and pollution. You outlined very nicely the modernist conception of purification as ordering chaos, as creating a clean, organized, material, spatial, and social environment. In looking comparatively at various case studies, however, including the ones in Israel, I recognized in the conceptions of purity and pollution in Greece a religious undertone or substratum in operation which, at the same time, incorporated ideas of aesthetic as well as ethical and moral value: Aesthetic because certain ruins were seen as ugly, as eyesores that needed to be removed. They were not seen as aesthetically pleasing, and they were often juxtaposed to the beauty of the antique; but they were also polluting in the moral sense because they are, as you said, filth and dirt that defile and contaminate the pure, moral, and respectable body of the nation. I will elaborate on these themes in relation to Greece below, but I wanted to ask you if Judaic, religious traditions about purity and pollution come into play here, even in an indirect way. In the vein of the Latourian thinking you mentioned earlier, I am implying here a move away from modernist and problematic dichotomies between sacred (pre-modern), and profane (modern), to trace the hybrid conception of official archaeology as a quasi-religious apparatus, which despite its claims, has never been completely modern.

RG: We are skirting deep waters here, given the long history and extensive study of the Jewish attachment and affective relation to the

Holy Land, but I would expect that secular Zionists, who set the tone during the pre-state and early state era, would not have habitually invoked traditional Jewish concepts of pollution and purity. Nonetheless, those conceptions were certainly there in the religious substratum (and we should keep in mind that most secular Zionists were raised in orthodoxy); the land is intrinsically holy, and the gentiles occupying Palestine during the 2000 years of Jewish diaspora and exile have polluted it. Of course, this applies to the ancient Greeks as well: The attempt to introduce their religion, or at least their icons, into the temple precinct in Jerusalem was said to have caused the Hasmonaean revolt as early as the 2nd century BCE. So, there's always been a thread in traditional Judaism of the land being defiled by idolators, that is, pagans and Christians. Muslims would not be in the same category since they are not considered idolators. Islam and Judaism, before the modern politicization of these two religions, would not have been in a state of binary conflict and, in fact, there are many recorded cases, in Palestine and in other Muslim countries such as Morocco,[13] of shared holy places – primarily tombs of saints and prophets. Even if it was not always easy going, there was a similarity in the way the past was integrated into the present in these communities.

This changed as nationalism took over the discourse: Religious sites began to be perceived as national heritage, and what was earlier a secular enterprise began to incorporate religious concepts. If, going back to what you said, there is a sense that part of the Jewish return is recovering the land and restoring its status as a place of destiny, then the *national* element would require it to be an exclusively Jewish destiny, and the *religious* element would add the idea of purification. This created a new dynamic, moving from sharing (though under Muslim hegemony), to contesting, and eventually to replacement. A good example for that would be the pilgrimage to tombs of venerated rabbis or biblical prophets. In earlier times such tombs might have been shared or contested by Jews and Muslims, but after Israeli statehood, when the borders were fortified and large numbers of immigrants and refugees arrived from Jewish communities in which traditional religion was still a way of life, replacement became the rule.[14] There was a need for a new, national–religious sacred geography, or ethnoscape, which has been constantly expanding. In many cases, religious authorities and unauthorized worshippers have taken Muslim and even pagan mausolea and shrines and renamed them or re-consecrated them. All that was needed was some historical thread, a record that a Jewish pilgrim or traveler had seen the tomb of Prophet X or Rabbi Y. This would be matched with a whitewashed tomb or shrine of a sheikh or *wali* (saint), often the only visible and undamaged remains of depopulated Muslim villages, and retroactively justified: "the Muslims took our rabbi's tomb, they turned it into a shrine, and now we're re-consecrating it as a Jewish saint's tomb." It is a melding of nationalism, religion, and the invention of tradition or collective memory, which bears, I think, an interesting relationship to the secular process that uses archaeology for a similar purpose. These are the things that come to mind in relation to ritual notions of purity and pollution.

YH: Another, perhaps minor, but to me very interesting, topic that you mentioned very briefly, is the idea of excavation as tunneling, as burrowing under the ground. This relates to notions of verticality and horizontality, but also visibility and invisibility, the sense of experiencing different worlds, some visible and some invisible, some belonging to the dead and some to the living, some to mortals and some to immortals. I know from your writings and from our discussions that a key strategy for the undermining, literally but also metaphorically, of the physical existence of the Palestinians today in Jerusalem and elsewhere is burrowing under their houses in doing excavations. So, what was all that about? I mean what's happening here with this process, and how does it relate to our themes of purity and pollution?

RG: Yes, as if taking a page out of Calvino's *Invisible Cities*, historic Jerusalem constantly wrestles with its verticality, that is, with the locus of reality and the seat of spiritual power – is it above or beneath the surface? If you take the current surface level as your datum point, virtually anything of significance above that datum is Muslim and Christian – Ottoman, Mamluk, Crusader, Umayyad or Byzantine; everything below that datum is ancient and could very well be Jewish. This relation took on a political dimension under the "Clinton parameters" back in 2000, when the US negotiators offered to divide the most contested parts of Jerusalem vertically, rather than horizontally. The idea of vertical separation was floated for other parts of the country – for example, a proposed bridge to connect Gaza and the West Bank, with the bridge being Palestinian territory and the land beneath it Israeli – and its use as an instrument of domination in occupied territories has been subject to a detailed critique by Eyal Weizman;[15] but in Jerusalem the usual power differential between "top" and "bottom" is reversed. It is, as we have already seen, a very old idea that can be followed back to Wilson and Warren's underground explorations of the 1860s, where you take an architectural mass that you cannot change and go beneath it, to reveal a prior reality that you consider more essential and powerful.[16] Because the odds are stacked against you – everything above ground is highly visible, is often quite beautiful and visually dominant: The golden Dome of the Rock being a case in point – you go underground to create an alternate reality that flies in the face of the physical one. You switch things around by saying that what is visible above ground is a mirage; reality lies beneath it. And you constantly develop and expand this subterranean world, where spaces and structures of different ages and functions are stitched together to create something akin to a theme-park "ride": Imagine a Disneyland ride into "the world of the future"? Here you provide a ride into the world of the past, whose passengers are invited to flow along and suspend their critical faculty: They may know that there's nothing behind the façade, just bedrock or layers of ancient refuse behind the walls of the tunnel, but, as long as they are on that ride they can imagine a different reality, free of unwanted intrusions (Fig. 4.2).

YH: This relates to a wider fascination with the invisible, the hidden, the underground. Archaeologist Julian Thomas, in his book *Archaeology and Modernity*, connects this fascination with Western modernity, including intellectual developments such as Freudian psychoanalysis.[17] But I think it goes beyond it: I have often encountered it in my own ethnographic work among communities living around archaeological sites who would wonder what's underneath the archaeological site being excavated and made visible in front of them; what tunnels and secret passages lie underground, where do

FIGURE 4.2. Sara Netanyahu with American and Israeli officials, political donors, and settlers in an archaeological tunnel beneath Silwan, June 2019. Photo, Haim Zach, Government Press Office.

they lead to, and what riches do they contain. In a recent study,[18] I have claimed, along with others, that there is an economy of hope at play here, a soteriological feeling, an occult economy relying on the notion that what's underneath and hidden will bring about salvation.[19] We know that occult economies are particularly powerful at moments of crisis,[20] and in the recent Greek financial "crisis," such feelings surfaced in connection to the excavations at Amphipolis in northern Greece which we discuss briefly in Chapter 2.

But to return to your points, are these spaces now open to visitors? Are they now heritage spaces for tourists?

RG: Yes, and they are complicated heritage spaces because the jurisdictions are composed of rabbinical jurisdictions and archaeological jurisdictions that meet and bleed into each other. You have rabbis digging as archaeologists and archaeologists using religious language to describe excavations.[21]

YH: So, by implication, if archaeologists are the masters of the underground in these cases of vertical separation of spheres, then from the point of view of the inhabitants, the Muslim, Arab, Palestinian inhabitants of Jerusalem, the archaeologists, in their various personas and guises, are the people who undermine their existence in many ways, not only metaphorically but also physically, in very concrete terms (apologies for the pun).

RG: Yes, archaeologists put a modern face on what is fundamentally a religious and moral claim to priority and superiority, and it goes back to the 19th century. It begins with Charles Wilson and Charles Warren. Wilson, as we mentioned, conducted an archaeological survey under the guise of philanthropic "water relief," while Warren, who had obtained a permit to excavate, nonetheless had to hoodwink the Ottoman officials by beginning to dig in one place and tunneling to another, unauthorized, location.[22] And this was okay. This was gamesmanship. It was permitted because it was just a battle of wills, between the clever Englishman and this slow-moving, ignorant, cold, and uncaring Pasha. Warren had, in his own eyes and those of his sponsors, complete moral justification to excavate by any means possible, and there's a direct line from him to the current excavators. Warren is the patron saint of the "dig we must" archaeologists and of the settlers who run this subterranean theme park, which by now is composed of miles of underground passages and spaces, synagogues, restrooms, exhibit halls, and concrete-lined thoroughfares. It is no accident that these spaces, more than any others in Jerusalem, have been adopted by some of the most militant Islamophobic Jewish and Christian nationalists, including several prominent members of the Trump administration and its evangelical supporters, as the bedrock of the "Judeo-Christian" alliance and as a setting for its apocalyptic vision of the battle between good and evil.[23] Their innate hybridity, the confusion of categories within them, generates strong patriotic emotions and provides an ideal setting for national–religious kitsch.

I see our discussion of purification has taken us to a visceral place where archaeology, nationalism, and primal anxieties about collective physical and moral hygiene meet: Can you see a resonance with the Greek case? And is there a religious dimension at work there as well?

YH: I will start from where you started, about the nature of modernity but also about the stories that the "moderns" tell about

Archaeology as Purification

themselves, the myths they live by. Like you, I am sympathetic to the Latourian idea that we've never been modern. You evoked his sense of purification as a modernist strategy of creating rigid, separate entities and dichotomies such as nature and society, while denying and masking at the same time their hybrid character. This reminds us of the concealing and masking work of the crypto-colonizing process, which we discussed in the previous chapter. But let's remember that Latour comes from Science and Technology Studies, and his writings are fairly weak on the historical specificity of phenomena we call modernity, as well as the political nature of such phenomena; Western modernity has been from the start racial, colonial, and capitalist modernity, something we rarely see being discussed in his work. This passage is an exception:

> Native Americans were not mistaken when they accused the Whites of having forked tongues. By separating the relations of political power from the relations of scientific reasoning while continuing to shore up power with reason and reason with power, the moderns have always had two irons in the fire. They have become invincible.[24]

In our discussion, we have elaborated on the notion of purification, and have explored its historically specific meanings and shades, conjuring up concrete material entities, specific "quasi-objects," to use Latour's term, and providing some depth to the notion of hybrids and hybridity. In a similar mode, I want to slightly elaborate on his famous book title and perhaps modify the dictum: I want to suggest that we have never been uniformly, homogeneously and absolutely modern. Latour says, in a rhetorically hyperbolic manner, that "No one has ever been modern. Modernity has never begun. There has never been a modern world".[25] With this statement, he erases historically situated processes such as colonization, capitalist commodification, and racialization, with their specific ontological and epistemic grounding on progress, hierarchy, and civilization. Despite the talk about asymmetry in his book, these highly asymmetrical processes did not feature much.

If modernity is meant as a temporal break, of course, he is right, and he rehearses the critique of historicism and temporal linearity elaborated upon by previous thinkers such as Bergson and Deleuze,[26] to stay within the French tradition. But my point is that the global, mythological conception of Anthropos as an individuated, omnipotent being, as a *homo autotelus*,[27] and the global process which reshaped the world after the Middle Ages did not develop uniformly in what we call the Western world; nor were they understood in the same way.[28] Coloniality as a logic and colonization as a material process were also active and had serious consequences in Europe, not just in non-European lands. Equally, what he calls hybrids, the proliferation of which Latour connects with modernity, were and are at the basis of indigenous, non- or alter-modern cosmologies, not only in non-European contexts[29] but also closer to "home." As I will discuss below, local, diverse communities in what we call the "European" lands developed ways of living and thinking that rejected the separation between sentient and non-sentient beings, between humans and things, and even between past and present. While colonization, racialization and commoditization shaped the phenomenon we call (Western) modernity, such complex phenomenon did not manage to completely erase alternative, "local" or indigenous cosmologies.

To flesh out these thoughts with reference to Greece, we saw how the constitution of the country was at least partly a process of crypto-colonial archaeologization, employing the vehicle of Western Hellenism. But Western Hellenism was progressively transformed into Indigenous Hellenism. This was a process both from "above," through the work of national historians, for example, who produced a new historical synthesis bridging the gaps in national time, and "from below," through popular beliefs and practices such as the ones merging antiquity and Orthodox Christianity. This new synthesis merged some of the modernist concepts of Western Hellenism with other ideas and practices which can be called indigenous, although the term is imperfect and carries its own problems of essentialism. In this process, Orthodox Christianity, through folk ideas and rituals as well as the Byzantine legacy, fused with Indigenous Hellenism to form Helleno-Christianism, a cornerstone of modern Greek identity.

To make this more specific in terms of purification, the arrival of modernist archaeology of Greece as an official apparatus and a set of ideas and practices embodying Western Hellenism, a colonial-cum-national enterprise, initiated a clash with what I call pre-existing, indigenous archaeologies. The definition of archaeology here is broader than the official, authorized, or professional one, and describes all discourses and practices involving things from another time. These indigenous archaeologies practiced by ordinary people as well as scholars, were in operation long before the arrival of official, authorized archaeology. People were collecting things such as inscriptions, statues, or architectural fragments, often exhibiting them in houses, in mosques, and in churches, following a certain logic about their assumed origins, agency, and power.[30] At the same time, they were telling stories about those things which were collected by travelers and folklorists, stories which were most commonly rendered, by travelers, as tales based on ignorance and superstition, or by Greek *laografi* (folklorists) as local wisdom indicative of national continuity with ancient Greece.[31] They were seen as having literary or folkloristic value but certainly not historical or archaeological worth. They were part of the domain of *laografia* or ethnology, not of archaeology, nor part of its history. I have proposed instead that these are archaeologies with distinctive epistemic value.[32] Furthermore, that they embody distinctive ontologies, recognizing, for example, sentient properties to things from another time, quasi-objects or quasi-subjects.

RG: This is parallel to what I earlier called the integration or continuum of past and present in traditional Palestinian – and indeed Jewish – communities. While we often treat this at the folkloristic level, theorizing about the material remains of the past has deep discursive roots in Islamic, Classical, Biblical, and even Mesopotamian literature. For example, the North African historian Ibn Khaldun, in his *Muqaddimah*, makes several observations on the stature of ancient people, based on the ruined remains of their houses; he also has a prescient take on archaeologists, stating that "many weak-minded persons in cities hope to discover property under the surface of the earth and to make some profit from it ... they try to get their sustenance by (persuading well-to-do people) to send them out to dig and hunt for treasure."[33] There has been very little systemization of the practical and theoretical knowledge of antiquities in Palestinian society, beyond the early ethnographic compilations of Tawfiq Cana'an and his circle.[34] The body of work undertaken by Salah al-Houdalieh and his students at al-Quds University provides an important new stage in this work, covering local traditions and commemorative practice as well as the impact that the commodification of antiquities has had in recent decades, in the form of unlicensed excavation and its accompanying knowledge base and vocabulary.[35] I suspect that a lot of information is buried in archived inspector's reports and in both published and unpublished narrative accounts of excavations and surveys.

YH: I am aware that others would find the description of these practices as "archaeology" problematic. For example, Alain Schnapp would prefer to use the term antiquarianism, perhaps vernacular antiquarianism in this case. Ben Anderson would rather use the term local interpreters to describe the social actors who are engaging in these practices. And my Brown colleague, Felipe Rojas, would rather use the term archaeophilia and archaeophiles.[36] I would insist on the use of the term archaeologies though, for several reasons, some epistemic, some ethical and political. First, because I want to valorize them against the colonial accusations of ignorance, superstition, and irrationality, but also to remove them from the domain of folklore studies; second, because I think that they constitute a rich body of ideas, discourses (often tacit), and practices that can fertilize our understanding and perception of antiquities, rather than a set of peculiar and exotic customs. To deny such a right to an alternative archaeology, would be to reproduce the colonial distinction between the "West" (in its various forms) which possesses science and scholarship, and the "rest" which possess custom, ethnological interest, and folklore. Third, because such valorization would benefit all of us who work within the domain of modernist archaeology; it could hold a mirror in front of us and ask us to question our own assumptions on materiality, time, and history. Fourth, I wish to continue calling them archaeologies because none of the other suggestions seem quite appropriate to me: Antiquarianism is heavily loaded but it also prioritizes knowledge and understanding, at least in the definition of Ben Anderson, who claims that "Antiquarianism is the attempt to understand the past through interaction with objects that exist in the present."[37] The term *local interpreters* equally emphasizes interpretation, whereas many local alternative or indigenous archaeologies are

Archaeology as Purification

much more complex, and go well beyond interpretation, especially when they involve active, often affective, and emotive engagement with and reworking of the material past. And archaeophilia, despite its appeal, sounds somehow pathological to me. As for the term indigenous, I am aware of its difficulties and problematic connotations, given that it is normally used in settler colonial contexts such as US, Canada, or Australia. But my use here (and elsewhere) is deliberate. I wanted to connect our discussion to the global debates on indigeneity but also colonization and decolonization.

RG: So you are suggesting that we cultivate the concept of an archaeology that precedes the modernist ones, and which might challenge or enrich them.

YH: Indeed. But you can see how these indigenous archaeologies clashed with official archaeology. Official archaeologies insisted these things don't belong here, in your garden, or in your house, or in your courtyard, or in your church and mosque but belong to the museum, to be appreciated by the sense of autonomous vision. That's a clash that played out, time and again, in many different instances. And some of these clashes are being actually recorded in travelers' accounts, especially when such "travelers" or antiquarians were implicated in that process of taking things away, either for their own personal gain or for specific institutions they were working for: Major Western museums, university collections, and other museums in the West. So, they would record how these people would actually not consent to them taking these things away and at times put up stiff resistance, which the travelers would explain away as the outcome of ignorance and superstition. The same written accounts would also record local beliefs on the power of these things, on their agency, on their sentient, affective and emotive properties, on what was going to happen if these things were to be removed: Statues who weep, others who guarantee the fertility of your land, inscriptions that can protect your house and your family. There is an alternative ontology of life and matter which emerges from these stories. This clash of archaeologies was both epistemic and ontological. In other words, these material things from another time were integral parts of specific indigenous worlds, livelihoods, cosmologies. They had formed part of the sensorial *assemblages of life* of these people.[38] Purification in this process meant the removal, the extraction of these "ancient" things out of their matrix, out of the sphere of ordinary life, and their transportation into more "appropriate" surroundings, in museums, universities, royal houses, and aristocratic estates. It also meant, for standing, immobile objects, the clearing away of polluting accretions, later additions and modifications. But it also entailed the destruction of these local worlds, of these assemblages of life, since some of their key components were taken away by Western "travelers," as well as national (and perhaps equally "foreign") archaeologists.[39] Indigenous Hellenism thus, took diverse forms and expressions, and it was understood differently by different groups such as official, "modernist" archaeologies, and local communities practicing their own indigenous archaeology from below. Barriers of class and educational status would surface in this contested field.

A theme that emerges in the travelers' accounts of these clashes is not only the more generic dichotomy between purity (linked to ancient art and to Western scholars and connoisseurs) and pollution (linked to modern life and to "ignorant" peasants) but also the encounter of precious ancient things amidst filth in general but also animal dung in particular. This is a trope that deserves closer scrutiny. The association here is not only with pollution, more specifically bodily pollution and its olfactory associations, but also with animality, with the beast. This has been a clash which is not only ontological, epistemic, aesthetic, and sensorial, but also a clash relying on anthropocentrism, on the fundamental incompatibility between animality and humanity, at the center of the Western modernist project.

RG: Is there a discourse of disease as well? Because both the accumulation of rubbish and modern, Roman and even biblical techniques of harnessing water and maintaining its purity are a thread that connects multiple archaeological discourses in Jerusalem, from the earliest 19th-century studies of its rock-carved aqueducts to 21st-century tours of its Roman drain. The purity of the city's drinking water must constantly be defended against the infiltration of waste, with the merging of natural and tainted water in Silwan (and elsewhere, in the rainwater reservoirs in and around the Old City) comprising a conspicuous threat to civilizational advance.

Archaeology as Purification

YH: Yes, absolutely. There is also a discourse about health and disease, and that in fact is seen all the way through to the 20th century, when major processes of purification, of cleansing, or clearing, like the Athenian Agora project which we discussed in Chapter 3, were also couched as health and hygiene projects: The neighborhood to be demolished to make space for the American excavation was seen by archaeologists as full of dirt, unhygienic, as a source of contamination and disease, so close to the Acropolis.[40] So, purification was a sanitation exercise as well as an epistemic, aesthetic, and ideological exercise. Here, it was not the Western antiquarians who were projecting these ideas of pollution and hygiene but the modernist archaeologists, some foreign, some not.

RG: So, this is something to flag, because the sanitation discourse – the hygienic disciplining of the colonized – returns again and again.

YH: Absolutely. To return to the matter of animality and filth for a second, let me cite a couple of passages and discuss them briefly. The first is from the travelogue of the French antiquarian, diplomat and academician Choiseul-Gouffier who would travel to Greece in 1776 and who would write, in 1782, about a Roman sarcophagus which he encountered on the island of Sifnos:

> This tomb is finely executed ... Made perhaps to commemorate a hero, the barbarity of the inhabitants has consigned it to the vilest of uses. All the monuments of Greece experience the same fate: even stables are constructed with the finest remains ... One cannot take a step in this country without coming across masterpieces, remains of what she once possessed and testaments to what she has lost.[41]

Besides being another example of a clash of different archaeologies, the reference to stables in the passage above, and the depiction of a dog next to the sarcophagus in the accompanying image, partake of the theme of animality and animal filth which characterize the modern fate of these ancient works, according to their Western admirers.

The second passage was written in 1878 by Lyssandros Kaftantzoglou, an architect who was one of the protagonists of the demolition of any remaining post-classical buildings and monuments on the Athenian Acropolis. Responding to a criticism for the demolition, in 1875, of the medieval tower of the Propylaia (by the Athens

FIGURE 4.3. A photograph of the Propylaia on the Athenian Acropolis taken by Bonfils (c. 1865–70), showing the medieval tower a few years before its demolition. Felix Bonfils Photographs Collection. Manuscripts Division. Department of Rare Books and Special Collections. Princeton University Library. Reproduced with permission.

Archaeological Society, and paid for by none other than Heinrich Schliemann) a prominent, highly visible landmark in 19th-century Athens (Fig. 4.3), he would write:

> But the badly-built Turkish minaret, once sited on the pediment of the Parthenon, and the barbarian tower, which was used to inappropriately occupy the Propylaia, were unnecessary shameful additions like the droppings of the birds of prey flying over it, and which were left on the venerable Feidian masterpieces as evidence of their pitiful state ...
>
> In such a sacred place, we consider it to be impious and improper to preserve the dark relics of the passing waves of barbarism.[42]

I have discussed this passage elsewhere[43] but in this context I want to emphasize something different: Not only the theme of filth with its sensorial, olfactory associations but also the specter of animality, in this case, birds of prey, a metaphor for Ottoman and Western foreign invaders. The tower of the Propylaia was built, after all, by the Acciaiuoli, an aristocratic family from Florence which ruled at the Duchy of Athens from 1388 until 1458.[44] Interestingly, in the context of Indigenous Hellenism which was formed in the mid to late 19th century, foreign barbaric invaders were no longer only the oriental others, the Ottomans (and before then the Persians), as was the case for the Bavarian classicists who initiated the cleansing in the 1830s,[45] but also the Western occupiers and rulers of Athens who were, after all, Christians but not Orthodox. But the broader point here is the anthropocentrism of this purifying logic, seen both in Western and in Indigenous Hellenism. Consider animality versus humanity, consider barns and stables versus museums and salons, consider the olfactory presence of dung, versus the olfactory neutrality of the museum.

RG: And how does this passion for the cleansing of the past manifest itself nowadays?

YH: It seems that these attitudes are still prevalent among some key players today: In 2020–2021, the world of archaeology, in Greece and internationally, was shaken by a public and increasingly acrimonious debate around the extensive interventions on the Athenian Acropolis, which included cementing over large parts of the space of the main plateau, building a series of terraces, and constructing a monumental staircase leading up to the Propylaia (Fig. 4.4).[46] Among others, these interventions would bury the rock itself and plentiful human traces from diverse moments in time under tons of (at places) reinforced concrete. It turned out this was the materialization of the long-held dream of Manolis Korres, the celebrated architect in charge of the Committee for the Conservation of the Acropolis. He made it clear in various public appearances that he wanted to restore the "correct perception" of the monument as it was in the 5th-century BCE, a view that was also adopted by the Ministry of Culture.[47] He had outlined this vision in a 2002 conference speech, which had, even then, caused serious concerns, recorded in the proceedings. To respond to the concerns, especially about the other phases in the history of the monument, he stated:

FIGURE 4.4. Extreme purification and the revenge of animality: the new, concreted-over Acropolis. Photo, Yannis Hamilakis, 28 March 2021.

Imagine a book written, say, by Dostoyevsky, which has some spider's cobwebs on it that prevent you from reading it, and because of some kind of sentimentality, you attribute greater importance to these cobwebs than to the reading of the masterpiece. This would mean that you are using a cultural-spiritual work in an arbitrary manner. This is what romanticism did once. But these things should not escape us, assuming we possess elementary theoretical thought.[48]

This seemed to be a response to one specific, female commentator, the classical archaeologist Ch. Tsirivakou-Neumann who noted that with this idea we will be getting "a very classicizing impression of the Acropolis." In Korres's reaction, it is clear that he does not see the monument as a multi-cultural and multi-temporal one but rather a masterpiece representing one point in time. Further, in his thought we encounter again the notion of remnants of certain historical periods as filth, as pollution; more pertinently, the specter of animality emerges yet again: Not the droppings of the threatening raptors this time but the filthy and disruptive works of insignificant insects which prevent us from appreciating the masterpieces that are the classical buildings. But there is more: Note the chastising of "sentimentality" and of "romanticism" by a male authority responding to a female colleague; nationalist archaeology and anthropocentrism meet patriarchy and Western "rationality." Nevertheless, Korres does not, of course, propose to paint the Parthenon in bright colors, to bring it closer to its classical original; and it is obvious that we cannot inhabit the bodies of the 5th-century BCE people, so we cannot experience the Acropolis as they did (which was not a homogeneous perception anyway). What this purifying delusion creates is not the Acropolis of the 5th century BCE but the Acropolis of racialized, sanitized modernity, the Acropolis of whiteness. This is the same celebrated author and public intellectual who would reveal his orientalist attitudes in an interview for a popular magazine, saying that "the Parthenon contains a sense of eternity, as happens with the Cheops's Pyramid. Its sight, however, does not hypnotize you as happens with the sight of the pyramid. Instead, it wakes you up, it has a stimulating effect on you."[49]

It is clear though that this is not just about the Acropolis. The iconic monument at the core of Western psyche can be seen as a metonymy or better synecdoche for society in general, in Greece and the West as a whole: A cleansed Acropolis for a cleansed world, without the sentient and non-sentient beings and things that pollute it, without otherness. Was this the nightmare that haunted Freud during his 1904 visit to the site, the nightmare that he attempted to banish through writing, interestingly, in the dark year of 1935?[50]

There is a lot more than can be said in relation to purification: For example, on how in the late 19th century the cleansing of archaeological sites went hand with hand with the cleaning of the Greek language, and the introduction of *katharevoussa* (or the "purifying" form) which aimed at instituting, through education and officialdom, the use of archaic linguistic types, and at removing words and other linguistic forms which were seen as foreign or too vulgar and thus polluting. As with the cleansing of archaeological sites, the cleansing of the language was also seen as another way of becoming modern in the western European sense – archaization and purification as modernization.[51] Equally, as we already saw, the cleansing of the landscape from the indigenous, non-Greek place names, a project that started in the first years of the Greek state and continued throughout its history, is part of the same logic.[52]

RG: Amazing: This all-absorbing and yet hopeless task of purifying the language and the landscape of "foreign" elements consumed huge national energies in Israel and modern Turkey as well. And, to echo your earlier question to me, is there a religious dimension to the pollution associated with foreign intervention?

YH: Well, as we saw in Chapter 2, the Greek War of Independence which led to the foundation of the state was, to a large extent, a religious clash, a revolt of the Christian *millet*, a fight mostly between Christians (of different ethnicities) and Muslims. Ethnically and linguistically diverse people were united by religion against the Muslim other. As we saw, the war was seen as a clash between Christianity and Islam also by some orientalist, philhellenic Westerners, some of whom were fighting with the Christians themselves. This battle was fought on the "Greek" side mostly by deeply religious local people, not the scholars, diplomats, and politicians, several of whom aspired to a secular state guided by the principles of Western humanism and classicism. The Filiki Etaireia, the secret,

Archaeology as Purification

transnational society which was instrumental in propagating the ideas of nationhood in the early 19th century and organizing politically for it,[53] had strong and clear religious references in its oath, its texts, and its symbols, while some of its most prominent founders and leaders were enlightened clergy. More importantly, for hundreds of years a number of soteriological, oracular prophecies were circulating widely among the Christian population of the Hellenic peninsula in oral and written form which gained political currency in the last decades prior to the War of Independence.[54] In them, the fate of Christians was presented as a story of Fall due to past sins, Redemption, and eventual Resurrection, perceived in a teleological manner. This occult political theology was often ambivalent toward the Ottoman Empire but it did provide a powerful vehicle for the reception of national ideas and the creation of a national–religious synthesis. *Epanastasi*, the Greek word for revolution, is very close phonetically and grammatically to *Anastasi*, resurrection, with its Christian connotations. In this vernacular Christianity, you needed to be cleansed and purified of your sins to achieve redemption, so that divine providence can grant you liberation from the Muslim yoke.[55]

Religion thus, both as an organizing imaginary and as a vehicle for prophetic beliefs, was fundamental in the process of nation building and in the foundation of the state, but it became also crucial in the later years. The Church of the new state gained its autonomy from the ecumenical Patriarchate of Constantinople in 1833, which allowed it to align itself more closely with the Greek national project.[56] It also enabled the Church to progressively dominate the national project and the State itself, securing the status of orthodox Christianity as the official and prevailing religion of the state, with immense powers over education, state rituals, human rights, and religious freedoms for other denominations, all the way to the present. The link to the Patriarchate became mostly a matter of tradition and spiritual allegiance, although many Christians would recognize it as their religious center due to the symbolic weight of Byzantine heritage.

RG: Is it is still that way?

YH: Yes, it is still that way, with the exception of some new territories which joined the national body in the 20th century, such as Crete, for example; the Church in these areas is subjected to the authority of the Patriarchate.

RG: And all Greek Orthodox communities, are they considered a diaspora? Does, for example, the Greek Orthodox Church in Chicago, have some relation to Greece as a nation?

YH: They definitely have a relationship to Greece as a nation, since these communities are considered *apodimos ellinismos* (or diasporic Hellenism); the communities there, even when the links to the motherland are tenuous, are seen as important lobbying forces for national issues, but the Churches in these countries are linked directly to the Patriarchate in Constantinople, not to the Church of Greece. It is only in that sense that the Patriarchate is Ecumenical. Given that many/most people in these diasporic communities are citizens of their country of residence, and many of them do not even speak Greek, religion is one of their strongest links with the fatherland. As you can tell, there are close parallels with Israel here, as the political scientist Mavrogordatos has noted: "The Greek situation is perhaps most comparable with that of Israel and the Jewish diaspora. In both cases, religious freedom and state neutrality cannot be addressed simply as an internal question, confined to the borders of the state, and indifferent to coreligionists throughout the world."[57]

Why is all this important for our discussion? Because it is crucial to understand the processes through which modern Greek national imagination gave birth to a Helleno-Christian synthesis. In other words, it was not only classical heritage and Hellenism in its Western or Indigenous versions which shaped such an identity but Orthodox Christianity too. And while Byzantine (mostly religious) monuments came to be valued as heritage fairly late compared to Classical monuments (the Christian Archaeological Society, established to protect such monuments, was founded in 1884, and a decree to establish a state Byzantine museum was issued only in 1914), the Christian component in the Greek national imagination had a long pedigree, and it did not have to wait for such state or official, top-down moves. It was sustained and fertilized by the vernacular Christian, popular messianic beliefs, in circulation for centuries. When the prominent national historian Spyridon Zambelios launched, in 1852, the term *Ellino-Christianikos* (Helleno-Christian) to define the new synthesis in modern Hellenic imagination, he was naming an already established phenomenon, he was not describing an emerging one.[58] At the level of state ideology and national scholarship, such synthesis required various strategic realignments, modifications, and syncretic moves. For example, the fusion of ancient Greek, pagan heritage and modern Christian tradition required an emphasis not on dogmatic principles but on the continuity of geography and place, the sanctity of certain localities for both the ancients and the moderns; under every Christian church, the popular saying goes, there existed an ancient temple.

RG: So Greece too is, in some senses, a Holy Land?

YH: Absolutely! Zambelios, by the way, called, in 1852, Greece "έθνος άγιον" (*ethnos agion*, saintly or holy nation).[59] Greece became, in some senses, a Holy Land not only as a consequence of the sacralization of classical antiquity in national imagination, which was helped by the fact that some of the key landmarks in this imagination are ancient temples, but also because of the merging of antiquity and Orthodox Christianity, especially in the synthetic construction of Indigenous Hellenism. It is also, in many, perhaps more metaphorical ways, a Holy Land and a place of pilgrimage for Western Hellenism.

To return to the issue of purification, what I'm trying to say is that in addition to the themes we already debated and discussed, social and spatial order, pollution, or perceptions of health and hygiene, there is also the polluting/sinful and purifying/redemptive elements in the vernacular/religious substratum. One way of purifying the remnants of classical antiquity beyond the strategies we have already discussed is to make them sacred, to render them holy relics of the ancestors but also (almost) Christian relics at the same time, worthy of veneration due to their double holiness. Zambelios, the prophet of Helleno-Christianism would declare in 1852 that "antiquity's vital juice has not vanished, it's rather subjected to cleansing".[60] Not just its material remnants thus but the classical past overall needed to be purified, remade in other words to suit the present. Sacralization has been a key effect through which antiquities were and are perceived and interacted with in the Hellenic national imagination,[61] although increasingly, within the regime of neoliberal commodification, this sacralized effect causes at times severe tensions – how can you sell the ancestral holy relics, the bodies of the ancestors themselves?

Museums are a good case in point; national pedagogy is one of the key roles of archaeological museums, but it seems that the main didactic method is based on the embodied submission to the sacred space of the museum, and on communion through veneration. Loud speaking, laughing, any signs of joy and exuberance, specific bodily postures, are often seen as highly inappropriate inside archaeological museums, and they are actively discouraged by the guards. This has led commentators to call these spaces, disapprovingly, temples or churches, rather than schools for learning, as they would prefer to see them. The 19th- and early 20th-century museums, with their often neoclassical façades, resembled in form such ancient temples, and even the most recent ones, despite their often innovative architectural and museographic design, have not completely broken out of this sacralized tradition. Even the new Acropolis Museum, with its highly innovative architectural design grounded on the politics of vision, on inter-visibility with the monument, and on mirrors and reflections, evokes a site of pilgrimage and veneration. You slowly ascend to the top (as you would to the "Holy Rock," the Acropolis), to the most sacred and precious exhibit, the Parthenon marbles, a pilgrim who comes to pay respect to the most famous of the ancient Greek temples, not a visitor who comes to learn something about the diverse and multi-temporal lives of this world-famous locality.[62] The whole Western world, of course, venerates the classical moment of this site, you only need to look at the logo of UNESCO, yet veneration inside this museum relies on the power of place, and on the direct visual contact with the monument itself. This applies to all visitors, but it is more potent and affectively powerful for the Greek national subjects who not only commune with and venerate the ancestors in a modern monument which has gained international prominence and earned wide praise for this design, but who also partake, through their presence there, of the national campaign for the return of the Parthenon marbles. Veneration here gains the additional efficacy of a political ritual, the emotional weight of national crusade to bring home not the feats of the ancestors, but the ancestors themselves, not as objects but as national subjects, as members of the national body who were abducted by Elgin, were exiled in London, and had to suffer imprisonment in the British Museum for 200 years.[63] This affect co-exists, however, with the increasingly intense commodification of museums and archaeological sites, causing at times strong reactions from certain members of the national body.

RG: A few things sprung to mind as you spoke. There are certainly differences: The concept of the museum – and especially the museum of antiquities – as being a formal and sacred space is not particularly marked in Israel. Despite the interest in some elite circles, archaeology never really became that significant in popular culture or in the educational system. Archaeology was never a formal part of the school curriculum, other than anecdotally. I would say that it was less integrated into the fabric of the state. Even the Shrine of the Book in Jerusalem, sacralized by its very name,[64] is not a state institution, and it often seems to me that the shrine and the Dead Sea scrolls that are exhibited in it have a more prominent role in Israel's foreign policy and its TripAdvisor rating than in Israeli culture. But I was very intrigued by the parallel ties between State and Church in Greece, and the State and Rabbinate in Israel. In Israel, these ties contribute to increasing sacralization of antiquities. It's evolving and difficult to nail down, but it's becoming, at least in Jerusalem, more pronounced. Earlier, I spoke of the tunnels near the western wall of the Temple Mount, where religious and archaeological jurisdictions have become entangled. Another thing that comes to mind is the proclivity among a certain segment of professional and amateur archaeologists to seek out ritual purification baths (*mikva'ot*), considered a hallmark of Jewish presence during the later centuries of the Second Commonwealth (the Judean kingdoms of the 2nd and 1st century BCE and the 1st century CE). You have many installations in towns and across the countryside that are identified as ritual baths, and it's quite popular to point them out because they are supposed to register the presence of pious Jews who were anxious to maintain ritual purity. This enthusiasm has led to misidentifications (in one case that I am familiar with, an elaborate winepress – nearly identical to one that I had excavated in the Rogem Ganim community project – was touted in the media as a *mikveh*), but it is much more pronounced now than it would have been twenty or thirty years ago. So, that's a case of literal purification, and I think it connects to your question from a few minutes ago about religious conceptions of purity. There they are, insinuating themselves into the discourse.

YH: An interesting issue we may want to discuss briefly is what happens to spaces that were created by an Other, a national Other or religious Other, and are continuously inhabited and transformed as sacred spaces of the national Self. And that's pretty common in Greece for some monuments, primarily mosques that have become churches. In many cases, buildings built as mosques are used primarily today as heritage spaces, either as monuments open to visitors which may also house cultural activities or as spaces for the archaeological service to house museum collections or store antiquities. But there are a few cases where the building built as a mosque has become a church. So, in that case the ideas of pollution and purification become more complicated. It's a process of material appropriation which poses its own problems; it may lead, for example, to what Yael Navaro-Yashin has called *material melancholia*,[65] the recognition that one occupies, perhaps illegitimately, a space that belonged to the Other, and as such it embodies a sense of loss, the loss of the purity of the Self. There are strategies to avoid such material melancholia, however. Very often, one strategy is to claim that the building in question may have been built as a mosque but, in fact, it was built on a spot where a church used to be, the claim here being that the locality itself, the earth, was sacred to start with, it was polluted with the building of the mosque, and it was now re-sacralized with the change of use of the building from mosque to a Christian church. Such claims may or may not have a factual basis.[66]

Another strategy, less discursive and more material, is to erase all the visible and tangible reminders of the Other. For example, it was very common for the mosque towers, the minarets, to be demolished while maintaining and reusing the main building. The minarets are the most visible and imposing features of a mosque complex, but they are also the ones that are linked directly to the broader auditory–sensorial as well as community and religious impact of the buildings: These are the towers from which the muezzin issues the call to prayer, creating a sonorous landscape, a zone of inclusion, participation, and command. The demolition of the minarets dismantles such a field of religious sensoriality while its replacement by the bell tower creates a new sensorial–religious field. At the same time, this demolition and new building activity act as a purification process, reminiscent of the Byzantine practice of *sphragis*, of carving a cross onto an ancient, pagan relief and embedding it into the fabric of a Christian church.[67] There were of course, other less visually impressive modifications in both the exterior and the interior of these buildings. Ironically, the first parliament of the new Greek state was housed in a mosque, in the city of Nafplio, in 1825. The building was modified of course: Its domes were covered, the walls were plastered over inside and outside, and they were whitewashed with two layers of lime.[68] Such strategies of cultural appropriation and purification were also practiced by the Ottomans, involving churches which were turned into mosques in conquered lands, and this approach intensified following the exchange of populations between Greece and Turkey after the 1923 Lausanne Treaty.

RG: In Palestine and Israel, this re-sacralization of heritage or ritual spaces – like the saints' tombs I mentioned earlier – converges with a more totalizing project of replacement, the re-naming of places, which began as a scholarly project before it became one of conquest and settlement. When Robinson and Smith began their "Biblical Researches" in the 1830s, they started a process of appropriation based on biblical and colonial concepts, according to which attaining a thorough knowledge of a land is the means of acquiring a moral or divine right to it. This can be illustrated by two notorious statements, the one by Raymond de Verninac Saint Maur, who stated that "Antiquity is a land that belongs by natural right to those who cultivate it in order to harvest its fruits,"[69] and the other by William Thomson, the Archbishop of York, at the 1865 inauguration of the Palestine Exploration Fund: "This country of Palestine belongs to *you* and *me*, it is essentially ours ... We mean to walk through Palestine in the length and in the breadth of it, because that land has been given unto us."[70]

In the process of creating their biblical geography of Palestine, they relegated the local Arab communities to unknowing "stewards" of the past: Just as their lifestyles preserved those of antiquity, their place-names performed the service of preserving the names of antiquity. I think the line between these 19th-century concepts and the creation of the Hebrew map by the newborn state of Israel, which has been described vividly by Meron Benvenisti,[71] is a direct one, as is the line between defining the role of the Palestinian Arabs as place-holders and Ben-Gurion's statement to the committee charged with replacing Arabic place-names: "Just as we do not recognize the Arabs' political proprietorship of the land, so also do we not recognize their spiritual proprietorship and their names."[72]

Even nowadays, among West Bank settlers, it is common to hear, where a site is identified with another religion, whether as a church or a mosque – "Oh, there must be a synagogue beneath it."

Notes

1 Douglas 1966.
2 Cf. Hamilakis 2013b.
3 Cf. Herzfeld 2006.
4 Latour 1993: 68.
5 Latour 1993; 2013.
6 Hamman (2008) uses this term to describe ritually and culturally "untimely" objects as expressions of "chronological pollution" in pre-colonial and early colonial Mesoamerica and Iberia; the tenets of archaeological stratigraphy, prescribed and formalized in excavation manuals and algorithms, certainly seem to retain a strong sense of pollution anxiety! Cf. Beverley Butler's (2020) retrospective description of Kathleen Kenyon's excavations at Jericho as the scene of a ritual drama, replete with acts of possession and dreams of redemption.
7 Anderson 1995.
8 Wilson 1871; the tactics of misdirection continued for nearly the entire duration of British archaeological activity in Ottoman Palestine.
9 Melman 2020.
10 Halevy 2018.
11 Glock 1994; Abu El-Haj 2002.
12 Mbembe 2019.
13 Bar 2018; Levy 2003.
14 Bar 2008; 2018.
15 Weizman 2002.
16 Greenberg 2018.
17 Thomas 2004.

18 Hamilakis 2016.
19 See also Charles Stewart's ethnography of dreaming as a history-making process and a way of relating to things hidden underground, the discovery of which may bring salvation (2017); on the dialectics of concealment and revelation in Greece, see Sutton 2014.
20 Cf. Comaroff and Comaroff 1999.
21 Mizrachi 2017.
22 Warren 1871: 38.
23 Greenberg 2021.
24 Latour 1993: 38.
25 Latour 1993: 47.
26 Bergson 1991; Deleuze 1991.
27 Buck-Morss 1992.
28 Cf. Chakrabarty 2000.
29 Cf. Todd 2016.
30 Cf. Hamilakis 2011b.
31 Cf. Herzfeld 2020.
32 Ibid., n. 27.
33 Ibn Khaldun, *Muqaddimah* V, 4.
34 Tamari 2009.
35 E.g., Al-Houdalieh 2010, 2012a, b.
36 Schnapp 1996; Anderson 2015; Rojas 2019.
37 Anderson 2015, 186.
38 Cf. Hamilakis 2017.
39 For a related argument, see Azoulay 2019.
40 Hamilakis 2013a.
41 Choiseul-Gouffier 1782: 13; cited and translated by B. Anderson 2015: 450.
42 Schliemann 1878: 302.
43 Hamilakis 2007: 92–93.
44 Tanoulas 1997: 139.
45 Klenze, for example, was in favour of preserving some mediaeval buildings on account of their picturesque value, including this tower (Papageorgiou-Venetas 2001: 64; Tsiomis 2021).
46 See Smith 2021, Hamilakis 2021.
47 See for example, Sotiris 2021.
48 Korres 2002: 434.
49 Archimandritis 2019: 220.
50 This is what Papagiannopoulos seems to suggest, in his perceptive essay (2019). Freud's text is titled, *A Disturbance of Memory on the Acropolis*.
51 Cf. Mackridge 2010.
52 Cf. Dimitropoulos 2020.
53 Cf. Yakovaki 2014.
54 Hatzopoulos 2011.

55 Cf. Theotokas 1992, 2021.
56 Cf. Kitromilides 1989; Matalas 2002.
57 Mavrogordatos 2003: 112.
58 On Zambelios and his ideas see Svoronos 1992, and more recently, and from a critical point of view, Vallianos 2018.
59 Zambelios 1852: 296.
60 Ibid.
61 Hamilakis and Yalouri 1999.
62 Hamilakis 2011c; Plantzos 2011; on the conflict around the construction of this museum, see Fouseki 2006; Gazi 2021.
63 Cf. Hamilakis 2007.
64 Roitman 2001.
65 Navaro-Yashin 2009.
66 Scholars of the politics of the past may recognize here echoes of the heated debates around the destruction of the Babri Masjid mosque in India, and the deadly violence that accompanied it. The literature is extensive but for a recent, comprehensive discussion see Avikunthak 2021.
67 See Kiilerich 2006 for a discussion of this practice in the church of the Little Metropolis in Athens.
68 Amygdalou and Kolovos 2021: 95.
69 Cited in Bahrani et al. 2011: 16.
70 Cited in Bar Yosef 2005: 7–8.
71 Benvenisti 2000.
72 Cited in Benvenisti 2000: 14.

CHAPTER 5

Whitening Greece and Israel
Nation, Race, and Archaeogenetics

We explore the inherently racialized premises of colonial–national modernity and of imperial and national archaeologies, juxtaposing them with the contradictions and fluidity inherent in "Greek" and "Israeli" identities. This is followed by a brief critique of the reductionist, and often self-serving, roll-out of ancient DNA studies and of their political cooptation.

YH: As we have stated from the start, one of the aims of our dialog is to foreground issues and themes that have eluded the discussion on archaeology and the nationalization of societies, due to epistemic as well as political reasons. Some of these issues had to wait for the right historical moment: Race is a case in point. As we write these lines, in the midst of the global uprising spearheaded by the Black Lives Matter Movement in the USA, it seems that it is timely and appropriate to explore the links between nationhood and race in the two national contexts, both historically and historiographically. We need to probe the more traditional understandings of race as developed in the 19th and the 20th century, as well as contemporary attempts to return to a biological discourse on individual and social identity – exemplified by the current flourishing of archaeogenetics – that are reminiscent of the earlier racial paradigm. Would you like to start?

RG: The intersections of race, ethnicity, religion, and class in Israel are challenging to unravel, but, insofar as archaeology and its relation to colonialism and nationalism are concerned, I would like to focus on the duality of Jewish and Israeli self-identification as European or, effectively, as White, and at the same time as "Middle Eastern" or "Levantine" in origin, and on how archaeology is used to advance these seemingly contradictory aims. We have already spoken about the wish secular European Jews had to escape the racially stereotyped Jewish body, and we know quite well that, in places like the United States, Jews (including expat Israelis of varying ethnicity) have acquired whiteness; that is, they have – for the most part and often, it seems, conditionally[1] – become racially accepted into the White community by learning the ways of the White middle class (that is, by "Americanization") and by self-identifying as White – something that wasn't a foregone conclusion in the 1880s and 1890s, when the huge immigration of mostly impoverished Yiddish-speaking Jews from Eastern Europe began.[2] In fact, as I have recently discovered while reading diaries written by my grandparents, who each spent several months in 1920s Palestine in preparation for their roles in public Jewish–American life, Zionism served as a model of Jewish regeneration and authenticity even for those never intending to colonize Palestine, offering them a secure foothold in American middle-class modernity without requiring them to relinquish their religious tradition or their diasporic relation to the homeland.

In Israel itself, however, the issue of European or White self-identification is fraught, not least because there are many Jews of Asian and African origin – naturalized citizens under Israel's Law of Return – who have suffered a similar kind of discrimination at the hands of Jews of European descent as do people of color in Europe and America, and because these are only the top rungs of a discriminatory ladder that creates effective ethnic and class divisions between and within Jewish and Arab communities (divisions that are implicitly, rather than explicitly, racialized).[3] Now we have already discussed, and I think agreed upon, the integration of archaeology in the construction of Greece and Israel as crypto-colonies, as buffer-states between the Judeo-Christian West and the Islamic East. We have also defined the modern archaeological gaze as a historically and culturally determined way of seeing, measuring, and valuing the landscape while defining local people as a cultural and racial Other. I would suggest that this is so deeply ingrained as to equate the practice and high cultural valuation of archaeology with being modern (that is, "secular") and culturally European. It is this principle that is so often invoked by political figures, like former Prime Minister Netanyahu, of accentuating the European affinity of Israel, setting up modernity and the "Judeo-Christian ethic" as the bases of that affinity. But if that is the case, where does that leave the majority of Israelis, who are of Middle Eastern and African origin, and what does it do to the claim of Jewish indigeneity in Palestine?

For 19th and early 20th century colonial explorers, the racial inferiority of natives of the Ottoman Levant was self-evident: In a memoir published in 1889, Claude Conder, the leader of the Palestine Exploration Fund's Survey of Palestine, writes at length on the racial origins of the inhabitants of Palestine, including recommendations for scientific research: "If peasants are to be asked to have their heads measured, we must know something of their genealogies also. If skulls are to be collected, we must find out what skulls they are."[4] W. M. F. Petrie, an enthusiastic promoter of eugenics in Britain, writes in his manual of archaeology: "The Egyptian is good at steady work, but the Syrian is very different ... In Greece ... rational regular hard work cannot be reckoned upon ...,"[5] and subsequently expands on the physical and mental characteristics of potential laborers, in language that sounds not much different from that used in slave markets. The same attitude is painfully evident in the 1936 Oriental Institute documentary film *The Human Adventure*, where, in almost every locus of American archaeological activity in the Near East, but especially in Palestine, local laborers are characterized as ethnological "specimens," infantile, undisciplined, ignorant, and ruled by their passions. As an aside, both the "ethnological" gaze and Petrie's eugenicist aspiration to populate his excavation with classes of laborers temperamentally suited to their place in the workforce have had a long afterlife in archaeology.[6] Excavation camps might be described as heterotopias, or zones of exclusion writ small, where the workforce is characterized in terms – usually gendered and often racialized – of their "natural" fitness for various types of archaeological work. Thus, in Yadin's popular 1975 illustrated volume on the Hazor excavations of 1955–1958, recent immigrants from North Africa – men and women recruited as laborers from a nearby "development" town – are presented either as exotic human "types" of another time, or as naturally suited to perform domestic labor in a Bronze Age kitchen (Fig. 5.1). And in contract excavations, even to this day, laborers on consignment from the employment service (often in work-for-welfare schemes) are regularly stereotyped by ethnicity and gender as fit for certain types of tasks.

YH: How was that essentializing, racialized discourse deployed in the construction of Israel, internally, and especially in relation to Palestinians?

RG: That's where it becomes complicated: Israelis and their Zionist precursors could not adopt this supremacist posture in its entirety, not only because it had been used against Jews in Europe, defining them as Semitic outsiders, but because the chief selling-point of fulfilling Zionism in Palestine, and not elsewhere on the globe, was the claim to indigeneity: The Jews were a diaspora whose authentic, never-abandoned homeland was in Palestine. Outlandish

FIGURE 5.1. Photograph from Yadin's popular book on the excavations at Hazor, with the caption "A girl from North Africa felt 'at home' operating the two grinding stones, which are over 3,000 years old." Yadin 1975: 34, reproduced with permission.

as it may sound in the 21st century, Jews were widely viewed in 19th-century Europe as a distinctively inferior physical type, akin to black Africans. By mid-century, writes Sander Gilman,

> being black, being Jewish, being diseased, and being ugly come to be inexorably linked. All races, according to the ethnology of the day, were described in terms of aesthetics, as either "ugly" or "beautiful." ... And being ugly ... was not merely a matter of aesthetics but was a clear sign of pathology, of disease. Being black was not beautiful. Indeed, the blackness of the African, like the blackness of the Jew, was believed to mark a pathological change in the skin, the result of syphilis. (And, as we shall see, syphilis was given the responsibility for the form of the nose.) One bore the signs of one's diseased status on one's anatomy, and by extension, in one's psyche. And all of these signs pointed to the Jew's being a member of the "ugly" races of mankind, rather than the "beautiful" races.[7]

Jews were considered to possess a peculiar way of speaking and devious use of language that could not be overcome, a peculiar gait that symbolized physical degeneracy, a pathological gaze that indicated psychological trauma, and they were widely associated with sexual deviancy. There was no escape from Jewish moral and physical inferiority: Conversion or assimilation were inadequate, and even medical interventions – modern cosmetic surgery was invented in 1898 by Jewish physicians as a way to rectify the "Jewish nose" – could not overcome the fear of being outed as Jewish. The only antidote to the hopeless task of "passing" for European would therefore be the attaining of true indigeneity in the historic homeland of Palestine.

But in practice, how would a recently arrived colonist "become indigenous" in Palestine, and how quickly could this be accomplished? One route was by the mere fact of being born in Palestine: This was sufficient to be dubbed "native-born" (a conceit shared by other settler-colonial collectives; Zreik 2016). Another route, which complemented and fortified the first, was by showing that the Jewish settler collective (as a nation) was originally of the land, that its absence was temporary, that its return is natural, and, finally, that the Palestinian Arab claim to indigeneity is weak or fabricated. In this manner, the new Hebrew collective could be imagined as of the land, yet – and this cannot be stressed too strongly – distinct from the deficient "Levantine" or "Oriental" Other.

Archaeology was recruited to support the concept of Jewish indigeneity in direct and in symbolic ways. The direct use – which Israeli archaeologists, in their professional persona, tend to deny or disown – was based on selective citation of finds (and, recently, of ancient DNA, which we will get to later) to both show Jewish continuity in the land and imply that the current non-Jewish inhabitants are latecomers to it. In the study on Israel Exploration Society meetings that I mentioned earlier, Michael Feige showed that while politicians used the meetings as a platform for orations that recruited archaeology to support the myth of direct continuity between the ancient past and the present, the scholars in those same meetings usually confined themselves to highly technical papers, often incomprehensible to any but the most devoted amateurs in the audience. Yet, even as they were engaged in a sort of small-bore archaeology, the very context of their participation and the fact that the debate remained an all-Jewish one, fulfilled the overtly political aims outlined by the political and military leaders.[8]

The indirect or symbolic exploitation of archaeology for the indigeneity project was through its very practice: The knowledge, field skills, physical exertion, and ability to interpret what one found depended on the quality of being not only in the land but of it. This was a combination of the colonialist precept that detailed knowledge is nine parts of possession, with an ambition to emulate and even surpass native practical knowhow and survival skills.[9] Seasoned archaeologists will be, on the one hand, representatives of modern European and Western values – archaeology being one of those modern values – and on the other, weathered and authentic locals (at least to Western eyes, accustomed to the orientalizing pastiche of explorers "going native"), trekking the desert, gathering herbs by the wayside or baking their own flatbread. In recent decades, with the disappearance of traditional Palestinian lifeways, with the advance of technology, and with the advance of consumer capitalism, the performative aspects of indigeneity in archaeology have receded, but not disappeared.

These racialized aspects of archaeology obviously touch on unresolved anxieties surrounding national, religious and cultural identity.[10] Insofar as Israel aligns itself with Europe and the West, there's the anxiety of being outsiders in the Middle East and of creating rifts within Israeli society, much of which is barred from adopting or disinclined to accept a European identity – whether on religious, cultural or racial grounds. Insofar as indigeneity is claimed, the prospect of "Levantine" self-identification can provoke anxiety over the fate of Israel's affinity to Europe, to modern nationalism, and to diasporic Jewish communities in the West. As Israelis move away from the western European model of secular nationalism and toward a religious nationalism, archaeology is either sidelined (in favor of more easily manipulated heritage practices) or asked to contribute overtly to the cause, by providing proof of Jewish priority and exceptionalism in Palestine (*Make us indigenous, but like no others; prove that we were here first, but scientifically!*). I think that an important part of squaring the circle, of making Israel both indigenous and European, is through the trope of Judeo-Christianity, which makes the Jews in Israel constituents of Europe while relegating the Palestinians to the status of intruders. This certainly resonates with European anxieties over Muslim migration, while successfully obscuring the intermingling of people and ideas that always existed between Islamic, Christian, and Jewish worlds.

In regard to this final point, which merits a much broader discussion, I would just like to mention briefly that new investigations of pre-Great War Zionism and Palestinian nationalism point to a broad range of "potential histories" for these movements and for Palestine itself. An "alternative Zionism" could have, for example, melded the Jewish quest for indigeneity and racial dignity with non-binary conceptions of Jewish–Islamic and even Jewish–Christian relations, in the spirit of mediating Jewish–Arab figures such as Shimon Moyal and Nissim Malul.[11] I think it would be most instructive to imagine a non-imperial, non-national pan-Levantine or pan-Mediterranean archaeology that might have emerged from such forms of interaction.

YH: Your points remind me of the debates on the definition of Greek citizenship which are, in fact, mostly debates on who has the right to be a member of the national body. Already in the first year of the War of Independence there was a need to "make Greeks," and the definition which was adopted relied on territory and religion: Greeks were the inhabitants of Greece who were Orthodox Christians. Greece was, of course, still an imaginary entity, an evocation of the ancient Hellas, mapped onto the territory of the southern Balkan peninsula, an imaginary topography that was made real through the remnants of classical antiquity. Autochthony, that is proof that you come from the area, was soon added to the criteria, to deal with the diverse origin of people who were involved in the national struggle, and rules for naturalization were also adopted for non-local inhabitants. But Orthodoxy seemed to be the most important feature. This, relative inclusive, definition did not last long, as since at least 1827 and more formally since 1844, *jure sanguinis*, or the law of the blood, became the primary criterion: You had to be born to Greek parents to be recognized as Greek. Only very recently, in the last five years or so, have substantive legal reforms allowed the right of citizenship to second generation migrants.[12]

I am thinking as you speak, that both Greece and Israel have been constructed and are often thought of, by others and by themselves, as borderlands, and their people as people of the border, as Gershom Scholem noted once, for the Jews.[13] They have been often produced by Western colonial discourses as areas lying on the fault-lines of East and West, hence their buffer role. But the border, and the bordering process itself, result in the continuous making and remaking of sameness and otherness, and often in the racialization of difference. Since 2015, with the so-called "refugee or migration crisis," Greece has become again a major borderland, resulting in a spectacular process of othering and racialization, which we can discuss further in the next chapter. But the discourse and the practices of race are not new in the political and social history of the country. Their spectral presence has been there all along. As with the case of crypto-colonialism, however, there has been a reluctance to discuss them openly, and only recently has such a discussion been initiated, partly because of the rise of parties that advanced explicitly racialized policies such as the neo-Nazi Golden Dawn.

Race has been seen as a category that is not relevant to the case of Greece, and whiteness has been treated as a self-evident, essentialist attribute of the country, since ancient times. In some ways, this is a deliberate attempt to avoid a thorny and very difficult issue. Only in Greek diasporic, multi-racial contexts has whiteness become a matter of public negotiation and debate, and recently, also a matter of academic exploration.[14] The discussion about race in Greece is being displaced into discussions about geopolitics, for example (whether Greece is East or West), or it is contained within and masked by other analytical categories, including ethnicity and religion. The increasing visibility of recent migrant communities in Greece and the impact of global movements that challenge white supremacy, as well as the echoes of theoretical, intellectual discussions on the construction of blackness and whiteness, have forced the issue into the foreground. The second-generation migrants of African descent, for example, have recently claimed their stake in the public arena and have projected the identity of the Afro-Greek as one of the constituent parts of the Neo-Hellenic. The global celebrity status of the NBA player Giannis Ugo Antetokounmpo, born in Greece to Nigerian parents, has done much to help their cause: "The most famous Greek today is black," some note with amazement.

Yet, we tend to forget that African communities existed in Greece in the past, not only in ancient times but even as recently as the late 19th and the early 20th century CE, partly due to the population movements in the Ottoman Empire. The Muslims among them were serving the empire in various roles, and the non-Muslims were brought in as slaves. Popular memory, as well as academic study, speak even today, often in exoticist language, of the black communities in Crete, some of whom were brought in as slaves in Ottoman times, and who, after gaining freedom, established their own neighborhoods and organisations, and some performed their own, African rituals. They were subjected to all sorts of discrimination and persecution by Christian populations and Ottoman authorities alike, and most of them were forced to leave and resettle in Turkey, a country they did not know, following the unification of Crete with Greece and the population exchange of 1923, which happened along religious lines.[15]

Historical references to the African communities of Greece are also becoming more frequent. For example, Kotsonis mentions the sizable populations of Africans in areas in mainland Greece, such as Preveza, Patras, Gastouni, or in Koroni around the slave bazaar, and notes that the memory of their presence is maintained not only in folk tales but also in toponyms such as *Arapohori* (village of the Arap – see below) or *Sklavohori* (slave village).[16] Earlier references by travelers are also telling. The British topographer and military man Leake who traveled in the Peloponnese in the early 19th century, would write of the coastal town of Mothoni/Metheni, and its extensive trade in black slaves from Africa.[17] And the British physician and traveler Henry Holland would pass through the Thessalian city of Larissa at the same time and would be surprised in seeing "the large amount of negro population which was much greater than I have remarked in any other Turkish town."[18] Athens had its own share of black people, emancipated slaves, who used to live around the Acropolis, especially on its north side, coming possibly from Ethiopia. Some black figures are depicted in antiquarians' drawings of Athens, while even today the place name, Abyssinia Square, in this very same area, may echo their presence.[19]

And here is a link to archaeology worth exploring further: Folk tales from 18th- and 19th-century Greece maintained the memory of people of black skin in the figure of Αράπη (*Arapi, Arap* in Turkish), a word that denotes the black person although some sources such as travel accounts would translate it as *Arab or Arabim*.[20] This figure, which embodied both positive and negative attributes, was exoticized as a mysterious, *jinn*-like creature which could act as the guardian or spirit of a house and which often inhabited ancient places or possessed ancient statues. Such a spirit would either express emotional reactions, and lament, for example, the mutilation and loss of statues or would act as a guard for hidden treasures linked to the ancient past. When the antiquarian Dodwell visited Athens, in 1805–1806 he was wandering among the ruins of the temple of Olympian Zeus with his camera obscura when he encountered an old Albanian woman who fearlessly confronted him:

> "You know where the sequins are – but with all your magic you cannot conjure them into your box! For a black watches them all

Nation, Race, and Archaeogenetics

day; and at night jumps from column to column." She then proceeded gravely to assure me that the brick building upon the architrave was the repository of grave treasure and the habitation of a black.[21]

Let me tell you another, related story. In Candia, which is the Venetian name of present-day city of Iraklio in Crete, in today's Kornarou Square, there is a fountain constructed by the Venetian governor of the island, Bembo, in 1552. In that fountain, a headless Roman statue was embedded, you can still see it today. That's not so unusual, a typical example of spolia, you would say. But what comes next is directly connected to my argument: Following the conquest of the city by the Ottomans in 1669, this became the fountain of the nearby Valide mosque, which was previously the catholic church of San Salvatore. At this time, or some time later, it seemed that this statue became the center of attention and a focus for worship among Black/African Muslims, especially women. In the 19th century, Western travelers note that these Muslims believed the statue to be an "Arab" or Ethiopian saint who was mutilated by Christians.[22] They would suspend pieces of rag from it as votive offerings, and would burn a lamp in front of it, a syncretism, it seems, borrowing from Christian practices. But something even more interesting seemed to have been happening, which we have evidence for in the early 20th century: During certain rituals, they would also paint the exposed part of the torso black; they imagined this saint as black-skinned as they were. The custom would survive to be photographed by Giussepe Gerola, the Venetian scholar who came to Crete from 1902 to 1904 to record its Venetian monuments and produce his monumental work (Fig. 5.2).[23] Hasluck, who would write a few years later on local practices involving antiquities, would note:

> The statue is still (1915) as Pashley [a late 19th-century traveler] saw it, except that the flesh parts and lower draperies have been *painted black*, evidently to shew that the saint was an 'Arab': [T]he cult is discontinued, though the lighting of lamps and candles at the place by negro women is still remembered.[24]

Antiquities and ruins here provided the material anchoring for the expression of ethnic diversity and for the production of self-identity

FIGURE 5.2. The Venetian Bembo fountain in Candia (Heraklion) in Crete, with the embedded Roman statue painted black, in a photograph taken in 1900–1902. Gerola 1938/1940, p. 42, fig. 16; reproduced courtesy of the Istituto Veneto di Scienze, Lettere ed Arti.

and otherness, including otherness based on skin color. As in the ethnographic context of Delhi analyzed by Taneja where *jinn* inhabit ruinous palaces, such stories challenge "the magical amnesia of the state" and of the nation.[25]

RG: Palestinian scholars have also written about the prevalence of *jinn*, including many described as black, in natural and manmade caverns, wells, springs, ruins, and so on, according to village lore. They seem to function as shape-shifting portals to worlds that are just beyond our grasp, which makes their role in protecting ancient treasures logical.[26] As in Greece, the presence of sub-Saharan Africans in Ottoman Palestine and in earlier historical periods has received little attention, especially as it raises the specters of slavery and racism within Palestinian society.[27] But beyond this important reinsertion of Africans into the Greek cultural fabric, where else did race and racial anxieties assert themselves in the context of Greek nation-building?

YH: We have already described in this book the transformations that such ethnic and religious diversity underwent with the advent of national ideas; we also spoke of the key role of antiquity and of antiquities, but we also mentioned the crucial role of religion in this process as a key vehicle of nationalism, and even talked of the Greek War of Independence as, in some ways, a religious conflict. But race has been hardly discussed with regards to the Greek War of Independence. Was race also a factor in the War and in the foundation of the new state? And if so, in what ways? Let's recall that the War took place in a globalized world in which slavery, and the question of race, were central, and permeated every facet of society, from economics and politics to art. Most scholars, including myself, have so far explored the Greek national project, at least its early conception in the late 18th and 19th century, as a matter of culture and ethnicity, not race, especially since the biological and physical anthropological connotations of the term, and an overt racial hierarchy, were developed and theorized explicitly several decades later.[28] But if we are to follow Foucault for a moment and think of race as a discursive, biopolitical, and cultural category, and not purely as a biological one, then perhaps the matter is of direct relevance to our discussion here.[29] Foucault, in his posthumously published lectures developed a biopolitical conception of race which is not simply about blood and biological attributes such as physiognomy and skin pigmentation, but also and perhaps mostly about life and death, about whose lives are deemed livable and whose are not, thoughts that were explored further by scholars such as Achille Mbembe, especially in relation to necro-politics.[30]

Furthermore, while most scholarship has treated race and racial thinking as a feature of modernity, recent, thorough accounts have started tracing and reconstructing older histories and contexts where racialized thinking often merges with religious thinking. I have in mind, for example, the work of Geraldine Heng on the invention of race in the middle ages where she emphasizes "multiple locations of race," including "religion, the state, economic interests, colonization, war, and international contests for hegemony."[31] These multiple locations are still generative of racialized modes of thinking and action such as essentialist constructions of sameness and otherness, demonization of difference, hierarchization, and mostly biopolitical and necro-political thinking. She says, for example, with reference to the crusades and Christianity that:

> [I]n holy war, concepts of religious race expediently emerged: Christians were theorized as a *blood race*, linked by the shedding of Christ's blood and by the blood suffering of Christian bodies at the hands of the Islamic foe. That Islamic foe was an infernal race, a race incarnating evil, whose extirpation would be a form of *malicide*.[32]

What happens if we start rethinking the emergence of modern Greek nationhood along similar lines? Many texts and pronouncements prior and during the War of Independence would speak of *φυλή (fili)*, as in *elliniki fili*. *Fili* is translated as race in modern Greek, but at the time it was often used interchangeably with *genos* (which is perhaps closer to the Latin *natio*), and was more likely to refer to the Greek-speaking Christians as an ethno-religious category and as an aspiring nation-to-be. To make matters more complicated, *fili* is also an ancient Greek term to denote tribes or clans. The term *fili* was increasingly used in mainstream, official and popular discourses, to denote the community of the nation, especially from the mid-late 19th century and up until WWII. We see ambiguity and polysemy, as well as semantic slippage here,[33] but also perhaps a discursive ground for the biopolitical and hierarchical as well as exclusionist connotations of race to develop, especially since the War of Independence was an all-out war which glorified sacrificial death, and a war of complete annihilation of the enemy.[34]

Let's see for a moment a couple of key texts, more like "call to arms" for the Greek War of Independence. In his 1797 patriotic poem, *Thourios*, the radical thinker and revolutionary Rigas Feraios, would dream of a free, multi-ethnic and multi-faith Hellas, inspired by both ancient Greece and the French Revolution, while at the same time ask all fighters to take an oath to the Cross and to the Christian faith. He would also encourage "Blacks and Whites [to fight] with a common zeal," a passage that has received scant attention to date, and which denotes both the impact of racial thinking and categorization, as well as a clear awareness of social diversity, in this case based on skin pigmentation.

The other key text, "*Salpisma Polemistirion*" ("War Trumpeting"), was written by Adamantios Korais, the most prominent Greek intellectual of the phenomenon called "Greek Enlightenment." It was published in 1801, twenty years before the outbreak of the War of Independence, and in it, things become even more interesting. The text is not simply a call to arms, based again on the notion of ancient glory, of the resurrected Hellas, and of the descendants who needed to prove worthy of their glorious ancestors. More than that, it called for a nation that needed to embrace not only ancient Greece as its ancestral heritage but also the new global order of Western powers, mostly the French, which were at that very moment marching against the Oriental Others: Korais was explicit in his support for the colonial expedition of Napoleon to Egypt, which he saw as liberation. For him the common enemy was not only the Ottoman administration but the "heartless," the "inhuman race (or nation) of Muslims" (*apanthopon genos ton Mousoulmanon*). "The heartless race of Muslims is used to feed on blood, lying and tossing in blood. Blood and more blood is needed to quench the thirst of Hagarenes, who are wilder than wolves," he would further add, using another common term denoting Muslims. According to him, ancient Greece united Greeks and French who had embraced its heritage and who are now defeating the enemy, "the race of Muslims." This is the moment for Greeks to revolt too, against the common enemy. Korais uses the idiom of biological kinship ("Mother Greece") to talk about ancestry and continuity, an idiom that implies affection and proximity as well as, if mostly in metaphorical terms, a blood relationship.[35] Indeed, as Korais stresses, it is Mother Greece who issues this call, and the one who is illustrated in the front of this pamphlet, not the author himself (Fig. 5.3).[36] Moreover, and perhaps more importantly, it is racialized religion and common Western interests that provide the ground upon which this call to arms is based. The plentiful references to death and to blood-thirsty Muslims allows for a broader, biopolitical–cultural conception of race to be inferred here. When reading such diverse constitutional texts of Greek nationhood, scholars tend mostly to foreground the calls to liberty and egalitarianism (in relation to the rule of law) but turn a blind eye to racialized inferences and to the calls for the complete annihilation of the Muslim Other.[37]

FIGURE 5.3. The front plate from A. Korais's, *Salpisma Polemistirion* (Unknown artist, Paris, 1801). Note the fragmented antiquities and the papyrus with the word OMHPOC (Homer) upon which the human figure, the personification of enslaved Greece, stands.

RG: It's probably worth mentioning that Napoleon Bonaparte has a cherished place in Jewish history, both as an emancipator of Jews in France and the conquered territories and as a purported proto-Zionist, who contemplated enlisting Jewish support for the conquest of Palestine during his campaign in Egypt and the Levant. While his proto-Zionism was probably anecdotal, his offer to accept Jews as part of modern Europe certainly had far-reaching effects on 19th-century Jewish communities, including those in French territories – especially in North Africa. French conquest opened a route to becoming European and distancing oneself from the Muslim environment. But to get back to Greece, do you see a transition, at the start of the 19th century, from a long tradition of Christian–Muslim religious and ethnic enmity to a form of opposition rooted in biological determinism, establishing "whiteness" as inherently superior?

YH: I will get to the transition in a minute. But first, I want to suggest that through the Greek War of Independence, through this nationalization process, and through this constitution of the country as a modern European–Christian kingdom – born as it was out of a fight against oriental backwardness and barbarity, which went all the way back to the Persians – the Greek-speaking Christians who started calling themselves Hellenes and who were joining a fight against "the race of Muslims" secured their place in whiteness as well as Europeanness. Whiteness, in the broadest, cultural sense, and the anxiety over racial battles and racial boundaries were the subtle themes that underscored these developments, and shaped some of the reactions, especially by Western politicians, intellectuals, and artists. Look again at depictions such as the orientalist, philhellenic paintings of Delacroix (on which more below) and notice how "Greeks" and "Turks" were represented, to see it surfacing explicitly – closely entangled with notions of gender and sexuality – as a visual discourse.[38]

Orientalist authors and artists joined in this anti-Muslim, "philhellenic" campaign, fighting not only for the liberation of the Greek-speaking Christians but also for the triumph of Christian Europe and its ideals, however variously conceived. Appeals to help the Greek revolution in the name of Christianity (as well as Greek antiquity and civilization) were common in western European and American press, and bottom-up philhellenic societies would also project the Christian character of their initiative. This was the case of French philhellenic movement which was initially organized around the *Société de la Morale chrétienne* and whose second secretary would declare in 1822 that "[I]f there is a cause in the world more deserving the support of all people who believe in Christianity and justice, that is the cause of the liberation of Greece."[39] From the point of view of western European, philhellenic audiences, the Greek War of Independence can be in some ways seen thus as the most recent chapter of the Crusades, although in this case a key aim was the liberation of the other Holy Land, Classical Hellas, alongside the expansion of Christian Europe.

The "whitening" of the modern nation went hand in hand with the whitening of ancient Greece, carried out by classicists, archaeologists, and other scholars, and both were discursive, scholarly, and artistic, as well as political and biopolitical projects, taking place on a global stage.[40] It rested on a fertile substratum and the notion of the "superiority of Greek art beyond that of other nations," as Winckelmann, the founding figure of classical archaeology, would state in 1764, relying on physiognomy and environmental determinism, among other factors. The well-known, white marble sculpture by Hiram Powers, *The Greek Slave* – various versions of which were executed between 1844 and the 1860s and were reproduced in several media – is an interesting case in this respect (Fig. 5.4). Art historians still consider it the most famous American sculpture of the 19th century, with mass popular appeal. The artist, an American expat living mostly in Florence, wanted this work to be a homage to the Greek War of Independence, but also to connect it to the American Revolution. The reactions and interpretations that this work inspired, however, were many and diverse. First, it is a work of neoclassicism, so the connection to the material culture of Greece, ancient as well as modern, is direct, not only through formal similarities but also through the medium of white marble. The naked, female body in chains may have referenced the capturing and the enslavement of women by the Ottomans following events such as the Massacre at Chios (1822), but the addition of the cross as a sculptural feature at the low pillar and the emphasis on whiteness (denoted by

FIGURE 5.4. View of the exhibition, *Sculpture Victorious: Art in an Age of Invention, 1837–1901* (held at Yale Center for British Art, New Haven, 2014), showing Hiram Powers' *The Greek Slave*, 1847. Note the cross near the top of the low pillar. Photograph by Karl Thomas Moore. CC-BY-SA-4.0

material as well as bodily features) have helped portray modern Greek nationhood as a racialized project and as a crusade of Christendom against the Muslim Other. Moreover, the naked, white marble flesh evoked not only the purity and virginity of the woman but also the sexual violation to come, in the hands of her captors.

In the American context, at a time in which debates on the abolition of slavery were raging, this extremely popular work and its connotations were bound to be widely deployed in many and diverse ways. It was seen as an abolitionist work, bringing to mind especially the fair skin offspring of enslaved black women, victims of sexual violence committed by their owners.[41] But it was also deemed highly hypocritical, as it made no direct reference to black, enslaved people in North America. In the 1851 Crystal Palace exhibition where the sculpture was prominently exhibited, formerly enslaved African Americans and abolitionists marched into the gallery, parading a cartoon from the magazine *Punch*, and even depositing a copy next to the sculpture. The cartoon depicted *The Virginian Slave*, a figure of an African American woman in chains (Fig 5.5). Who is slave and who is not? And how hypocritical of neoclassical artists to forget the most crucial matter of the day, while appropriating a term from the African American struggle![42] Not to mention the fact that the term slavery was appropriated by both Western Philhellenes and Greek-speaking national intellectuals and local elites to talk about the status of Greek-speaking Christians in the Ottoman Empire. While various forms of unfreedom (included forms of slavery) existed in the Ottoman Empire, and while some Christians were enslaved, most Christians were subjects, not slaves. They enjoyed relative autonomy, and their status was far from the brutality of transatlantic slavery.[43]

It is often heard that the Greek War of Independence promoted the cause of black slave abolitionism, and there were certainly people who championed both causes. But what if something very different and very sinister has been happening at the same time? What if some key Western champions of the Greek cause highjacked the abolitionist rhetoric to project a specter of "white slavery," of which the Greek-speaking Christians of the Ottoman Empire were seen as the most prominent example, and the one in need of liberation? In fact, the art historian Darcy Grimaldo Grigsby notes that, especially in

FIGURE 5.5. *The Virginian Slave* by John Tenniel, published in the *Punch* magazine in 1851.

Restoration France, this is exactly what has been taking place. In the aftermath of the victorious Haitian Revolution, even liberal authors and politicians would turn their attention to the "white slavery" in the Mediterranean; they would even juxtapose it to the black slavery of the Caribbean, in the maintenance of which, France had a vested interest.[44] Here is what Chateaubriand, the philhellene, would write in 1816, following the abolition of the slave trade in England, in 1807: "The parliament of England, in abolishing the trade of Blacks, seems to have indicated for our emulation the object of a more beautiful triumph: let us end the slavery of whites."[45] The same author would comment, in his 1825 philhellenic manifesto (*Note sur la Grèce*), the very same year that Haiti declared its independence:

> Bands of enslaved negros, transported from the depths of Africa, hasten to conclude in Athens the work of the black eunuchs of the seraglio. The [enslaved negros] come in their force to knock over ruins, which at least the [black eunuchs], in their impotence, had left standing. Will our century witness hordes of savages suffocate civilization as it is being reborn in the tomb of a people who civilized the earth? Will Christians leave the Turks to slaughter, with no obstruction, Christians?[46]

The context here is the arrival of Ibrahim Pasha, leader of the Egyptian forces who landed in the Peloponnese in early 1825 to help the Ottoman army. But note the reference to Athens and to ruins, meaning classical ruins, as well as the references to Christian solidarity and to "black eunuchs," merging coloniality, racism, religion, and gender. In the same year, and for the same cause, he would publish a press editorial noting:

> We let Greece perish at our door, recognizing the sovereignty of the Great Turk in Morea, abandoning our [sovereignty] in Saint-Domingue for negro despotism under [the Egyptian leader] Ibrahim [Pasha]; for negro liberalism under [Haitian President] Boyer. Who knows if we will see one day, under the standard of the crescent and the liberty cap, African legions bringing to us from one side the Koran, and from the other, the Rights of Man.[47]

Here, it becomes clear that the anxiety is not about Greece per se, but about France, about the core of Europe, about whiteness, echoing our earlier discussion about Greece as a buffer country.[48] It is also an anxiety about "negros" appropriating European concepts such as "the Rights of Man" and thus threatening both whiteness and Christianity in Europe: The Haitian Revolution had clearly disturbed the sleep and challenged the "liberal" credentials of many in Europe. But these developments also make clear that not only was Greece entangled directly with coloniality, race, and Atlantic slavery, but also that its own "independence" movement became a springboard for asserting white superiority and supremacy.

The perceived whiteness of ancient Greek sculptures and temples, a not-so-innocent myth long debunked (and on which more below) contributed further to the simultaneous whitening of ancient and modern Greece, while it will be classical, Greco-Roman sculpture again which will be chosen to stand for the white, superior race in the various, racialized anthropological handbooks that will be produced in the later part of the 19th century. You could say, paraphrasing Shakespeare, that the Christian, Greek-speaking people of the country we now call Greece were not born white, nor did they earn whiteness, but had whiteness thrust upon them, thanks to the conscious efforts of key national intellectuals such as Korais and philhellenic artists and authors.

RG: Here's an interesting divergence: Because Greece has been appropriated by "Europe," extracted from its Mediterranean and eastward- and southward-looking milieu, its antiquities become a vehicle for establishing an essential whiteness or "occidentality"; the antiquities of Palestine and Syro-Mesopotamia, on the other hand, defined as part of the "Near East," are used by Jews of European descent as a vehicle for their own "oriental" indigeneity!

YH: Yes, but this status, both in terms of Europeanness and in terms of whiteness, was not without ambivalence. Indeed, it was fraught and contested (by Greeks and non-Greeks) from the start and would continue to be so, to the present day. It had to be fought and proven, time and again. Let's stay on this point for a moment, and return to the example of Delacroix's orientalist paintings, especially the *Massacre at Chios* (1824; Fig. 5.6). This highly complex work is often assumed to depict the sorry state of Christians, following yet another barbarian atrocity by the Turks. Yet, although similar

FIGURE 5.6. Eugène Delacroix, *The Massacre at Chios* (1824), The Louvre Museum, reproduced with permission.

paintings by the same artist such as *Greece on the ruins of Missolonghi* (1826; Fig. 5.7) with only two human characters which depict a physiognomically and phenotypically black Turk juxtaposed against a much larger in scale white woman who stands for Greece. This Chios painting tells a different story. It is a story about coloniality, gender and sexuality, heterosexual prowess, and anxiety about

FIGURE 5.7. Eugène Delacroix, *Greece on the Ruins of Missolonghi* (1826), Museum of Fine Arts of Bordeaux, reproduced with permission.

race and miscegenation.⁴⁹ There is no unified mode of representing the victimized Christians here, but an amalgam of different types. Moreover, if the model for the central male figure in the middle of the painting is Aspasie, a woman of color or rather a "mixed blood" female ("la nera," Delacroix used to call her), then the painter seems to be expressing a view on the racial ambiguity of the people who, at the fault-line between Europe and Asia, were emerging as Greeks. To quote Grigsby,

> Delacroix was making visible the recently repressed arguments that the Greeks were no more than a pot-pourri of peoples: Slavs, Albanians, Turks, Arnautes, and so on. For these philhellenic critics, Delacroix's Greeks were an aesthetically repugnant accumulation of persons, parts, and pigments in utter disarray.⁵⁰

Critics, especially the ones aligned with the philhellenic cause, were not happy at all. Two years later, when *Greece on the Ruins of Missolonghi* was painted (Fig. 5.7), the racial lines were depicted in more clear terms (and note also the similarities with Fig. 5.3). The role of the Egyptian army (which, as we saw earlier, was perceived as an army of "negros," at least by some notable writers) in the siege and the eventual fall of Missolonghi to the Ottomans must have surely been in the mind of the painter when he depicted these figures. Still, Grigsby's points are pertinent:

> Delacroix had learned his lesson. In this later fundraising picture, the painter chose to conform more closely to his audience's preconceptions about Greeks. Here, in a single female body, Delacroix finally constituted not only the discrete and cogent Greek identity he had dispersed and disassembled in his multi-figured history painting, but also Hellenic beauty as well as whiteness ... As coloristic and symbolic foil, the black warrior in *Missolonghi* proposes the very bifurcation of racial identity that the trope of the mulatto had so effectively undermined in the paint handling of *Chios*.⁵¹

RG: How long did such crude racialization persist, with respect to modern Greeks?

YH: In the middle 19th century, the national narrative faced the challenge of Fallmerayer, the German-speaking Tyrolian scholar who claimed, already in 1830, that "not even a drop of noble and undiluted Hellenic blood flows in the veins of the Christian population of present-day Greece." While initial responses to his thesis would focus on refuting Slavic presence in Greece, Konstantinos Paparrigopoulos, who would become the national historian, would shift the debate away from blood and toward culture, the superior spirit and the qualities of Hellenism and mostly its ability to absorb "inferior" cultures, to "civilize" them.[52] Direct racialization subsided as part of this discourse, although race was still implicitly present, and more directly biological and physiognomic conceptions of race will resurface in the later decades of the 19th century. This followed similar trends in Europe, including the publication of Gobineau's 1853 manifesto, *Essay on the Inequality of the Human Races*. Anthropometric and physiognomic studies would appear in Greece too,[53] although perhaps with less impact than in other Western countries: The spiritualist and culturalistic dimensions of Hellenism would seem to dominate.[54]

Whiteness and race in the broader sense, however, never went away. They are the unspoken assumptions and the "truths" in the background which hold national imagination together. They are often expressed in the terrain of religion, mostly as antisemitism as well as Islamophobia. In the late 19th and mostly in the 20th century, they would be reframed as the dilemma on whether Greece is East or West. By East here is not meant the Orient of the orientalist thinking, nor the East of the Arab cultures. The expression *"kath' imas Anatoli,"* meaning literally the East that is closest to us, and culturally, the Christian Orthodox and Greek East of Byzantium and Anatolia (and perhaps of Orthodox Russia), has been deployed by a discourse that rejects both Western Hellenism (including Western Christianity) as well as the Muslim Orient, in favor of a mostly imaginary, Hellenized-Byzantinized East.

The accession of the country in the European Economic Community (which became the European Union) in 1981, delivered a blow to this ambivalence. The architect of this accession Konstantinos Karamanlis famously declared, *"Anikomen eis tin Disin."* The phrasing here is interesting: He did not say we are part of the West but "we belong to the West," expressing thus an ownership relationship, in a turn of phrase and a slip which revealed once again, perhaps accidently, Greece's crypto-colonial status. At the same time, it moved Greece decidedly further away from its Balkan context, a geographical affinity that was the cause of further anxiety for various reasons, including the fear of being tainted with the stereotype of Balkanism,[55] and the ethnological or other associations with the "Slavs," and since the mid-20th century, with the communist north.

So, that was, I think, the moment when discussions about East and West, and its racial undertones, actually subsided. But race is back with the new millennium, as more and more migrants from Asia and Africa cross the border on their way to western Europe or make Greece their new home. In the 1990s, migrants from the Balkans and the Soviet Republics, seemingly "white" and mostly Christian, did not pose a major challenge to the implicit assumptions about race and racial hierarchies, despite the racism that these communities suffer. Things have now changed with the migrants from Asian and African countries, and one reaction has been the growth of racist, neofascist parties, whereas another is the realization among both scholars and the public, that race as a social phenomenon needs to be confronted head on.

As for archaeology, the implicit popular assumption on the whiteness of the prominent icons of classical material culture, despite the plentiful specialist studies that demonstrate the key significance of polychromy, remains largely unchallenged. It is partly reinforced by the phenomenological–sensorial impact of the white marble of the temples and sculptures, from the Bronze Age Cycladic figurines to classical statues. The Bronze Age Cycladic figurines in particular are often shown and exhibited against a blue background, evoking the national colors, becoming thus both, nationalized *and* inscribed in the aesthetic of whiteness. The perceived whiteness of classical legacy is also partly reinforced by the accidents of preservation: Marble is an extremely robust material, and the white marble used in classical times has mostly lost its colored surfaces with time. On the other hand, very few of the plentiful bronze, dark-colored statues survived, as their raw material was recycled. As for the broader classical cultures and their legacy, Martin Bernal's *Black Athena* was received in Greece mostly with scorn and contempt, and it was seen as the baseless excesses of Afro-centrists. The critics of Bernal, on the other hand, were welcomed as heroes, given honorary degrees, and their critiques were translated into Greek while the "Black Athena" books were not.[56]

RG: I'd like to revisit a few things that you brought up, in relation to Israel: The position between East and West of course is always relevant to the Levant, and as you spoke, I was reminded of another arena in which the internal contradictions of Israeli society are playing out, with implications for archaeological research, and that is the cultural one. Well into the sixties, the cultural elite was almost entirely oriented toward Europe. Popular music was modeled first on Russian folk songs and later French chansons and Italian pop, most translated literature was European, even the ideal countryside was imagined as European. At some point a backlash began, with people who came from other parts of the world – who are actually a majority in Israel – demanding space for their own stories, music, and languages in the public sphere. This has become a vibrant and fractious debate in Israel. But there was a phase – I would put its high point between the mid-eighties, which you mentioned earlier as a pivotal moment for Europe, and the mid-nineties, when liberal optimism crested in Israel – in which Greek and Cypriot music offered Israelis a "Mediterranean" middle ground. This offered a new localization or regional identity, as East Mediterranean; not too Arab, but not entirely of the West, and it was mediated by the large Ladino-speaking community of Jews from the Balkans and the coastal Levant who emigrated to Palestine and Israel. The anchor of "Mediterranean" culture was Greek music, and that's when Greek performers like Yorgos Dalaras and Glykeria (along with the Israeli songwriter Yehuda Poliker [born Leonidas Polikaris]) attained peak popularity.

In the search for an Israeli identity, mediating the deep internal rifts between communities of North African, Middle Eastern, and European origins, the Mediterranean seemed like a very convenient place to be, on the cusp, committed neither to East nor West. It allowed us to say, "we too have the sky and the sea, olives and wine, and blue and white," which are of course the colors of the Israeli flag as well. This affinity, this sense of shared destiny between Greeks and

Israelis, had, I suggest, a resonance in archaeological research, expressed as a preference – shared primarily with the secular Israeli community – for being coastal, for looking westward and not eastward. To look eastward is to look back, to look westward is to look ahead, and that feeds into an archaeology of the Mediterranean: An archaeology of sea-borne trade and maritime colonization. There was a surge in marine archaeology, in the excavation of coastal sites and harbors, and in regional collaboration with Cypriot and Aegean archaeologists. Major excavations began at sites associated with the so-called Sea Peoples (Tel Dor in 1980; Tell Muqanna/Ekron in 1981; Tel Ashkelon in 1985), and the study of the putative Philistines became quite popular, not in biblical terms, but as Western migrants to the East; as people who brought new aesthetic into the Levant. I see a connection between this archaeological attraction to the Mediterranean and the optimism of the "post-ideological" late 20th century, which crashed to earth in the wake of the 1995 Rabin assassination and the "9/11" attacks and their aftermath. We see a remnant of this optimism, or at least of the hope that it could engender, even among the besieged Palestinians of Gaza City, in Nicholas Wadimoff's film *The Apollo of Gaza*, which describes the reaction of a cross-section of Gazan society to a purported Archaic bronze statue found in the sea by a local fisherman. It's as if living on the Mediterranean coast allows them to say, "we're fine with the Romans, we're fine with the Greeks; that's us as well." You can see where this competes with religious nationalism, which has put its stamp on the archaeology of this century. It might also point to an alternative to the "bastion of the West" and "we are the real indigenes" narratives: Instead of manning the forts along the border with the East or West, Israelis and Palestinians might consider the possibility of a more fluid and fractured identity.[57]

YH: The Mediterranean as a third space: If we are to reflect on Mediterraneanness as a concept, we will encounter various modern and contemporary uses, often entangled with the notions of a selective, ancient past. In the early- and mid-20th century, for example, fascist Italy was constructed on the notion of *Romanitas*, appropriating the imperial past of ancient Rome, and the Mediterranean became "mare nostrum," our sea, expressing the imperial ambitions for North Africa and the Eastern Mediterranean. Moreover, racist intellectuals conceived of a "Mediterranean race," which helped to counter the glorification of the Nordic, Aryan race of their Nazi allies.[58] More recently, post-colonial scholars such as the Naples-based Iain Chambers would project the Mediterranean as a site of an alternative modernity, a hybrid, multi-cultural and multi-faith modernity, halfway between Africa and Europe, exemplified by the diverse and vibrant spaces of cities like Napoli.[59]

As for Greece, the notion of Mediterraneanness is present in the evocation of some archaeological narratives, most prominently in the ones about the "Minoans" and the "Mycenaeans" which are arbitrary and anachronistic ethnonyms for the people of the Bronze Age, but it is often conceived of as "thalassocracy," as rule over the sea, as proto-imperial domination. Here, the empirically attested, intense material and social connections among the people of the Eastern Mediterranean are recast as relationships of domination. And while the "Minoans" and "Mycenaeans" are firmly embedded within the national self and the national narrative, such proto-imperial legacies feature less prominently, compared to later and more widely known episodes, such as the legacy of Alexander the Great, and the establishment of Hellenistic polities in places like Egypt or the Levant. The story of the "Minoans" and the "Mycenaeans" is interesting nevertheless with regards to the archaeogenetic conceptions of race which will be explored below.

As for the conception of the Mediterranean in the modern political history of Greece, such a notion as a space of shared identity will feature only rarely, given the westward orientation of the country, especially after the collapse of the imperial dream of the Great Idea, following the defeat in the Greco-Turkish War of 1919–1922. Two such episodes are the 1980s PASOK government's dogma of the "Third Way" (neither the capitalist West, not the Soviet East), which led to temporary alliances with the Arab states of North Africa and the Middle East; and the recent alliances among Greece, Egypt, Cyprus, and Israel in the commercial exploitation of the natural gas resources of the Eastern Mediterranean, aimed also at isolating Turkey.

But it is time for us to turn to ancient DNA studies and how they are reshaping understandings of race.

RG: Yes, let's get into that, and see how this supposedly cutting-edge research recreates the very same categories that we had hoped to put behind us: Many of these ancient DNA studies are couched in terms of "population movements," reproducing Minoans, Mycenaeans, Canaanites, Phoenicians, and so on as primordial, sociobiological categories, and then comparing them with modern population groups, also seemingly primordial and self-evident: "Ashkenazi Jews" (as if we can really define them),[60] or "Lebanese."[61] They've been creating, or recreating, maps that we thought had gone out of fashion: The old maps offered clearly delineated geo-racial boundaries and explained cultural change by drawing thick black arrows extending from one region to another;[62] this has suddenly become legitimate again through ancient DNA studies, which use more sophisticated graphics to say pretty much the same thing.[63] I see the problem here embedded in two types of discourse: One is that which wrongly establishes genes as the predominant or indeed sole determinants of heritable traits, rather than as components of broader developmental systems. Gabriel Motzkin put it quite starkly: "It is clear ... that the purely genetic analysis of biological development is no longer tenable, that the invocation of genetic drift is just as prone to mysticism as the idea of genes as subject to complete control by phenotypical developments."[64] The second discourse is that which characterizes clear-cut genetic "populations"; the assumption of a systematic congruence between group identity, settlement patterns, shared material culture assemblages, and a definable genetic package. The conception of identity is a unity, purified of admixtures, rather than a multiplicity. We know – and geneticists know too – that the thrust of their work reveals how people and species come together and impact each other; how evolution is history.[65] But they allow their work to be presented in almost diametrically opposite terms: As a study of what sets people apart; a scientific demonstration of what makes people inherently different.

YH: Beyond our two cases, we see globally how biology has become a meta-science, the source of pronouncements about history, identity, life. Books such as the one by David Reich, *Who We Are, and How We Got Here*, set the tone.[66] He is the director of Harvard's ancient DNA lab, perhaps the most powerful center in archaeogenetics in the world right now, and one which has been heavily critiqued for its aggressive and expansive policies in sourcing archaeogenetics data.[67] The title and the preface of the book alone give the game away. "Our idea was," Reich writes, "to make DNA industrial – to build an American style, genomics factory...."[68] Your DNA will tell you who you are, this book claims, and will write your history, the history of humanity. You do not need to know details; they are too complicated anyway. This black-boxing of the scientific, analytical process adds to the mystified and authoritative status of science. It is this mystification which the anthropologist Stephan Palmié has called "racecraft." This is what he writes with reference to DNA testing, a lot of which can also apply to archaeogenetics: "[T]he function of DNA testing as a divinatory practice designed to visualize and give materiality by evidentiary proxy to entities whose ontological characteristics include the crucial feature of invisibility."[69] And while ancient DNA work can produce interesting archaeological results at the micro-scale, in exploring genetic connections among the inhabitants of a community or neighboring communities, for example, most archaeogenetics studies, and the ones that have received the most public attention, operate at a large scale, and as you say, work within an interpretative framework of "mass migrations." They return to a notion of "culture" as a bounded essentialist, ahistorical entity which is transplanted from place to place through population movement, but also through "population replacement." In the same book, we read that "we discovered that the population of northern Europe was largely replaced by a large migration from the Eastern European steppe." Note the language here, and recall how white supremacists today speak of the danger of "replacement" of white Europeans by "colored" people.[70]

Equally problematic is their use of various ethnonyms such as the ones you mentioned. There is no understanding nor any acknowledgment of the rich anthropological discussion on ethnicity, and these labels such as Minoans, Mycenaeans, or Phoenicians, stand for discrete, ethnically homogeneous "cultures," reminiscent of the culture history approach of the 18th and early 19th century, and of Gustav Kossinna, the 19th- and early 20th-century German diffusionist–nationalist archaeologist who proposed an isomorphic relationship between material culture and ethno-national identity. His ideas and their clear racial connotations, which formed the basis of the fascist and Nazi archaeology of the 20th century, were widely influential until recently. While on the decline, they seem to have found a new lease of life in archaeogenetics research, powered by "sophisticated" but black-boxed, analytical methodologies. And while a lot can be said on specific facets of such methodologies, from sample size to the naming of the social units that these samples represent, to the role of archaeologists in these studies (who operate mostly as the suppliers of samples, not the contributors in the interpretation process), the huge lacuna is to do with the theoretical naïveté, evident in most such studies.

In addition to the points we have raised and the examples given so far, we should perhaps add two more: The lack of any reflection on kin and human relationality which, as Marshall Sahlins and others have shown,[71] are mostly about the mutuality of being, not any genomic connection seen purely as a biological given; and the equally astonishing contempt for the abundant studies which have shown that genes themselves are shaped by relationality and its histories. They are based on and give rise to multiple assemblages of beings, some organic and some not, some human some not. They are not isolated and autonomous entities with no histories of their own; they cannot be understood within a framework of binary separation between "nature" and "culture."[72] In other words, human DNA is not purely human DNA but a hybrid, heterogeneous assemblage, a snapshot of our connections and relationships with plants and animals, other humans, with life, and the world.

RG: I would like to add that this research is evolving rapidly across the Levant, and while it began with studies that might be considered innocuous, that is, that don't have any clear contemporary relevance – looking at very early hominin and human populations, or at the possible admixture of Neanderthals and Homo Sapiens (which again reifies the separate strands of humanity as autonomous units) – it now extends to historical and modern populations.

Let me tell you a brief anecdote that illustrates both the power that genetic narratives hold in the public imagination and the ease with which they are adapted to racist conceptions. A short time ago

Nation, Race, and Archaeogenetics 143

I received a call from a journalist who was working up a brief story on my excavations at Tel Bet Yerah. Because we posited the presence of a migrant community at our site, the reporter asked if this was the same population that had been identified genetically as "the blue-eyed northerners who brought the Chalcolithic culture to Israel" (at about 4500 BCE). She was citing popular reporting of a genetic study published in 2018 that claimed to provide "an example of how population movements propelled cultural changes," and to show, based on a study from a single site, that "the blue-eyed phenotype was common" in the Chalcolithic Levant.[73] This study was presented under the following headline in the liberal-leaning *Ha'aretz* newspaper: "Mysterious 6,500-year-old Culture in Israel Was Brought by Migrants, Researchers Say: Genetic analysis shows ancient Galilean farmers warmly embraced blue-eyed, fair-skinned immigrants from Iran and Turkey in the late Copper Age."[74] When I asked her if she didn't think there was a tinge of racism in this characterization, she bristled at the suggestion; she could not see where the reporting on the paper published in *Nature* directly reproduces colonialist tropes in which superior northern cultures bring the light of civilization to a southern cultural *terra nullius*.

As the volume and speed of these analyses has increased, with numerous postdoctoral researchers from Israel and other countries ending up in the big European and American labs (especially in Harvard), the network of sample-acquisition is reaching more and more excavations. So now they have begun to bridge the gap, defining who *in the present* has a higher percentage of shared genes with some ancient population. And that's been perfect fodder for the groups who are perhaps the most insecure about their own identity: Lebanese can say "we're Phoenicians," Palestinians can say "we're Canaanites," Israelis will say "we're more Levantine than European, similar to each other and different from others." It's being bandied about and used in such loose ways that undermine almost everything that we try to do in the archaeology that we practice, which talks about identity being a construct, something that is imagined, negotiated and re-evaluated.

YH: And also, a matter of habitus and experience.

RG: Yes, and what they're telling you is that you don't know who you are; *they've* got the secret to who you are. You might think you're

X, but you're actually Y, and the same goes for the skeleton that you found in the ground: You might think it's Egyptian, but they know that it's not (as if archaeologists are required to call out the identity of every excavated individual!). And this reinfuses archaeology with all the reductive thinking, with its 19th-century colonial origins, that we have tried to get away from. As you said, it provides a very crude way of thinking about identities with the aura of high technology, available to the privileged few. There's a mystique around genes: They determine your character and can't be controlled. But treating people as the sum of their genes ultimately underlies racial stereotypes; you can't get away from your race (or your "blood," as it used to be characterized), no matter how hard you try; you'll never be what you want to be, you'll always be what your genes are. The biologization of identity is both misguided and dangerous, as it seems to offer a "neutral" measure of ethnic characterization while it is in fact – as Snait Gissis has described in a series of studies – completely caught up in a web of social, medical, genetic, and epidemiological conceptualizations.[75]

YH: In the case of Israel the politicization actually reached all the way to the Prime Minister, right?

RG: I guess you are referring to the *Jerusalem Post* headline "Netanyahu: Archaeology, DNA prove Palestinians not native to Land of Israel,"[76] which is of course a farce and a deliberate distortion of the intent of the Harvard University investigators, yet was nonetheless based on their biblical framing of the ancient DNA study. I have a rather self-punishing habit of looking at the public comments in online newspaper reports about archaeology and archaeogenetics. We all know the kinds of people who write comments, but nonetheless it is telling that the responses immediately become a racial battleground, testifying to the successful marketing of these genetic studies as pure clickbait. Based on the interactions I have had with PR officers in the organizations I have worked in, this is done intentionally, accompanied by headlines that will make those studies red meat for politicians. We know this is happening, not only in Israel, but, as I said earlier, in Lebanon, in Greece, in India. It's happening in almost every part of the world where there's some sort of struggle over ethnic identities and origins.[77]

YH: I want to give a brief example, to show how such phenomena are expressed in the case of Greece. Curiously, several ancient DNA studies on material from Greece do not seem to be satisfied with exploring questions about the past, but want to delve into "genetic" links between people of the past (even the remote Neolithic or Bronze Age past), and the contemporary inhabitants of the country. Let's take a study published in *Nature*, titled, "Genetic origins of the Minoans and the Mycenaeans."[78] Some of the authors of this study, based in the USA, have Greek surnames and they were presented as "Greek" by the media, and given its theme and conclusions, the article played very prominently in most mainstream Greek media. It was not so much the story, genetic or other, of the people of the Bronze Age that the pundits were interested in, however, but the genetic proof of continuity between such people and contemporary Greeks. I want to zoom in for a moment at how such a study was used by the most notorious neo-Nazi party of Europe, Golden Dawn.

The study featured on the front page of the Golden Dawn's website (Fig. 5.8), the day it was announced to the Greek press. The photograph that accompanied it was a collage by the photographer Nelly, produced as propaganda for the Metaxas's dictatorial regime (1936–1939) and displayed in the Greek Pavilion at the 1939 New York World's Fair.[79] There's a ruined temple in the background, and in the foreground the ancient bronze statue known as the Artemision Zeus or Poseidon, next to an elderly man, assumingly a modern Greek shepherd who looks remarkably like the classical god. The message of racial continuity between ancient and modern Greeks that the Metaxas regime was keen to project, alongside its tourism campaign, could not have been more obvious.

The Golden Dawn headline above the picture claims that "the 4000-year racial continuity of the Greeks has been proved." This is slight modification of the line taken by other media: The neo-Nazi site makes the reference to race explicit, whereas most other media talk of genetic and cultural continuity. The subtitle makes a direct reference to Fallmerayer, claiming that this study by "two Greek geneticists" delivers one more blow to the "descendants of Fallmerayer." Are the media and especially the neo-Nazis abusing a sophisticated scientific study here? Are these scientists to blame for

FIGURE 5.8. Screenshot from the webpage of the Greek neo-Nazi party, Golden Dawn (August 3, 2017).

how their work is used? The paper takes "Minoans" and "Mycenaeans" as truthful ethnic categories, representing coherent groups of people who identified themselves as such, whereas they are in fact archaeological constructs originating in the late 19th and early 20th century. They were coined by the likes of Heinrich Schliemann, Arthur Evans and their predecessors, a remnant of the racialized archaeology known as "cultural history," as we discussed above. One of the questions the researchers set out to answer was: "Do the labels 'Minoan' and 'Mycenaean' correspond to genetically coherent populations or do they obscure a more complex structure of the peoples who inhabited Crete and mainland Greece at this time?" But they'd already answered it in the affirmative by their choice of categories, by the labels they attached to the sampled skeletons.

The researchers say they "generated genome-wide data from nineteen ancient individuals," classed as "Minoan" or "Mycenaean" depending on their dates and whether they came from Crete or mainland Greece. Leaving aside the context and the size of sample here, it is their starting assumptions on ethnicity in the past as a bounded, static whole, and their initial labeling of samples that made this a study prone to racialization, and allowed for the readings we saw. Furthermore, these scholars also wanted to answer the question of "continuity," a question at the center of Greek national narrative and imagination, hence their decision to include in the analysis DNA from thirty "Modern Greek" individuals from mainland Greece, Cyprus, and Crete. Why was this important, in a study on the Bronze Age? How were these modern individuals selected, and how was their "Greekness" proved? Who is "Modern Greek" today? Is a modern Greek citizen, born in Greece of Albanian or Nigerian parents and living there all her life, a legitimate "specimen" for this study? "Modern Greeks resemble the Mycenaeans," they conclude, "but with some additional dilution of the Early Neolithic ancestry." The results of the study "support the idea of continuity but not isolation in the history of populations of the Aegean, before and after the time of its earliest civilizations." But it's hardly surprising that a few modern individuals living in the Eastern Mediterranean should share genetic material with a few individuals who lived in the same region in the Bronze Age; it's a big jump from there to the neo-Nazi fantasy of 4000 years of "racial continuity," which also assumed whiteness in the Bronze Age as well as today. It's not just the media thus and the neo-Nazi agenda which is to blame here. The study itself was founded on racialized grounds, and its research questions were inscribed primarily into a nationalist framework.

While the neo-Nazi website alluded to physiognomy and craniometrics, well known features of 19th-century racial anthropology, the geneticists updated the tool kit but did not depart from the ideological and conceptual framework of racial anthropology without referencing the term itself. Such framework which was implicit in their starting questions, narrative, labels, and methods, was made explicit in a crude manner in the media examples above.[80]

Zooming out and reflecting on earlier conceptions of identity and national continuity in the Hellenic national narrative, we can see how the 19th-century discourse which emphasized the cultural–spiritual continuity of Hellenism, and its ability, as a superior culture, to absorb and "civilize" others, despite the "admixtures," is being biologized today with the help of ancient DNA studies. In the past, the racial undertones of the previous national dogma were concealed in other terms and schemes, re-surfacing and becoming explicit in specific moments, such as under fascist dictatorships, but today they are fast becoming more direct, explicit, and mainstream.

Notes

1 Levine-Rasky 2008.
2 See, e.g., Gordon 2015.
3 Khazoom 2003; Shenhav and Yonah 2008; Sasson-Levy 2013.
4 Conder 1889: 230.
5 Petrie 1904.
6 Cf. Quirke 2010.
7 Gilman 1991: 173–174.
8 Feige 2001.
9 Zerubavel 2008.
10 Abu El-Haj 2012.
11 Gribetz 2014.
12 Christopoulos 2019; Kontiadis 2021; Vogli 2018.
13 Scholem 2003: 31. Cf. Papagiannopoulos 2019: 92.
14 E.g. Anagnostou 2009.
15 E.g. Ferguson 2008; Spyropoulos 2010; 2015.
16 Kotsonis 2020: 61, 144–145.
17 Leake 1830, vol. 1: 431.
18 Holland 1815: 266.
19 Kambouroglou 1889: 312; Travlos 2005: 221; Sakorafas 2019.
20 E.g. Hobhouse 1817: 1.288.
21 Dodwell 1819: 390; Kambouroglou (1899: 312) mentions that the same locality was used for prayers by the Ethiopian community of Athens, and it is well known that an open-air praying ground for Muslims, a *musalla*, had been established next to the ancient columns; Christians also used this area for prayers, making it a truly inter-faith space; see Fowden forthcoming, for a fascinating cultural biography of this locality.
22 Pashley 1837: 194; Spratt 1865: 44.
23 Gerola 1932–1940: 42.
24 Hasluck 1916: 68, n.1, emphasis in the original.
25 Taneja 2013.
26 Canaan 1922; Tamari 2009; Al-Houdalieh 2012a.

27 Beckerleg 2007.
28 Cf. Trubeta 2013.
29 Foucault 2003.
30 Mbembe 2019.
31 Heng 2018: 181.
32 Heng 2018: 149, emphasis in the original.
33 On discussions of the concept of *fili* in the Greek concept and its various connotations, see Lefkaditou 2017; Trubeta 2013; and papers in Avdela et al. 2017.
34 Cf. Ploumidis 2012.
35 On kinship as a way of expressing national bonds in Greece, see Sutton 1997.
36 See Kokkonas 2018: 134–137.
37 See Ploumidis 2012 for a rare exception, and Kotsonis 2020, esp. 49–64.
38 Cf. Grigsby 1999.
39 Cited in Karakatsouli 2016: 268.
40 Cf. Jockey 2013.
41 Green Fryd 201.
42 Volpe 2016.
43 As Leonidas Moiras notes (2020: 104), "The Ottoman administration, therefore, must have felt awkwardness in seeing a group of subjects characterizing the political framework of the Empire, within which they were living for centuries, as 'slavery.'"
44 Grigsby 2002.
45 Cited in Grigsby 2002: Chapter 6.
46 Chateaubriand 1825: 7–8.
47 Cited in Grigsby 2002: Chapter 6.
48 In fact, Chateaubriand is explicit about this future buffer role for Greece: A free and armed Greece, as any other Christian nation, can become a naval power, he would state, and "can guard the east of Europe" (1825: 24).
49 Grigsby 1999.
50 Op.cit., 698.
51 Grigsby 2002: 284; on the broader topic, see also Athanassoglou-Kallmyer 1989.
52 Fallermayer 1830: iv; Hamilakis 2007: 155–116. On Fallmerayer and the impact of his hypothesis in Greece, see among others, Papagiannopoulos 2020; Skopetea 1997; Veloudis 1982.
53 Trubeta 2013.
54 See Avdela et al. 2017.
55 On this stereotype, see the insightful analysis by Maria Todorova (1997).
56 This mirrors the reactions to the challenge by Fallmerayer in the 19th century: Here too, critiques of his thesis were immediately translated into Greek but his own books had to wait until the end of the 20th century.

57 Ohana 2012.
58 Cf. Pizzato 2017.
59 Chambers 2007.
60 Agranat-Tamir et al. 2020.
61 Haber et al. 2017.
62 Ambridge 2012.
63 Hakenbeck 2019.
64 Motzkin 2011: 7.
65 Gissis and Jablonka 2011.
66 Reich 2018.
67 Cf. Lewis-Kraus 2019.
68 Reich 2018: xviii.
69 Palmié 2007: 214.
70 Reich 2018: xxi; for powerful, broad critiques of such approaches see TallBear 2013; Marks 2017; Nelson 2016.
71 Sahlins 2012.
72 Cf. Crellin and Harris, 2020.
73 Harney et al. 2018.
74 David 2018.
75 Gissis 2008. See also Abu El-Haj (2012) on Jewish genomics.
76 Jaffe-Hoffman 2019.
77 Gannon 2019.
78 Lazaridis et al. 2017.
79 Cf. Hamilakis 2007: 167–204; Zacharia 2015; and on Nelly and her photography see also Kalantzis 2019: 85–86, 98, and elsewhere.
80 Cf. Kapsali 2017 on this article, and Lefkaditou 2017 for a further critique of archaeogenetics and their racial connotations in Greece.

CHAPTER 6

Decolonizing Our Imagination

In view of the enduring colonial and nationalist legacies that permeate current archaeological practice, we reflect here on ways to reimagine archaeology as decolonizing action.

YH: We are coming toward the end of our discussion, and it is important to reflect on what it means to decolonize our imagination – both our archaeological imagination and our broader social imagination – in the two contexts. I guess both of us have been involved in various attempts at decolonization, so I see this final chapter as a way of exchanging experience and talking about successes and failures, and perhaps developing some thoughts and ideas that may actually guide us, but also others, on how to continue engaging in this ongoing process.

RG: I agree, but with an important qualification, at least on my part: What we are trying to imagine is so far removed from our training, our experience, and the institutional structures in which many of us operate, that it should be taken neither as a manifesto nor a "guide to the perplexed," but a report on stages in a journey to an unrecognizable destination that is not only decolonized but denationalized and perhaps decapitalized. So where would you begin?

YH: Decolonization is not a metaphor; as you say, it will have to be both broad and specific at the same time, countering the ideological but also the material colonizing forces, including race, nation, and capital. Archaeology and academia are only two specific arenas in which we should be acting, and it's important to see this work as one facet of the global decolonizing movement which gained new vitality and force during the 2020 global, anti-racist uprising. We can gain inspiration, theoretical and methodological insights, and encouragement and support from that movement. Interestingly, and crucially for us, this anti-racism movement has identified statues, monuments, and sites of commemoration as key focal points and as localities that embody and perpetuate white supremacy. The activists and the public who have been protesting around and modifying such sites recognize the histories of forgetting that underpin their making, they can see clearly how monuments have been often weaponized in the ongoing battles around race and nation.[1]

For me, the decolonial process starts with the reflexive moment, the moment of realizing that you've been colonized, that everything you do within archaeology, operating within a specific modernist regime, a specific national-cum-colonial regime, is part of a long process of colonizing ideas, knowledge, but also institutions and practices. And we have to remember that we may be talking here about two specific, crypto-colonized (and colonizing) national contexts, but there is the broader regime of modernist archaeology within which we both operate, and which conditions our beings and our work as archaeologists and scholars. Specific ideas about the body, about time and experience, and domineering binaries such as subject and object, or nature and culture or even past versus present have colonized our imagination and shaped our thoughts and actions. Modernist archaeologists, for example, have bought into notions of temporal linearity, exemplified by our stratigraphic sequences, and are accustomed to separate past and present, a dichotomy with important consequences on how we see our role, our relationships to communities today, but also on how we tell stories about what we call "the past." I have written elsewhere on multi-temporality and duration and on time as co-existence rather than succession,[2] and I may say a bit more, later on.

Following on from the moment of reflexivity and the recognition of the colonial relationship within which we are entangled, the critical, historiographic as well as sociological–anthropological analyses of this relationship, in which both of us have been engaged for years, is the next step toward decolonization. These are decolonizing

Decolonizing Our Imagination

writings which also send the signal that the decolonizing of the archaeological apparatus is intricately linked with the decolonizing of the country as a whole, as social reality and as imaginary. Given the key role of archaeology in the constitution of these two colonial–national projects, the decolonization of archaeology can contribute to the broader project of the decolonization of these two societies. The two need to proceed in tandem, and the one can reinforce the other.

This process also calls for a historical anthropology of archaeology, both the modernist archaeology we practice, but also, the alternative, pre-modern archaeologies practiced by various groups and people prior to the establishment of the nation-state. Retrieving their own ontologies about time and matter, and their own engagements with things from various times, will help us historicize and relativize our own archaeology, "de-link" it from the epistemologies, the geo-politics and body-politics of coloniality,[3] unlearn the canon,[4] "un-discipline" modernist archaeology.[5] Such retrieval will also expose a series of ideas and practices which we can find inspirational today and which are hidden in plain sight in the various 18th and 19th century travel accounts and folk tales, as we have discussed in previous chapters.

Let's recall what we have already stressed in this book, that crypto-coloniality as a condition relies on the idea of concealing and masking colonial relationships. In colonies proper, things are more explicit; you know you're here to be governed by the colonial power and its apparatuses. In crypto-colonial projects, that dependence and the articulation of coloniality with knowledges and practices are being concealed. So, a lot of what we're doing is to actually show, first of all to us, then to others, that kind of relationship of colonial dependence. And, of course, this involves clashes, very often clashes against institutions.

For me, a key factor for the perpetuation of colonial relationships and practices in Greece is the power of specific institutions, structures which were founded within the crypto-colonial regime at its very beginning, but which continue operating today in different guises, largely unreconstructed. Such central institutions and structures are the archaeological service, the central archaeological council, which takes final decisions on almost everything to do with archaeology, the archaeological law, the universities (which, despite recent attempts, have not managed to undermine the colonial–national archaeological regime),[6] and the institution of foreign archaeological schools, which is a key component of the whole apparatus.

To take the archaeological law as an example, its first, systematic iteration was written by the Bavarians in 1834 and the later versions, all the way to the present one (2002), are, in essence, modifications and updates of that first law. Of course, there are many changes and additions, especially regarding harmonization with international heritage legislation and UNESCO practices, but the basic underlying principles remain mostly the same.[7] Take the definition of the law's object of protection and management and the understanding of temporality it reveals: The entity at its center is the antiquities, *arheotites* (*αρχαιότητες*) in Greek. The English or Latin version of the term refers to things of old, things prior to us, a term which interestingly, from the 15th century onward, came to be linked, at least in Europe, to the classical antiquities of Greece and Rome, an indication of the impact of classical legacy. The Greek version refers, etymologically, to the earliest things, to an originary moment. Moreover, *αρχή* (*arhi*) has a double meaning, the beginning, chronologically speaking, but also the authority, the institution which is in command.[8] Antiquities thus are the things that reference an originary moment and at the same time the things that embody an authority, moral and national. At the center of both protection and study thus are not the material traces of various pasts, material heritage in general, or entities of historical value, including places and landscapes, but originary material references of the nation, things that are the visible and tactile truths of the nation's golden age. True, the most recent archaeological law references not only "ancestral heritage," as was the case with earlier laws, but monuments connected historically to the country, a significant improvement. Yet, the other provisions and principles, and the implicit conceptions of value and temporality, weaken this move significantly; witness the dozens of abandoned Islamic monuments in ruinous state, scattered all over the country. Needless to say, the entities to be protected were originally meant to be works of art and historical documents; that's why in the earlier versions of the law it was specified that they were meant to be sculptures, buildings, inscriptions, and so on.

In more recent versions, the definition was expanded to material artefacts more broadly and to their "immediate surroundings," although the notion of art retained its pre-eminence. More importantly, archaeological and historical landscapes and natural features, are by definition excluded, reinscribing into the law and thus into archaeological consciousness the binary separation between nature and culture. As for the foreign schools, we have discussed how they constitute a crucial node in the whole assemblage of archaeology in Greece and how their relationship to other nodes and institutions is not simply one of colonizer-colonized but is entangled tightly with all other components in a framework of coloniality, with deep roots in the 18th and 19th centuries. The effort for the decolonization of archaeology in Greece will need to include these institutions, starting with the radical, reflexive thinking and study of their histories, currently in short supply, and their opening to critical institutional ethnographies.

RG: Hearing your critical analysis of the very language of antiquities and its enshrinement in law, and recalling that the enactment of antiquities laws in the Ottoman empire and in the states that succeeded it was a product of European intervention, it seems that a necessary basis for any decolonization should be both a radical revision of the laws regulating archaeological activity on the ground and a dissociation of archaeological thought from the concept of "antiquity," as suggested, among others, by Nativ and Lucas.[9] But getting back to Greece, you mentioned implicit conceptions of value and temporality – are these made explicit in the Greek antiquities law, in the same manner as the year 1700 was enshrined in the British Mandatory antiquities law – and in all its subsequent reincarnations – as the cut-off date for protected antiquities in Palestine and Israel?

YH: Under the current archaeological law, all material things that are older than the foundation of the state (1830) are automatically declared antiquities. After that date, things can be declared as modern monuments if deemed by the archaeological service and the various heritage bodies as possessing historical, scholarly, or artistic value. There is also a moving, one-hundred-year cut-off point from any given present date: Things older than this point can be potentially declared as monuments and worthy of protection, but not antiquities, the designation, value, and ownership status of which are fixed. There is a third landmark date, 1453, the date of the conquest of Constantinople by the Ottomans. "Antiquities" older than this date belong automatically to the state, whereas "antiquities" dated between 1453 and 1830 can be owned by individuals and non-state entities. You can own a 16th-century Christian icon, for example, despite its antiquity status, and in fact most surviving antiquities dated to this period are primarily ecclesiastical, and often owned by the Church. Taken together, these two fundamental principles (on what is worth protecting, and on how time is conceived) shape the ways through which material things from other times are imagined and managed by state and many non-state actors. Moreover, they embody the crypto-colonization of modern Greek imagination regarding material culture and material history. They establish a hierarchy of value: "Antiquities," a chronologically fixed category and corpus, are much more important than other material things, whatever their historical or scholarly weight; they tie material history to the national narrative and its chronological, commemorative landmarks: the "fall of Constantinople," the "resurrection of the nation," and the establishment of the modern Greek state; and they connect worthiness primarily to "art" or human-made things, and to pastness, to how old a thing is. The notion of "antiquities" thus is a major obstacle in our efforts toward decolonization. The performative iteration of archaeological routines and practices guided by this modernist archaeological framework reproduces the colonization of imagination, the ways we imagine materiality and time, heritage, and history, in the same way that the national narrative is being performatively reproduced in education, in national rituals and commemorations, or even in the staging of classical Greek plays, especially in restored ancient theaters, despite the at times ferocious challenges and heterodox readings: The continuous, banal nationalization meets banal colonization.[10]

RG: From where I stand, it seems that many of the enduring colonial residues that you have described exist, or might have existed in the past, in Israel/Palestine. The Israeli Antiquities Law of 1978, grandfathered by the mandatory law that we have already discussed, certainly preserves statist assumptions and European concepts of value, establishing the antiquities site as a *locus separatum* and granting an extensive franchise to the holders of excavation licenses. Moreover, it goes so far as to empower the Director of Antiquities with absolute discretion in determining what objects, structures and landscapes deserve or do not deserve protected status, and, as a gesture to the global community of wealthy collectors and the common practice of tax-deductible donations to large museums, traffic in antiquities is permitted, with the proviso that items of "national value" be offered first for sale to the state. In fact, it is so similar to colonial legislation that there is hardly any daylight between the law in Israel proper and the 1986 Antiquities Decree that governs archaeological activities in areas under Israeli military occupation.[11] Insofar as the crypto-colony goes – the continued embeddedness of colonial formations in the way archaeology is practiced, the presence of foreign schools – these things are obviously all present in Israel, but their impact is less pronounced than in Greece: There are not many foreign archaeologists dashing about, setting standards or running their own labs. Schools were founded before World War I by the Americans, British, Germans, and French, to serve as a home base for excavators in Palestine. Although they became quite prominent during the British Mandate (we've mentioned how the terms of the Mandate encouraged international participation), they never achieved the status of those in Greece. And nowadays, because they are in a liminal space, in occupied East Jerusalem, they barely make an impact. The British school serves mainly as a hostel for visiting scholars. The American school has fared better: It has carved out a niche which preserves some orientalist coloring as a sequestered garden oasis but is also trying to reinvent itself as a place of dialogue. It has a library and some facilities that serve American scholars, as well as Palestinians and Israelis who want a place to study or to interact. Nonetheless it is true that projects like the archaeogenetics projects we mentioned earlier, where big labs monopolize research, comprise an imperial legacy. The global North remains *the* source of prestige, wielding its stamp of authority. So, even while Israeli archaeologists fiercely defend their autonomy and claim local indigenous knowledge, they still need that approval in the guise of impact factors and international citation indexes, abdicating their cultural independence in favor of Anglo-American sources of scientific prestige and the values of neoliberal meritocracy.

But there are other, more pressing, matters that command attention in the Israeli context, that is, the context of Israeli colonization. Much of my own energy and reflection has been devoted to the role of archaeology in colonizing – that is, westernizing – the Israelis themselves, and in colonizing Palestine, whether you're talking about historical Palestine or the current – and perhaps future – political entity of Palestine. All the things you talked about exist and, or, have existed in one form or another, but they are crowded out or pushed aside because of the elephant in the room, the broad issue of Israel's constitution as a settler colony (which is a significant difference between Israel and Greece).[12] and the more immediate issue of the military occupation in the West Bank.

You talked about Greece as a crypto-colony, and about decolonization as a recognition of the impact of this colonization and the work of ridding oneself of some of its impositions and its attitudes. But in Israel we have a subsequent project that builds on the European one – the colonization by Israelis of Palestine; and then one wonders sometimes – I don't suppose one need wonder too much – how the lessons learned from the original colonizers are used in our continuing colonization. We've got the tools, the language, the laws – an entire structure – inherited from the British administration, that can be imposed on Palestinians and achieve the same kind of results that the original imperial regimes wanted to achieve. So when I think about decolonization of archaeology in Israel, I have to think, first, about changing ourselves, as archaeologists, redefining what archaeology is and what it does, and second, about rejecting our role as occupiers and as enforcers of injustice or inequality vis-à-vis Palestinians in Israel, where the legal framework is that of the state, and in the West Bank, where the legal framework is that of military occupation.

It is more complicated than the Greek case, because an Israeli archaeologist cannot appropriate the voice of the oppressed. If you're saying, "let's rid ourselves of the colony in our mind," I assume you mean, "let's do this in solidarity, we archaeologists of Greece." But in Israel, I am partly of the group that is colonized in its mind, and partly of the group that is oppressing others; I cannot represent the oppressed. That's why we have to talk about the Palestinians, and specifically Palestinian archaeologists, as a group that is a witness, an interlocutor, and a partner to this process of decolonization. They too are in a position of having accepted some of the tenets of colonization, because they have been educated in the Western tradition and they work within the same frameworks that we talked about. Like Israelis, they have accepted the regime of value associated with antiquities and linear temporality, the monetization of this value through tourism, and the leverage it affords through the allocation of excavation franchises. They have also, by and large, accepted what Laurajane Smith has termed the Authorized Heritage Discourse,[13] which takes as given the superior standing of large international organizations like UNESCO, the treatment of culture as a resource, and the naturalization of globalist interventions in local communities. At the same time, they've developed their own discourse, which rejects colonization, whether by the Israelis or by previous regimes. They give us some pointers toward what a decolonized Palestinian archaeology would look like.[14]

Among these still-hesitant steps toward an alternative archaeology, I am especially impressed by the recent work of Tawfiq Daʿadli on the Palestinian town of al-Ludd in the early 20th century, which combines multi-sited ethnography, deep dives into little-known archives, and contemporary and historic archaeology. Whether following an itinerary of religious pilgrimage and of industrial establishments in the town (see Fig. 6.1), or unraveling the philanthropic activities of a wealthy widow, he shows how archaeologies of contemporary Palestine can avoid the pitfalls of instrumentalist "ethnoarchaeological" studies or demonstrations of historical teleologies. They do not have to serve as mediators between east and west or past and present, but stand on their own, highlighting important transitions in

FIGURE 6.1. A Soap-factory of early 20th-century Ludd. Photos courtesy of Tawfiq Da'adli.

Palestinian society and exposing an unfamiliar Ottoman imperial geography, where movement in and through the Levant was unremarkable and crossed no strongly marked boundary.[15] Still, these studies have yet to set forth a complete archaeological program, from the planning stage through methodology and performance in the field, that can be said to be independent of existing models.

The question is, can there be such a thing as a decolonized *Israeli* archaeology? The position that I've come to after a lot of thought – and it's not only a question of what one thinks, but of what one can, in fact, accomplish, of whether there are potential allies traveling the same route – the conclusion that I've come to is that we – Israelis and Palestinians – have to decolonize along parallel paths and, to some extent, *together*. Since, ultimately, Israel/Palestine is a single historical and geographic entity, we will have to find a way to decolonize the archaeology of Israel/Palestine independently of any political regime. We don't know where things are headed: Two equal or unequal states? A single apartheid-like ethnocracy? A single democratic state, in which all people have equal rights? All these are possible futures. Can we imagine a decolonized archaeology to which we might aspire in any eventuality? An archaeology that could avoid serving as a tool of hegemonic domination or of globalized capital? To achieve that end, what is it in archaeology itself (wherever it is practiced) – in the origins of archaeology, in its methods, in the way archaeologists think and act – that should be reimagined and redesigned? What do archaeologists have to unlearn? How do we remain consistently "untimely" and avoid settling into "comfort zones"? And how do we align archaeology with a local vision of public interest?

YH: This is important. But let us recall that, key historical differences notwithstanding, Greece, having been crypto-colonized, itself acted in colonizing projects too, some successful and some unsuccessful. The decolonial project in both cases, Greece and Israel, thus entails the dismantling of the colonial framework which engenders colonial effects, whatever the specific roles in any given moment. It also demands the "loss of innocence": Coming to terms, in other words, with the hard truths that certain social groups, social agents, and institutions have benefited both from the crypto-colonized status of Greece, from its buffer role in global geopolitics, and from the country's crypto-colonizing endeavors; and accepting that race and white supremacy have been instrumental in the constitution of the Neohellenic and of Greece as an entity.

To follow up on what you are saying, one major difficulty that prevents people who practice archaeology in Greece – whether they are from Greece or other countries – from engaging with this process of decolonization, is the fear of the loss of the symbolic capital of Greek classical antiquity, broadly defined to include also the Bronze Age (the "Minoans" and "Mycenaeans"). Given the weight and power of Western Hellenism and its pull in the Global North, any attempt to deconstruct it, or even to actually unpack it, to demystify it, to make it historical as a phenomenon, as opposed to metahistorical or mythical, is extremely difficult. It means that you have to accept that you are not somehow special because you excavate and study classical Greece, you're not special because you study the Parthenon. You have to accept that monuments such as the Parthenon have been construed as works of mythical value under certain conditions of racial, colonial capitalism from which you yourself still benefit. That's a huge step that many, perhaps most archaeologists – and Greece as a whole – are not willing to take.

That symbolic capital may have somehow decreased in value, but it still brings in dividends, academic, social, political, economic. For many in Greece, this symbolic capital, beyond the sense of national pride it engenders, continues to allow people to claim that Greece may not be financially an important country, but culturally, it is a super-power. And I think many people still buy that, many people accept that, and this is going to be a huge stumbling block in the efforts of decolonization, even if the dividends of that symbolic capital are unevenly and unequally distributed, both symbolically and financially; some groups benefit much more than others, while some are clearly disadvantaged: people who are cleared away to allow excavations to happen, for example.

How can you respond? One response to this will be to say that you can demystify and historicize this phenomenon, and at the same time show that it is important to understand and study why this specific moment in history became such a powerful foundational myth. The fact that you accept it as a myth and demystify it doesn't mean that it's not interesting. Myths can be fascinating, so you can actually recoup some of that capital (assuming you want to think in those terms), seeing it not as an eternal value, a moral authority that you need to venerate and worship, but as a cultural and historical phenomenon that requires understanding and exploration vis-à-vis other cultures, vis-à-vis other people, vis-à-vis other kinds of connections. Another response could be to say that the epistemic decolonization of archaeological thinking and the engagement with the full richness and diversity of the material world would allow us to produce alternative stories about the past, free from nationalized teleologies, free from the mythical tales about glory, death and sacrifice: Potential histories that can leave open many alternative scenaria about the present and the future.[16]

So I can see a way out of this conundrum, this symbolic capital trap, but it's not easy to convince many people, and very often the efforts at decolonizing archaeology and countering the various myths come up against stereotypical views on what globalization is, on what postmodernity is, or against material realities that people call postmodernity, globalization or new world order. So very often, people, including some of my colleagues, would say to me that "what you're doing now is actually accepting a new world order of "postmodern" globalized entities, whereas I want to keep my own distinctiveness, I want to keep my own identity, my national identity; and I want to still believe that my heritage is important, and you want to erase all that, or you want to level it, and you would deprive us of something we are proud of, despite our marginal global position today. And this allows major, global Western imperial powers to dominate the rest of the world, because we don't have any defenses if you take away my symbolic capital of classical antiquity." You could see how the symbolic capital of classical antiquity is presented as a kind of anti-imperial weapon. Some would claim that, in theoretical terms, this is strategic essentialism. So, it's difficult to argue against it, but I think it is worth doing so, worth probing the meanings of globalization, as well as exposing the imperial and racial–colonial roots of that symbolic capital. And perhaps adding that a relational understanding and connection with previous, diverse peoples and cultures based on sharing a place and a landscape, and perhaps, for many, partaking of a similar language, is more appropriate than a sense of "ownership" implied by the words "my heritage;" a sense of ownership grounded in essentialist genealogical notions of cultural or even genetic continuity.

So what can be done in practical terms, today? For me, a key moment for decolonizing archaeology, heritage, and the country as a whole, is the contemporary moment of intensified global migration, of what I have called, the new nomadic age.[17] "Migration crisis" is often the name used to describe this moment. If indeed this is a crisis, it's not a migration crisis, but a reception crisis of the Global North which is finding it difficult to deal with its own imperial past and present, and their contemporary effects. It can be argued that border crossers today embody the return of the colonized who have been haunting the Global North for centuries. Further, I want to suggest that this moment can be seen not as a crisis but as an opportunity. I do not mean that we should instrumentalize the lives of border crossers for the benefit of the countries in the Global North, both destination countries and largely transit countries, such as Greece. I mean that border crossers, rather than being a threat to these countries, offer them huge benefits; they perform an important service. Besides economics, demographics, and everything else, they hold a mirror in front of us all, asking us to reflect on the histories of colonization and crypto-colonization. They also offer an opportunity to countries like Greece that have been, forcibly and brutally, ethnically, and racially homogenized, to declare, openly and proudly, their ethnic and cultural diversity, and perhaps rediscover their multiple, entangled histories. More importantly, they invite the country and its people to reflect on their own position in the history of whiteness, their contribution in the constitution of racialized global order. Migrants and border crossers, or rather people on the move from Asian and African countries, by their very presence in the country, say to the people of Greece: You can no longer take your whiteness as a given and naturalized fact, you need to historicize and problematize it.

RG: And you can leverage this realization to promote another, decolonized archaeology.

YH: As far as archaeology, material culture, and material heritage is concerned, border crossers and the whole assemblage of migration create new material realities on the ground, from refugee camps to detention centers and discarded life vests, a transient materiality that requires care and attention, a materiality that tells stories and speaks of truths that cannot be found elsewhere and cannot be told in other ways.[18] For a start, thus, contemporary border crossing invites border countries, countries that operate as buffer zones between the Global South and the Global North, to expand their own definition of archaeology and material heritage; to diversify and enlarge the material archive; to accept these material realities, these new ruins, these transient things, as worthy of attention, potential collection, study and imaginative exhibition.

Valorizing such material traces as "archaeological" counters xenophobic discourses that portray border crossers as polluters, not only of the national body but also of beaches and seashores, of the landscapes they traverse and the localities they inhabit during their journey. But they also challenge conventional modernist understandings on materiality and temporality, on worth and value, on permanence and transience, on what is trash and what is collectable. They invite us to appreciate ephemerality, and to think of different ways of engaging with transient matter, beyond the modernist conventions of conservation and permanence, and of aesthetic, vision-oriented appreciation, akin to distant and disembodied veneration. This nomadic materiality invites us to embrace a nomadic thinking which undermines the colonial logic of nationhood, and lays bare the workings of the border, as material reality, as an assemblage and an apparatus, as a relationship, and a method which produces otherness, violence, and profit, as well solidarity and a transcultural space of co-habitation.[19] This is what I have attempted to do with my project of an archaeology of contemporary forced and undocumented migration in the Mediterranean, taking the border island of Lesvos as a key fieldwork locality. In this context, sites such as Moria, the largest refugee camp in Europe, which was completely destroyed by fire in September 2020, become important archaeological sites, the study of which engenders both knowledge and affectivity on contemporary border regimes and segregation, as well as on resilience, ingenuity, and practices of place-making (Fig. 6.2).

Furthermore, people on the move re-energize, enliven material objects linked to previous historical moments, to multi-ethnic and multi-cultural realities. Let's take the rich Islamic material heritage of the country as an example: mosques, baths, cemeteries, fountains, public buildings, all over the country. This is just a small sample of the ones that used to exist, of course. Some of them survived, despite the systematic process of erasure which we talked about in previous chapters. For centuries, most of them were left to rot or they were repurposed and reused as churches, museums and museum storerooms, concert halls, cinemas, or private dwellings. More recently, some of the prominent ones were declared monuments, were restored as such, and were opened for tourist consumption. While Christian ecclesiastic monuments were allowed to operate both as heritage and as living buildings for ritual use by the community of the faith, this did not apply to Islamic religious monuments: Not only did they embody otherness, they were also seen as disconnected from a living community of faith since, legally and bureaucratically, the only substantial recognized minority in Greece, the Muslim minority, is confined to Thrace in the northeast of the country and to some islands in the Dodecanese. But that has not always been true, as there

FIGURE 6.2. Moria, Lesvos: The largest refugee camp in Europe, following its destruction by fire in September 2020. The ubiquitous plastic water bottles have been used here to lay out a sitting or sleeping platform. Photo, Yannis Hamilakis, 5 October 2020.

was also a small number of people of Muslim faith in other parts of the country, whereas new migration has meant that there are now hundreds of thousands of such people, not only in the major urban centers, but also, as agricultural or service workers, all over the country.

Now, it may be hard to accept that until the end of 2020, there was no officially recognized mosque in operation for these people. There were and are, of course hundreds of underground mosques with the full knowledge and tacit acceptance of the authorities. This speaks of a dual process of denial, denial of the new social realities of the country, and denial in terms of the politics of vision: Underground mosques, in poorly ventilated and often dangerous basements, with no prominent signs and, of course, no minarets, maintain a façade of national and religious homogenization, keeping at the same time the official Christian Orthodox Church happy. Athens got its first, officially recognized mosque in late 2020, but even that has no minaret and its architecture resembles a warehouse, as any visual connection to Muslim religious architecture had to be avoided.

Leaving aside the human rights issue here, these new communities, many of them Arabic speakers, can connect to the Islamic material heritage of Greece and can be invited to embrace it. Some mosques dating to the Ottoman times can operate again as places of worship, at least for certain ceremonies and times, if not more regularly, to serve the religious needs of these communities, sending also at the same time a powerful symbolic message of acceptance and integration, especially since many of them are located at the centers of modern cities. Some members of these communities can read the Ottoman Arabic inscriptions which are unintelligible to most inhabitants of Greece, and can even act as guides, explaining to others the ritual and religious significance of architectural and sculptural features in such monuments. But even the most sacred monuments of the Hellenic national imagination and of Western Hellenism, starting with the Parthenon, have their own connection to Islam, acting as mosques for centuries. Retrieving these largely erased or deliberately forgotten histories will enrich the monuments themselves, and more importantly, they will engender a sense of shared material heritage, a shared past of co-existence and co-habitation.

RG: And how will this intersect with archaeological practice "on the ground"?

YH: Archaeologists have recently experimented with various strategies that aim toward decolonization. Some of them, including community archaeology or public archaeology, are often too vague and apolitical and, in any case, concepts such as community have already been co-opted by neoliberal capitalism. But I want to say a word or two about another strategy which I have been personally advocating for some time, archaeological ethnography.[20] More than just the addition of ethnographic methods to the archaeological apparatus, we have defined archaeological ethnography as a shared space of multiple, transcultural encounters, involving things, beings, and humans of diverse background. But perhaps the most important contribution of archaeological ethnography is that it helps us counter the idea of archaeology as absence. Many archaeologists, including some of the most interesting theoretically informed ones, still perpetuate the idea that archaeology is predicated on the notion of absence: We encounter things, which form the basis of our object of study, but we don't have the people; they are absent; they are gone; socio-cultural anthropologists encounter people, we do not, the argument goes.

You can understand where this is coming from: You excavate say, a Neolithic site, you have the buildings, you have lithic tools made of obsidian, but you do not have the people who made them and used them, not living people anyway, you will only occasionally encounter their skeletons. Some socio-cultural anthropologists would even joke that they like archaeology because people cannot talk back. On the other hand, you could argue that this is problematic on several grounds. For a start, establishing a rigid separation between things and humans is a modernist ontology grounded on objectification, and often on utilitarianism, instrumentalism, and commodification. Things can be seen, in some ways, as the material, sensorial extensions of human beings, their bodily, sensorial prostheses.

Moreover, the shared space of archaeological ethnography allows us to see clearly and recognize other human presences, in addition to the presence of dead people who are still there through their material, bodily prostheses. To return to our Neolithic site under

Decolonizing Our Imagination

excavation, during this process people would come and visit all the time (unless we keep them away with fences and wood boards), wanting to see what we have found, but also wanting to understand our work and how we produce knowledge about the past. These people have lived around the site all their lives, they possess an intimate knowledge of its landscape and often its features, and they have perhaps themselves collected things from the surface, as they would work the land or just walk around. To use a neoliberal term, they have a stake in this site, in addition to knowledge, but also an embodied, affective connection with it. In that sense, these people are very much present, and archaeological ethnography valorizes their presence, and invites them to be a key component of the assemblage of the site, learning from their experience and tacit, embodied knowledge. I can see presences where other people see absences. Archaeological ethnography can counter the myth of absence by engaging with those people and by reconnecting perhaps with the pre-modern archaeologies, with other ways of relating to materiality, ways which may not prioritize chronology and scientific analysis but affective connection, or agentic qualities. These are relationships that are now foregrounded within affect theory or memory studies or material culture studies and certain, non-European ethnographies, but which can be also found and studied within the framework of archaeological ethnography, even in European archaeological sites and communities. You can see how this is another way of decolonizing our archaeological imagination, valorizing at the same time local affective and embodied knowledge and experience, that crypto-colonial archaeology has banished as ignorance, or at best, folklore.

RG: This reminds me of Bev Butler's description of the Kathleen Kenyon excavations at Jericho – which have always been held up as the ultimate triumph of dispassionate method (Kenyon famously left flint blades protruding from her meticulously trimmed excavation profiles so as not to subvert the integrity of the baulk) – as a site of "dramas of possession," where archaeologists were as much possessed by the site as they were possessors of it. She says that while trying to maintain a rigid scientific discipline, we view our excavation as liminal space and constantly invoke imaginary encounters and play roles in a themed drama of discovery and reenactment. We therefore "need to re-activate our curiosity and fascination and transformation *vis-à-vis* encounters with the unexpected, liminality, and experiences of 'othering' that take us into alternative cosmologies and world-views."[21] In other words, we have indeed "never been modern," nor should we aspire to be.

I'll try to connect with a few more of the things you said, and then move on to what I think I would like to do in the future. If I were to translate the Greek attachment to Classical remains into our local idiom, you – and I as well – would be asking my colleagues to stop being biblical archaeologists in the traditional sense, or classical archaeologists in the traditional sense. This, naturally, would undermine their perception of their own symbolic capital, of the special value that what they're doing has in the world. They would accuse us of homogenizing and trivializing their archaeology by removing the holiness from the Holy Land. And what you might be suggesting to them is to stop for a moment, reflect on what has been done, describe what has been done and why it was done that way, why it was made significant that way. I think at the foundation is probably a realization that we have come to, and I hope I'm speaking for both of us, that we're not, as the younger archaeologist that I once was thought, excavating the past, or *representing* the past. What I've come to understand, just by observing myself and my peers, is that everything we're doing is in the present, and that what we're excavating is in the present; the things that we are producing may have been fashioned in the past, but now they are in and of the present and not in the past at all. We are making them present; *presenting* them. This understanding then allows us to ask what it is in this convergence around biblical and ancient historical themes that makes archaeology so powerful and attractive, that gives it such a central position in the colonial imagination. Once that is understood, we can seek a way out.

Now, an advantage that I might have is the presence of interlocutors on the Palestinian side who are free, or who can more easily imagine themselves as free, of that baggage, because they never took the position of being biblical archaeologists and ambassadors of Western civilization in the Holy Land. They are able to show me other things that they do – in ethnography, in conversation with local tradition, in appreciating the nonlinear temporalities of vernacular architecture or agricultural landscapes – all situated outside the old paradigm. When I try to think of a decolonized archaeology, then at one level, what will make it special is, as you said, the role that Palestine and its archaeology has played in the Western historical imagination. But we must also recognize that we have to get beyond that role and establish a new way of looking at the country; a path to a shared vision that would accommodate disparate communities, that would appreciate the land for what it is, for what it says about us – about our crimes of omission and commission – and not for the weight it carries in someone else's conception. We need to figure out what weight it carries for present and future generations, and what a critical archaeology can say about that.

I sometimes call this redefining the locus of archaeological passion. The stereotype of archaeological passion in the Holy Land is the discovery of "something that's in the Bible," or, if not actually in the Bible, something that might easily be associated with "ancient history," such as a relic of Pharaonic Egypt; So where is the passion going to be located now? I suggest that what should make us passionate about archaeology is its potential to offer everyone living in Israel/Palestine a new relationship between past and present, a new form of remembering that isn't based on these previous conceptions. Part of that is, of course, unlearning the hegemonic definitions of what is worthwhile, erasing that whole scale of values and establishing a new one, based on the sum and range of the histories and traditions of the people who are there now. So yes, the cut-off date of 1700 has to be abolished and the concept of antiquity has to be demoted, because the power of the past-made-present lies not in its age, but in the power it has to startle us; to make us recalibrate our understanding of the world. We are asking archaeologists to change their concept of themselves, the way they are seen or presented, and the way they're valued in society.[22]

The relatively new and burgeoning field of contemporary archaeology[23] can help us understand what archaeology – or to be more precise, the archaeological gaze – has to offer when the mere antiquity of an object is taken out of the equation. By focusing on what is hidden, covered up, made invisible and forgotten in the world of our own making – the places from which we avert our gaze, the objects that we cast away or make obsolete, the pace of obliteration of recent and distant pasts – we take on a task of memory-work that is vital to our wellbeing.

YH: We are asking archaeologists to get rid of the archaeo- in the word archaeology, the definition of one's mission as the study of antiquity.[24]

RG: We're asking them to make themselves significant in their ability to show everyone, and themselves, how we construct our worlds out of memories incorporated in temporally heterogeneous assemblages of things, places, and actors, human and non-human. Somewhere in there is a new definition of what archaeologists should be.

YH: A brief comment, here: In my own work, I have come to the conclusion, like you, that archaeology is not about the past, but neither is it about just the present itself in the absolute sense. It is practiced in the present, of course, but it's about multitemporal existences. Some archaeologists would claim that archaeology is a social practice of and in the present, and I can understand why they make such claim in their effort to counter conventional definitions of archaeology as an escapist, objectivist practice obsessed with chronometry. But in saying that archaeology is of and in the present, with no further elaboration and discussion, you run into various problems: You risk becoming presentist, you run the danger of temporal reductionism, of not appreciating the multiplicity and richness of temporal understanding in various contexts. You ignore the fact that people care about different conceptions of the past, about senses of history and senses of time and time depth. Finally, you also ignore the rich philosophical discussion on the link between materiality and duration, developed by a number of people, most notably Henri Bergson and Gilles Deleuze among others,[25] the idea, in other words, that duration is a fundamental property of matter, and that the same material entities partake in different temporal moments; they may be of the present but at the same time contain, virtually, all past moments. So, for me, every material thing, all material entities are multitemporal, they are present and past at the same time. All pasts are contained virtually in every material thing although only certain past temporal moments are recalled and enacted in a specific moment in the present. The politics of memory and the politics of sensoriality are key in this recalling, in this presencing, especially since the senses are multi-temporal themselves: Every sensorial perception is full of memories, Bergson has taught us.[26]

In the past, I have used various examples to illustrate this thesis. Here is another one from a recent visit to the Acropolis of Athens. We have talked how this context became the subject of massive ritual cleansing and purification since the early 19th century, in an effort to impose a temporal and cultural homogeneity, to establish the monochromy of the classical upon a rich multi-temporal, palimpsestic landscape, to produce a new sacred landscape for national veneration and commercial exploitation. There are things, however, which have escaped this systematic erasure. In Fig. 6.3, among the discarded rubble atop of this most sacred specimen of Hellenism, you can make out the rounded top of a Muslim tombstone, coming perhaps from the cemetery which existed on the foothill of the Acropolis in Ottoman times.

It is made of marble, and it is perhaps a reworked piece from an ancient classical monument, a widespread social practice at the time. The authorized and authoritative discourse on this site would have us believe that we are visiting a classical archaeological site. But the resistance of materiality, and the archaeological unconscious (to evoke the Benjaminian optical unconscious) shatter such archaeological orthodoxies, give rise to nearly erased pasts, enable them to become alive again, and to haunt us. An interesting juxtaposition here: The classical ruins, which are being continually restored, made whole, in order to reach their ancient grandeur again on the one hand, and the caged-in (seemingly for protection purposes), forgotten, un-signposted rubble, the pile of fragments, full of surprises and material agency and energy, on the other.[27] This is a piece of marble which contains the geological time, the time of the classical, the Ottoman time, and the times when it was a component in funerary and commemorative rituals, as well as the time of its re-discovery and haunted presence today. This is a multi-temporal fragment of a multi-temporal archaeology with much decolonial potential.

FIGURE 6.3. Rubble in the midst of heavily reconstructed ruins: Fragments from Muslim tombstones on the Acropolis. Photo, Yannis Hamilakis, 28 March 2021.

Decolonizing Our Imagination

So, as counter-modern archaeologists we are not interested in "antique" things purely because of their antiquity, and the glorious, sacred heritage they embody, we are interested in *all* things because of their multi-temporality and agency, their sensorial and affective affordances, and their ability to intervene in the present, containing at the same time multiple pasts. Our archaeology is cultural production in the present, a process of mediation between different worlds. We reassemble multi-temporal fragments to weave new stories and produce new material realities. In addition to the materiality of things, we also care deeply about the temporality of things, and the entanglement of the two.

RG: That's a very important qualification. Every object we study carries its own temporality or duration, making the assemblages that we study palimpsests. Nothing we see, whether an object or a building or a natural landscape, can be encompassed by a description of its present condition. They're all carrying with them something of the past, and yet, here they are now. This is what we're making of them now. When I thought about what kind of things archaeologists would get passionate about, I initially thought about the landscape: How the landscape affects those who sense it and move in it, how it is a palimpsest, and how its suppressed configurations haunt attempts to obliterate it in supermodern development. But in fact, the haunting of the present by the past might be one of the most powerful characteristics of town- and village-scapes as well. In rural Palestine I have much to learn from Palestinian partners for whom the landscape – a creation of natural and human agency – speaks with more immediacy and significance than for me, who came as an immigrant and has lived in an urban setting. In Tel Aviv, the natural and settled landscapes of urban Palestinian Jaffa and the villages around it refuse to disappear, haunting it from within, while in a town like Jerusalem it seems we all have a lot to learn about accommodating its complex temporality and keeping the ghosts at bay.

YH: Yes, and the same could be said of many other indigenous ontologies in other settler colonial contexts, such as the USA, South America or Australia, where we read and hear that history, time and memory are embedded in the land, and in plants and animals, beyond humans and their artefacts. These are contexts where chronometry is irrelevant, and multi-temporality and temporal co-existence (rather than succession) are central tenets of life for all beings. We referenced earlier continental philosophers in relation to these ideas, but we often forget that these ontologies have been fundamental in the life of colonized people, and it is about time we give them their due.[28] A decolonial archaeology of Greece, of Israel, or of any context cannot afford to ignore such ideas.

RG: And then, perhaps on the other end of the spectrum from the land itself, is the constant movement – forced and unforced – of people, as individuals and as collectives: Let's understand that dynamic, which is so powerful and important in our own world. Connected to that is the topic of memory work: How we use (or abuse) our physical surroundings to create anchors for memory or patches of intentional forgetting or suppression.

This brings me to the project that I have just begun, along with a group of colleagues, in the borderline Palestinian/Lebanese village of Qadas. Depopulated in 1948 (Fig. 6.4), it has been subjected to ongoing destruction from then to the present. At this stage in the project, our primary interest is in this ongoing "event;" recognizing the former village as a space of memory and continuous disaggregation. You talked about absence a moment ago: I had a discussion with a colleague in the project about the habit we have of describing such villages as blank spaces on the map (which they often literally are). We say that they've been excised from memory, that we Israelis have intentionally forgotten them. He insists that this is not, in fact, the case: That ruin, that "no man's land," that place that you try to avoid, is very much present, whether in a negative way for Israelis, who avert their eyes, or as a present and complete place, a living village, for the refugees and their descendants in Lebanon. So how can you say it is absent? It's not absent, but suppressed, or repressed. Israelis might avert their eyes, but even so it's present. That is precisely where we are directing our gaze: We are looking at how the village was made – through a series of superimposed material interventions – first into a battleground, then into a place to be avoided between 1948 and now. We of course use archival materials, as well as a very important component of oral histories collected from three generations from both sides of the divide, but the main thrust of

Decolonizing Our Imagination

FIGURE 6.4. Ruins of Qadas Village in northern Palestine/Israel. Photo, Raphael Greenberg, February 2021

the archaeological portion of our work (we are willing workers, if nothing else!) focuses on a methodic, or even forensic, examination of the material remains: How was the village transformed by war? How was it abandoned, looted, destroyed, and made un-visible? What evidence is there of surreptitious return or of material subtraction? How do we reintroduce it to view, and allow its material remains to do their work on affect and memory? This is something that archaeologists are uniquely qualified to do, both in terms of their multi-dimensional *modus operandi* and their willingness to put in the time and sheer physical effort. Not just any archaeologists, but Israeli ones, who have access to the site and who are members of a community that was complicit in its destruction (the abandoned village was surveyed in 1966 by archaeologists, who approved its complete destruction, with the recommendation that "[Roman] architectural items in secondary use be identified and collected").[29] Who else would do it? An ethnographer alone would not have the method or the tools to carry this out; written archives, compiled by interested parties, won't tell the story. Village oral histories end just before the destruction. We're the only ones who really have the opportunity and responsibility to do it; we can tell this story and we must tell this story; that is something that we can be passionate about, something that will have a palpable effect on our community, our colleagues, and ourselves.

YH: I think we both ended on an optimistic note, so that's a good way to bring this chapter to an end, before we wrap up our discussion.

Notes

1 On decolonizing archaeology along broader, antiracist lines see Omilade Flewellen et al. 2021. On the commemorative monuments as part of the global, antiracist uprising of 2020, see Hamilakis 2020, and the collaboratively produced syllabus, *"All Monuments Must Fall."*
2 E.g. Hamilakis 2013b, 2017; Hamilakis and Labanyi 2008.
3 Mignolo 2009, 2011.
4 Cf. Azoulay 2019.
5 On the concept of un-disciplining archaeology inspired by Amerindian ontologies, see Haber 2012.
6 Cf. Hamilakis 2000.
7 Cf. Voudouri 2010, 2017, for overviews.
8 For a related discussion with reference to the term αρχεῖον (archive) and the archival impulse, see Derrida 1996; also Herzfeld 1987: 40.
9 Nativ and Lucas 2020.
10 On the concept of banal nationalism, see Billig 1995.
11 Greenberg and Keinan 2007.
12 Veracini 2006.
13 Smith 2013.
14 E.g., Ziadeh-Seely 2007; Jubeh 2010, 2018; Bshara 2013.
15 Daʻadli 2019.
16 Azoulay 2019; for another, recent, radical and liberating attack on history-writing as teleology see Graeber and Wengrow 2021.
17 Hamilakis 2018a.
18 Cf. Hamilakis 2018b.

19 Cf. Mezzadra and Neilson 2013; and on nomadic, feminist thinking, Braidotti 2012.
20 Cf. Hamilakis 2011; Hamilakis and Anagnostopoulos 2009; Stefanou and Antoniadou 2021.
21 Butler 2020.
22 Greenberg 2019; Nativ and Lucas 2020.
23 Gonzalez-Ruibal 2019.
24 Cf. Ingold 2010.
25 Bergson 1991; Deleuze 1991.
26 Cf. Hamilakis 2013b.
27 Cf. Gordillo 2014.
28 E.g. Todd 2016; Ferguson and Colwell-Chanthaphonh 2006; Laluk 2017.
29 Qadesh Naftali Inspection File, Israel Antiquities Authority archives.

CHAPTER 7

Conclusion

> ... I do not know what meaning classical studies could have for our time if they were not untimely – that is to say, acting counter to our time and thereby acting on our time and, let us hope, for the benefit of a time to come.
>
> (Nietzsche 1997[1876]: 60)

We embarked on this dialog during the first wave of the Covid global pandemic, and we completed it at the peak of the second (or third, depending on how one counts them) but clearly not the last one. The onset of the age of pandemics happened in the midst of already troubled times. If there is one concept that has captured the anxiety of the moment among scholars, that's the idea of ruins and ruination. The term is increasingly encountered in the gloomy writings that narrate the environmental and planetary crisis but also in the ones that trace the lasting remnants of the colonial order of modernity.

By placing archaeology at the center of our inquiry here, we have invited the reader to take a close look at ruins, not only in their metaphorical sense but also in their directly physical, raw, multi-sensorial materiality. We have suggested that at this moment of trouble, it will be instructive and hopeful to conjure up the ruins that lie at the "ground zero" of modernity, the ruins of the "holy lands" that propped up and sustained the racialized, modernist colonial order. Athens and Jerusalem, Hellenism, and Judaism were, of course, closely linked well before the modernist phenomena we talked about, the nation-states we have scrutinized here[1]. Their early modern association may have been linguistic, scriptural and theological, and its effect perhaps emancipatory: The languages of the Old and the New Testament had to be learned, in order to counter the authority of Latin and of the Church. But that theological heritage seemed to have been carried through in later modernity and become its political theology; it was additionally nourished by Humanism and universalism, as well the "god of modernity," the nation and its trappings.

If holy books and sacred texts, be they classical Greek works or the Bible, were the key guiding forces that shaped the colonial projects of imagining these two respective holy lands, in both cases ruins, material remnants, buildings and objects were essential in grounding this work of imagination, in giving it topographic veracity, sensorial immediacy, and affective power. These ruins shaped the two national–colonial projects as much as they were shaped by them. Yet, while we have discussed extensively the crypto-colonizing features of this process, we have shown that self-colonization was also at play here; and while both Greece and Israel were constructed as the borderlands of the imaginary topos of the civilized West as well its buffer zones, both crypto-colonized nations had engaged, and in the case of Israel still engage, in their own, often brutal, colonial projects: It was the condition and the premise of coloniality that produced these two nation-states (and perhaps, all nation-states), and it was the very same condition of coloniality that turned these two crypto-colonized states into colonizers.

The 19th century is bookended by two nationalisms that have taken on almost transcendental significance in the eyes of both champions and detractors because of the centrality of Hellenism and Judaism in the modernist European project. Hellenism (in both its Western and its Indigenous, modern Greek versions) may have been part of the broader humanistic project, linked directly to the emergence of modern bourgeois morality, political consciousness, temporality, and aesthetic, embracing at the same time the rationale of citizenship, of the autonomous individual, and, of course, of property and capital. Judaism played a crucial role in conceptualizing enlightened, universal European modernity and providing it with a biblical ethos and telos, shared with Christianity. Despite the proclamations of secularism and rationalism, the political theology of orientalism, colonialism, and nationalism merged with directly religious, occult, messianic theologies. The elites in both national projects, in an act partly of self-colonization and partly of expediency, still hark back to these principles and to this modernist and humanistic heritage, seeing it as an emancipatory project worth celebrating. The 2021 Greek bicentenary celebrations of the Greek War of Independence are a case in point. Yet these laudatory performances conceal the racial and colonial grounds of such edifices. Indeed, for both national projects, race has been, for the past two centuries, the white elephant in the room, the specter that haunts us. Greece and Israel as modern states were both whitened, at the same time as the ancient pasts which had become their golden ages were Europeanized and racialized. The glorious ruins, be they the white columns of temples, the imagined transcendence of a subterranean city, or, increasingly, the DNA traces of proclaimed ancestors, still sustain this racialized order. The two national-cum-colonial projects, that of Greece and Israel, despite their historical idiosyncrasies and differences, form part of that broader global order; they are not exceptional cases, although self-proclaimed exceptionalism is one of the strategies of masking and misrecognition that the proponents of these national projects have adopted.

This order has been challenged, of course, time and again by diverse social actors. It is also being challenged, perhaps more ferociously, today, at a time when decolonization, at least as a word, is on everyone's lips, and uprisings against white supremacy spring up everywhere. We have suggested here that if these efforts are to succeed, we will have to counter purification with contamination, we will need to forge alliances with the colonized "others," be it the people on the move who are, right now, trying to cross national borders or the ones who continue to suffer due to settler colonialism, whether in the West Bank or elsewhere. As for archaeology, while it's undergoing its own decolonial moment, we should perhaps remember that its continuing value lies not only in showing that things could have been otherwise, and perhaps could *still* turn so, but also in the fact that the material remnants it cares for and valorizes (and sometimes attempts to suppress) harbor enormous, almost

Conclusion

revolutionary potential: They are both uncanny and untimely, as Nietzsche would put it; they can spring up from nowhere to unsettle us, untamed by our chronometry; in the linearity and teleology of progressivism, they will always be out of line, deeply affective and out of order at the same time, material memories which will always come from the future.

Note

1 Cf. Lambropoulos 1993.

References

Abu El-Haj, N. 2001. *Facts on the Ground: Archaeological Practice and Territorial Self-Fashioning in Israeli Society*. Chicago: University of Chicago Press.

Abu El-Haj, N. 2002. Producing (arti) facts: archaeology and power during the British mandate of Palestine. *Israel Studies* 7: 33–61.

Abu El-Haj, N. 2012. *The Genealogical Science: The Search for Jewish Origins and the Politics of Epistemology*. Chicago: University of Chicago Press.

Agranat-Tamir, L., Waldman, S., Martin, M.A.S., Gokhman, D., Mishol, N.,, Eshel, T., Charonet, O., Rohland, N., Mallick, S., Adamski, N., Lawson, A.-M., Mah, M., Michel, M., Oppenheimer, J., Stewardson, K., Candilio, F., Keating, D., Gamarra, B., Tzur, S., Novak, M., Kalisher, R., Bechar, S., Eshed, V., Kennet, D.J., Faerman, M., Yahalom-Mack, N., Monge, J.M., Govrin, Y., Erel, Y., Yakir, B., Pinhasi, R., Carmi, S., Finkelstein, I., Carmel, L., and Reich, D. 2020. The genomic history of the Bronze Age southern Levant. *Cell* 181: 1146–1157. https://doi.org/10.1016/j.cell.2020.04.024

Albright, W.F. 1949. *The Archaeology of Palestine*. Hammondsworth: Penguin.

Al-Houdalieh, S. 2010. The sacred place of Sheikh Shihab ed-Din. *Palestine Exploration Quarterly* 142.2: 127–141.

Al-Houdalieh, S. 2012a. Archaeological heritage and spiritual protection: looting and the *jinn* in Palestine. *Journal of Mediterranean Archaeology* 25.1: 99–120.

Al-Houdalieh, S. 2012b. Palestinian antiquities looters, their skill development, methodology and specialised terminology: an ethnographic study. *Palestine Exploration Quarterly* 144.2: 115–127.

Ambridge, L.J. 2012. Imperialism and racial geography in James Henry Breasted's *Ancient Times, a History of the Early World*. *Journal of Egyptian History* 5: 12–33.

Amygdalou, K. and Kolovos, I. 2021. Το τζαμί του Ναυπλίου που μετασκευάστηκε στο "πρώτον εν Ελλάδι βουλευτήριον" [The Nafplio mosque which was repurposed as the "first parliament in Greece"]. In *Πως Προσεγγίζουμε το 1821? Πολιτική, Κοινωνία, και Ιδεολογία στην Ελληνική Επανάσταση [How Do We Approach 1821? Politics, Society, and Ideology in the Greek Revolution]*, edited by I. Kolovos and D. Dimitropoulos, 77–105. Athens: Efimerida ton Syntakton.

Anagnostopoulou, S. 2021. Η διπλή ανάγνωση της Επανάστασης στο πλαίσιο της αυτοκρατορικής λογικής περί εξουσίας του Πατριαρχείου Κωνσταντινουπόλεως: Από τον οθωμανορθόδοξο πατριωτισμό στον ελληνικό αλυτρωτισμό [The double reading of the Revolution in the context of the Patriarchate of Constantinople's imperial logic about power: from the Ottoman-Orthodox patriotism to the Greek irredentism]. In *Πως Προσεγγίζουμε το 1821? Πολιτική, Κοινωνία, και Ιδεολογία στην Ελληνική Επανάσταση [How Do We Approach 1821? Politics, Society, and Ideology in the Greek Revolution]*, edited by I. Kolovos and D. Dimitropoulos, 165–188. Athens: Efimerida ton Syntakton.

Anagnostou, G. 2009. *Contours of White Ethnicity: Popular Ethnography and the Making of Usable Pasts in Greek America*. Athens, OH: Ohio University Press.

Anderson, Benedict. 1991. *Imagined Communities: Reflections on the Origins and Spread of Nationalism*. London: Verso.

Anderson, Ben. 2015. "An alternative discourse": local interpreters of antiquities in the Ottoman empire. *Journal of Field Archaeology* 40.4: 50–60.

Anderson, W. 1995. Excremental colonialism: public health and the poetics of pollution. *Critical Inquiry* 21: 640–669.

Archimandritis, G. 2019. Μανώλης Κορρές, "Ο Παρθενώνας συμβολίζει την τελειότητα" [Manolis Korres, "The Parthenon stands for perfection"]. *Blue Magazine (Aegean Airlines)* 79: 212–220.

Arvanitakis, D.D. 2020. *Η Αγωγή του Πολίτη: Η Γαλλική Παρουσία στο Ιόνιο (1797–1799) και το Έθνος των Ελλήνων [Civics: The French Presence in the Ionian Sea (1797–1799) and the Nation of the Greeks]*. Iraklio: Crete University Press.

Athanassoglou-Kallmyer, N. 1989. *French Images from the Greek War of Independence, 1821–1830: Art and Politics under the Restoration*. New Haven: Yale University Press.

Avdela, E., Arvanitakis, D., Delveroudi, E., Matthiopoulos, E., Petmezas, S., and Sakellaropoulos, T. (eds). 2017. *Φυλετικές Θεωρίες στην Ελλάδα: Προσλήψεις και Χρήσεις στις Επιστήμες, την Πολιτική, τη Λογοτεχνία και την Ιστορία της Τέχνης κατά τον 19ο και τον 20ό Αιώνα [Racial Theories*

References

in Greece: Perception and Use in Science, Politics, Literature and Art History in the 19th and 20th Centuries]. Iraklio: Crete University Press.

Avikunthak, A. 2021. *Bureaucratic Archaeology: State, Science, and Past in Postcolonial India*. Cambridge: Cambridge University Press.

Avineri, S. 1985. *Moses Hess: Prophet of Communism and Zionism*. New York: New York University Press.

Azoulay, A. 2019. *Potential History: Unlearning Imperialism*. London: Verso.

Bahrani, Z., Çelik, Z., and Eldem, E. (eds). 2011. *Scramble for the Past: The Story of Archaeology in the Ottoman Empire, 1733–1914*. Istanbul: Salt.

Baloglou, Ch. 2009. The diffusion of the ideas of Saint-Simon in the Hellenic state and their reception thereby (1825–1837). *History of Economic Ideas* 17.2: 155–179.

Bar, D. 2008. Reconstructing the past: the creation of Jewish sacred space in the State of Israel, 1948–1967. *Israel Studies* 13: 1–21.

Bar, D. 2018. Between Muslim and Jewish sanctity: Judaizing Muslim holy places in the State of Israel, 1948–1967. *Journal of Historical Geography* 59: 68–76.

Bar-Yosef, E. 2003. Christian Zionism and Victorian culture. *Israel Studies* 8.2: 18–44.

Bar-Yosef, E. 2005. *The Holy Land in English Culture 1799–1917: Palestine and the Question of Orientalism*. Oxford: Clarendon.

Beaton, R. 2013. *Byron's War: Romantic Rebellion, Greek Revolution*. Cambridge: Cambridge University Press.

Beckerleg, S. 2007. African Bedouin in Palestine. *African and Asian Studies* 6: 289–303.

Benvenisti, M. 2000. *Sacred Landscape: The Buried History of the Holy Land since 1948*. Berkeley: University of California Press.

Ben-Yehuda, N. 2007. Excavating Masada: the politics–archaeology connection at work. In *Selective Remembrances: Archaeology in the Construction, Commemoration, and Consecration of National Pasts*, edited by P.L. Kohl, M. Kozelsky, and N. Ben-Yehuda, 247–276. Chicago: University of Chicago Press.

Bergson, H. 1991[1908]. *Matter and Memory*. New York: Zone Books.

Billig, M. 1995. *Banal Nationalism*. London: Sage.

Bohotis, Th. 2015. *Ελέγχοντας τον Τόπο του Παρελθόντος: Η Γερμανοελληνική Σχέση Εξουσίας στις Ανασκαφές της Ολυμπίας, 1869 – 1882. [Controlling the Place of the Past: The Greek–German Power Relationship during the Olympia Excavations, 1869–1882]*. Iraklio: Crete University Press.

Boyarin, D. 1997. *Unheroic Conduct: The Rise of Heterosexuality and the Invention of the Jewish Man*. Berkeley: University of California Press.

Braidotti, R. 2012. *Nomadic Theory*. New York: Columbia University Press.

Brownell, S. (ed). 2008. *The 1904 Anthropology Days and Olympic Games: Sport, Race, and American Imperialism*. Lincoln, NE: University of Nebraska Press.

Bruchac, M.M. 2014. Decolonization in archaeological theory. In *Encyclopedia of Global Archaeology*, edited by C. Smith, 2069–2077. New York: Springer.

Bshara, K. 2013. Heritage in Palestine: colonial legacy in postcolonial discourse. *Archaeologies* 9.2: 295–319.

Buck-Morss, S. 1992. Aesthetics and anaesthetics: Walter Benjamin's artwork essay reconsidered. *October* 62: 3–41.

Butler, B. 2020. Jericho syndromes: 'Digging Up Jericho' as ritual dramas of possession. In *Digging Up Jericho: Past, Present and Future*, edited by R.T. Sparks, B. Finlayson, B. Wagemakers, and J.M. Briffa, 47–68. Oxford: Archaeopress.

Calotychos, V. 2004. *Modern Greece: A Cultural Poetics*. Oxford: Berg.

Canaan, T. 1922. *Haunted Springs and Water-Demons in Palestine. Studies in Palestinian Folklore and Customs II*. Jerusalem: Palestine Oriental Society.

Carabott, Ph., Hamilakis, Y., and Papargyriou, E. (eds). 2015. *Camera Graeca: Photographs, Narratives, Materialities*. Routledge: London.

Chakrabarty, D. 2000. *Provincializing Europe: Post-colonial Thought and Historical Difference*. Princeton: Princeton University Press.

Chambers, I. 2007. *Mediterranean Crossings: The Politics of an Interrupted Modernity*. Durham, NC: Duke University Press.

Chapoutot, J. 2016. *Greeks, Romans, Germans: How the Nazis Usurped Europe's Classical Past*. Translated by R.R. Nybakken. Berkeley: University of California Press.

Chateaubriand, F.A.R. 1825. *Note Sur la Grèce*. Paris: Le Normant.

Chatterjee, P. 1986. *Nationalist Thought and the Colonial World: A Derivative Discourse*. London: Zed Books.

Christopoulos, D. 2019. *Ποιος Είναι Έλληνας Πολίτης; Δυο Αιώνες Ιθαγένεια [Who Is a Greek Citizen? Two Centuries of Ithagenia]*. Athens: Vivliorama.

Christopoulos, D. and Spyropoulou, G. 2019. Buffer states: Greek–Turkish framing on the EU externalisation policy of refugee management. In *Greece and Turkey in Conflict and Cooperation: From Europeanization to De-Europeanization*, edited by A. Heraclides and G. Alioğlu Çakmak, 271–185. London: Routledge.

Close, D. 1995. *The Origins of the Greek Civil War*. London: Longman.

Comaroff, J. and Comaroff, J.L. 1999. Occult economies and the violence of abstraction: notes from the South African postcolony. *American Ethnologist* 26.2: 279–303.

Conder, C.R. 1878. *Tent Work in Palestine*, vol. II. London: Richard Bentley and Son.

References

Conder, C. 1889. *Palestine*. New York: Dodd, Mead & Company.
Crellin, R. and Harris, O. 2020. Beyond binaries: interrogating ancient DNA. *Archaeological Dialogues* 27.1: 37–56.
Crome, A. 2018. *Christian Zionism and English National Identity, 1600–1850*. London: Palgrave Macmillan.
Daʻadli, T. 2019. Remains of Ottoman buildings in the city of al-Ludd. *Der Islam* 96.1: 158–189.
Damaskos, D. and Plantzos, D. (eds). 2008. *A Singular Antiquity: Archaeology and Hellenic Identity in 20th c. Greece*. Athens: The Benaki Museum.
David, A. 2018. Mysterious 6500-year-old culture was brought by migrants, researchers say. *Ha'aretz*, August 20, 2018. www.haaretz.com/archaeology/MAGAZINE-mysterious-6-500-year-old-culture-in-israel-brought-by-migrants-1.6389513. Accessed August 4, 2021.
Davis, J. 2000. Warriors for the Fatherland: national consciousness and archaeology in "barbarian" Epirus and "verdant" Ionia, 1912–22. *Journal of Mediterranean Archaeology* 13.1: 76–98.
Davis, J. 2003. A foreign school of archaeology and the politics of archaeological practice: Anatolia 1922. *Journal of Mediterranean Archaeology* 16.2: 145–172.
Davis, J. 2021. "Metropolitan Transportation": Sardis, Colophon, and the Asia Minor Disaster of 1922. *From the Archivist's Notebook*, July 3, 2021. https://nataliavogeikoff.com/2021/07/03/metropolitan-transportation-sardis-colophon-and-the-asia-minor-disaster-of-1922/?fbclid=IwAR0V2VUewggoFPahTcE942BcR1USB3QvnLyUFbjhU-5OSD7k4E77A0yfovg (accessed July 9, 2021).
Davis, J. and Vogeikoff-Brogan, N. (eds). 2013. *Philhellenism, Philanthropy, or Political Convenience? American Archaeology in Greece*. Princeton: American School of Classical Studies at Athens (Hesperia 82.1).
Deleuze, G. 1991[1966]. *Bergsonism*. Translated by H. Tomlinson and B. Habberjam. New York: Zone Books.
Derrida, J. 1996. *Archive Fever: A Freudian Impression*. Translated by E. Prenowitz. Chicago: Chicago University Press.
Díaz-Andreu, M. 2007. *A World History of Nineteenth-Century Archaeology: Nationalism, Colonialism, and the Past*. Oxford: Oxford University Press.
Dimitropoulos, D. (ed) 2020. *Αλλάζοντας το Χάρτη: Ζητήματα Μετονομασιών στη Μεσόγειο, 19ος και 20ός Αιώνας* [*Changing the Map: Issues of Name-Changing in the Mediterranean in the 19th and 20th Centuries*]. Athens: Ethniko Idryma Erevnon.
Dobie, M. 2011. *Foreign Bodies: Gender, Language, and Culture in French Orientalism*. Stanford, CA: Stanford University Press.
Dodwell, E. 1819. *A Classical and Topographical Tour through Greece during the Years 1801, 1805, and 1806*, 2 vols. London: Rodwell and Martin.

Douglas, M. 1966. *Purity and Danger: An Analysis of the Concepts of Pollution and Taboo*. London: Routledge and Kegan Paul.

Doumanis, N. 1997. *Myth and Memory in the Mediterranean: Remembering Fascism's Empire*. Basingstoke: Macmillan.

Du Bois, W.E.B. 2007 [1903]. *The Souls of the Black Folk*. Oxford: Oxford University Press.

Dudinski, N. (dir.) 2006. Rogem Ganim: The Past on Our Doorstep. www.youtube.com/watch?v=ef3fPcrB11c

Dumont, S. 2020. *Vrysaki: A Neighborhood Lost in Search for the Athenian Agora*. Princeton: American School of Classical Studies.

Dyson, S.L. 2006. *In the Pursuit of Ancient Pasts: A History of Classical Archaeology in the Nineteenth and Twentieth Centuries*. New Haven: Yale University Press.

Elon, A. 1971. *The Israelis: Founders and Sons*. London: Weidenfeld and Nicholson.

Elon, A. 1979. A native on his native land" [review of Moshe Dayan, *Living with the Bible*], *New York Times*, January 14, 1979.

Emberling, G. 2010. *Pioneers to the Past: American Archaeologists in the Middle East 1919–1920*. Chicago: Oriental Institute Museum.

Fabian, J. 1983. *Time and the Other: How Anthropology Makes Its Object*. New York: Columbia University Press.

Fallmerayer, J.Ph. 1830. *Geschichte der Halbinsel Morea während des Mittelalters, 1. Untergang der peloponnesischen Hellenen und Wiederbevölkerung des leeren Bodens durch slavische Volksstämme*. Stuttgart and Tübingen: Cotta'schen Buchhandlung.

Feige, M. 2001. Identity, ritual and pilgrimage: the meetings of the Israel Exploration Society. In *Divergent Jewish Culture Israel and America*, edited by D.P. Moore and S.I. Troen, 87–106. New Haven: Yale University Press.

Feige, M. 2007. Recovering authenticity: West Bank settlers and the second stage of national archaeology. In *Selective Remembrances: Archaeology in the Construction, Commemoration, and Consecration of National Pasts*, edited by P.L. Kohl, M. Kozelsky, and N. Ben-Yehuda, 277–297 eds. Chicago: University of Chicago Press.

Ferguson, M. 2008. Enslaved and emancipated Africans on Crete. In *Race and Slavery in the Middle East: Histories of Trans-Saharan Africans in Nineteenth-Century Egypt, Sudan, and the Ottoman Mediterranean*, edited by T. Walz and K.M. Cuno, 171–195. Cairo: The American University in Cairo Press.

Ferguson, T.J. and Colwel-Chanthaphonh, C. 2006. *History Is in the Land: Multivocal Tribal Traditions in Arizona's San Pedro Valley*. Tucson: University of Arizona Press.

Fleming, K.E. 1999. *The Muslim Bonaparte: Diplomacy and Orientalism in Ali Pasha's Greece*. Princeton: Princeton University Press.

References

Fleming, K.E. 2000. *Orientalism, the Balkans and Balkan historiography. American Historical Review* 105: 1218–1233.

Fleming, K.E. 2010. Ο Χερτζλ στην Ακρόπολη. Μεγάλες ιστορίες, μικρά κράτη: Ελλάδα, Ισραήλ, και τα όρια του έθνους [Herzl on the Acropolis. Big Histories, Small Countries: Greece, Israel, and the limits of the nation]. *Athens Review of Books* 8: 32–37.

Foucault, M. 2003. *Society Must Be Defended: Lectures at the Collège de France, 1975–76*, translated by David Macey. London: Penguin Books.

Fouseki, K. 2006. Conflicting discourses on the construction of the New Acropolis Museum: past and present. *European Review of History* 13.4: 533–548.

Fouseki, K. and Dragouni, M. 2017. Heritage spectacles: the case of Amphipolis excavations during the Greek economic crisis. *International Journal of Heritage Studies* 23.8: 742–758.

Fowden, E.K. 2019. The Parthenon mosque, King Solomon, and the Greek sages. In *Ottoman Athens: Archaeology, Topography, and History*, edited by M. Georgopoulou and K. Thanasakis, 67–95. Athens: Gennadius Library and Aikaterini Laskaridis Foundation.

Fowden, E.K. Forthcoming. Rituals of memory at the Olympieion precinct of Athens. In *Remembering the Ancient City in the Post-Antique World*, edited by J. Martínez Jiménez and S. Ottewill-Soulsby. Oxford: Oxbow Books.

Franklin, C. 1998. Some samples of the finest orientalism: Byronic philhellenism and proto-Zionism at the time of the Congress of Vienna. In *Romanticism and Colonialism: Writings and Empire, 1780–1830*, edited by T. Fulford, 221–242. Cambridge: Cambridge University Press.

Gannon, M. 2019. When Ancient DNA gets politicized. *Smithsonian Magazine*, July 12, 2019. www.smithsonianmag.com/history/when-ancient-dna-gets-politicized-180972639/

Gazi, A. 2021. Heritage as obstacle or which view to the Acropolis? In *Contested Antiquity: Archaeological Heritage and Social Conflict in Modern Greece and Cyprus*, edited by E. Solomon, 245–271. Bloomington: Indiana University Press

Gazi, E. 2020. *Άγνωστη Χώρα: Ελλάδα και Δύση στις Αρχές του Εικοστού Αιώνα [Unknown Country: Greece and the West at the Beginning of the 20th Century]*. Athens: Polis.

Gekas, S. 2017. *Xenocracy: State, Class, and Colonialism in the Ionian Islands, 1815–1864*. New York: Berghahn.

Georgopoulou, M. and Thanasakis, K. (eds). 2019. *Ottoman Athens: Archaeology, Topography, History*. Athens: Gennadius Library and Aikaterini Laskaridis Foundation.

Gerola, G. 1932–1940. *Monumenti Veneti nell' Isola di Creta*, vol. 4. Istituto Veneto di Scienze, Venice: Lettere ed Arti.

Gilman, S.L. 1991. *The Jew's Body*. New York and London: Routledge.
Gissis, S.B. 2008. When is 'race' a race? 1946–2003. *Studies in History and Philosophy of Biological and Biomedical Sciences* 39: 437–450.
Gissis, S. and Jablonka, E. 2011. Introduction: Lamarckian problematics in the philosophy of biology. In *Transformations of Lamarckism: From Subtle Fluids to Molecular Biology*, edited by S.B. Gissis and E. Jablonka, 297–305. Cambridge, MA: Massachusetts Institute of Technology Press.
Glock, A. 1994. Archaeology as cultural survival: The future of the Palestinian past. *Journal of Palestine Studies* 23.3: 70–84.
Gonzalez-Ruibal, A. 2019. *An Archaeology of the Contemporary Era*. London: Routledge.
Gordillo, G. 2014. *Rubble: The Afterlife of Destruction*. Durham, NC: Duke University Press.
Gordon, J.A. 2015. What should Blacks think when Jews choose whiteness?: An ode to Baldwin. *Critical Philosophy of Race* 3.2: 227–258.
Gorenberg, G. 2002. *The End of Days: Fundamentalism and the Struggle for the Temple Mount*. Oxford: Oxford University Press.
Gourgouris, S. 1996. *Dream Nation: Enlightenment, Colonization, and the Institution of Modern Greece*. Stanford, CA: Stanford University Press.
Graeber, D. and Wengrow, D. 2021. *The Dawn of Everything: A New History of Humanity*. London: Allen Lane.
Green Fryd, V. 2016. Reflections on Hiram Powers's Greek Slave. *Nineteenth-Century Art Worldwide* 15.2. www.19thc-artworldwide.org/summer16/fryd-on-reflections-on-hiram-powers-greek-slave
Greenberg, R. 2015. Ethics in action: a viewpoint from Israel/Palestine. In *Ethics and the Archaeology of Violence*, edited by A. González-Ruibal and G. Moshenska, 19–32. Ethical Archaeologies: The Politics of Social Justice 2. New York: Springer.
Greenberg, R. 2018. One hundred and fifty years of archaeology and controversy in Jerusalem. In *The Routledge Handbook on Jerusalem*, edited by S. Mourad, N. Koltun-Fromm, B. der Matossian, 363–376. London and New York: Routledge.
Greenberg, R. 2019. Wedded to privilege: archaeology, academic capital, and critical public engagement. *Archaeologies* 15: 481–495.
Greenberg, R. 2021. Pompeo in Silwan: Judeo-Christian nationalism, kitsch, and empire in ancient Jerusalem. *Forum Kritische Archäologie* 10: 55–66.
Greenberg, R. and Keinan, A. 2007. *The Present Past of the Israeli-Palestinian Conflict: Israeli Archaeology in the West Bank and East Jerusalem since 1967*. Research Paper 1. Tel Aviv: S. Daniel Abraham Center for International and Regional Studies.
Greenberg, R. and Keinan, A. 2009. *Israeli Archaeological Activity in the West Bank, 1967–2007: A Sourcebook*. Jerusalem: Ostracon.

References

Gribetz, J. 2014. *Defining Neighbors: Religion, Race, and the Early Zionist-Arab Encounter*. Princeton: Princeton University Press.

Grigsby, D.G. 1999. "Whose colour was not black nor white nor grey, But an extraneous mixture, which no pen Can trace, although perhaps the pencil may": Aspasie and Delacroix's "Massacres at Chios." *Art History* 22.5: 676–704.

Grigsby, D.G. 2002. *Extremities: Painting Empire in Post-Revolutionary France*. New Haven: Yale University Press.

Gur, A. 2010. Political excavations of the Anatolian Past: nationalism and archaeology in Turkey. In *Controlling the Past, Owning the Future: The Political Uses of Archaeology in the Middle East*, edited by R. Boytner, L. Swartz Dodd, and B.J. Parker, 68–89. Tucson: Arizona University Press.

Haber, A. 2012. Undisciplining archaeology. *Archaeologies* 8.1: 55–66.

Haber, M., Doumet-Serhal, C., Scheib, C., Xue, Y., Danecek, P., Mezzavilla, M., Youhanna, S., Martiniano, R., Prado-Martinez, J., Szpak, M., Matisoo-Smith, E., Schutkowski, H., Mikulski, R., Zalloua, P., Kivisild, T., and Tyler-Smith, C. 2017. Continuity and admixture in the last five millennia of Levantine history from ancient Canaanite and present-day Lebanese genome sequences. *American Journal of Human Genetics* 101: 274–282.

Hackenbeck, S.E. 2019. Genetics, archaeology and the far right: an unholy Trinity. *World Archaeology* 51.4: 517–527.

Halevy, D. 2018. Toward a Palestinian history of ruins: interwar Gaza. *Journal of Palestine Studies* 48.1: 53–71.

Hamilakis, Y. 2000. Archaeology in Greek higher education. *Antiquity* 74: 177–181.

Hamilakis, Y. 2001. Monumental visions: Bonfils, classical antiquity and 19th century Athenian society. *History of Photography* 25.1: 5–12 and 23–43.

Hamilakis, Y. 2007. *The Nation and Its Ruins: Antiquity, Archaeology, and National Imagination in Greece*. Oxford: Oxford University Press.

Hamilakis, Y. 2011a. Archaeological ethnography: a multi-temporal meeting ground for archaeology and anthropology. *Annual Review of Anthropology* 40: 399–414.

Hamilakis, Y. 2011b. Indigenous archaeologies in Ottoman Greece. In *Scramble for the Past: the Story of Archaeology in the Ottoman Empire 1733–1914*, edited by Z. Bahrani, Z. Çelik, and E. Eldem, 49–69. Istanbul: Salt.

Hamilakis, Y. 2011c. Museums of oblivion. *Antiquity* 85: 625–629.

Hamilakis, Y. 2013a. Double colonization: the story of the excavations of the Athenian Agora (1924–1931). *Hesperia* 82.1: 153–177.

Hamilakis, Y. 2013b. *Archaeology and the Senses: Human Experience, Memory, and Affect*. Cambridge: Cambridge University Press.

Hamilakis, Y. 2016. Some debts can never be repaid: the archaeo-politics of the crisis. *Journal of Modern Greek Studies* 34.2: 227–264.

Hamilakis, Y. 2017. Sensorial assemblages: affect, memory, and temporality in assemblage thinking. *Cambridge Archaeological Journal* 27.1: 169–182.

Hamilakis, Y. (ed.) 2018a. *The New Nomadic Age: Archaeologies of Forced and Undocumented Migration.* Sheffield: Equinox.

Hamilakis, Y. 2018b. Archaeologies of forced and undocumented migration. In *The New Nomadic Age: Archaeologies of Forced and Undocumented Migration*, edited by Y. Hamilakis, 1–19. Sheffield: Equinox.

Hamilakis, Y. 2020. Learning from the "vandals": Histories of forgetting. *Los Angeles Review of Books*, June 26, 2020. www.lareviewofbooks.org/short-takes/learning-vandals-histories-forgetting/.

Hamilakis, Y. 2021. Για την Ακρόπολη του 21ου αιώνα [An Acropolis for the 21st Century]. *Avgi*, April 20, 2021.

Hamilakis, Y. and Anagnostopoulos, A. 2009. What is archaeological ethnography? *Public Archaeology* 8.2–3: 65–78.

Hamilakis, Y. and Ifantidis, F. 2016. *Camera Kalaureia: An Archaeological Photo-Ethnography.* Oxford: Archaeopress.

Hamilakis, Y. and Labanyi, J. 2008 Introduction: time, materiality, and the work of memory. In *Remembering and Forgetting on Europe's Southern Periphery*, edited by Y. Hamilakis and J. Labanyi, 5–17. Bloomington: Indiana University Press (Special issue of *History and Memory* 20(2)).

Hamilakis, Y. and Momigliano, N. (eds). 2006. *Archaeology and European Modernity: Producing and Consuming the "Minoans."* Padua: Bottega d'Erasmo.

Hamilakis, Y. and Yalouri, E. 1996. Antiquities as symbolic capital in modern Greek society. *Antiquity* 70: 117–129.

Hamilakis, Y. and Yalouri, E. 1999 Sacralising the past: the cults of archaeology in modern Greece. *Archaeological Dialogues* 6.2: 115–135.

Hamman, B.E. 2008. Chronological pollution: potsherds, mosques, and broken gods before and after the conquest of Mexico. *Current Anthropology* 49: 803–836.

Harloe, K. 2013. *Winckelmann and the Invention of Antiquity.* Oxford: Oxford University Press.

Harney, E., May, H., Shalem, D., Rohland, N., Mallick, S., Lazaridis, I., Sarig, R., Stewardson, K., Nordenfelt, S., Patterson, N., Hershkovitz, I., and Reich, D. 2018. Ancient DNA from Chalcolithic Israel reveals the role of population mixture in cultural transformation. *Nature Communications* 9: 3336. https://doi.org/10.1038/s41467-018-05649-9

Harvey, W.Z. 2016. The Judeo-Christian tradition's five others. In *Is There a Judeo-Christian Tradition? A European Perspective*, edited by E. Nathan and A. Topolski, 211–224. Berlin and Boston: De Gruyter.

Hasluck, F. W. 1916. Stone cults and venerated stones in the Graeco-Turkish area. *Annual of the British School at Athens* 21: 62–83.

References

Hatzopoulos, M. 2011. Oracular prophecy and the politics of toppling Ottoman rule in south-east Europe. *The Historical Review* 8: 95–116.

Heng, G. 2018. *The Invention of Race in the European Middle Ages*. Cambridge: Cambridge University Press.

Hering, G. 1994. Der griechische Unabhängigkeitskrieg und der Philhellenismus. In *Der Philhellenismus in der westeuropäischen Literatur 1780–1830*, 17–72. Amsterdam: Rodopi/Brill.

Herzfeld, M. 1987. *Anthropology through the Looking Glass: Critical Ethnography in the Margins of Europe*. Cambridge: Cambridge University Press.

Herzfeld, M. 2002. The absent present: discourses of crypto-colonialism. *South Atlantic Quarterly* 101: 899–926.

Herzfeld, M. 2003. *The Body Impolitic: Artisans and Artifice in the Global Hierarchy of Value*. Chicago: University of Chicago Press.

Herzfeld, M. 2006. Spatial cleansing: monumental vacuity and the idea of the West. *Journal of Material Culture* 11: 127–149.

Herzfeld, M. 2020. *Ours Once More: Folklore, Ideology, and Making of Modern Greece*. Oxford: Berghahn (2nd edition).

Hilprecht, H.V. 1896. *Recent Research in Bible Lands: Its Progress and Results*. Philadelphia: John D. Wattles & Co.

Hobhouse, J. C. 1817. *A Journey through Albania, and Other Provinces of Turkey in Europe and Asia*. Philadelphia: Carey and Son.

Holland, H. 1815. *Travels in the Ionian Isles, Albania, Thessaly, Macedonia, etc. during the years 1812 and 1813*. London: Longman, Hurst, Rees, Orme, and Brown.

Hummel, D.G. 2019. *Covenant Brothers: Evangelicals, Jews, and U.S.-Israeli Relations*. Philadelphia: University of Pennsylvania Press.

Ibn Khaldun. 1958. *The Muqaddimah: An Introduction to History*. Translated by Franz Rosenthal. London: Routledge and Kegan Paul.

Ingold, T. 2010. No more ancient; no more human: the future past of archaeology and anthropology. In *Archaeology and Anthropology: Understanding Similarity, Exploring Difference*, edited by G. Garrow and T. Yarrow, 160–170. Oxford: Oxbow.

Jaffe-Hoffman, M. 2019. Netanyahu: Archaeology, DNA prove Palestinians not native to Land of Israel. *Jerusalem Post*, July 7, 2019. www.jpost.com/arab-israeli-conflict/netanyahu-archaeology-dna-prove-palestinians-not-native-to-land-of-israel-594872 (accessed July 24, 2021).

Jockey, P. 2013. *Le mythe de la Grèce blanche. Histoire d'un rêve occidental*. Paris: Belin.

Jubeh, N. 2010. What matters? considering the future of cultural heritage in Palestine. *Present Pasts*, 2.1: 54–57.

Jubeh, N. 2018. Cultural heritage in Palestine: challenges and opportunities. In *Reclaiming the Past for the Future: Oral History, Craft and*

Archaeology – Adel Yahya in memoriam, edited by R. Bernbeck, A. Badran, and S. Pollock, 67–94. Berlin: Ex Oriente.

Kalantzis, K. 2019. Tradition in the Frame: Photography, Power, and Imagination in Sfakia, Crete. Bloomington: Indiana University Press.

Kalpaxis, Th. 1990. Αρχαιολογία και Πολιτική Ι: Σαμιακά Αρχαιολογικά 1850–1914 [Archaeology and Politics I: Samian Archaeology 1850–1914]. Rethimno: Crete University Press.

Kalpaxis, Th. 1993. Αρχαιολογία και Πολιτική ΙΙ: Η Ανασκαφή του Ναού της Αρτέμιδος (Κέρκυρα 1911) [Archaeology and Politics II: The Excavation of the Temple of Artemis (Corfu 1911)]. Rethimno: Crete University Press.

Kambouris, N. 2019. Greece begins celebrations for 2500-year anniversary of battles of Thermopylai and Salamis. Greek Reporter, October 16, 2019 (https://greece.greekreporter.com/2019/10/16/greece-begins-celebrations-for-2500-year-anniversary-of-battles-of-thermopylae-and-salamis/)

Kambouroglou, D. 1899. Μνημεία της Ιστορίας των Αθηναίων τ. 1. [Monuments of the History of Athenian People, v. 1]. Athens: A. Papageorgiou.

Kaplan, L.D. 2010. "Writing down the country": travelers and the emergence of the archaeological gaze. In Archaeology in Situ: Sites, Archaeology, and Communities in Greece, edited by A. Stroulia and S. Buck Sutton, 75–108. Lanham: Lexington Books.

Kapsali, K. 2017. Εθνοκεντρικές θεωρήσεις πολιτισμικής συνέχειας και άλλες φαντασιώσεις [Ethnocentric Views on Cultural Continuity and Other Fantasies]. Efimerida ton Syntakton, August 23, 2017.

Karakatsouli, A. 2016. "Μαχητές της Ελευθερίας" και 1821: Η Ελληνική Επανάσταση στη Διεθνική της Διάσταση ["Fighters of Freedom" and 1821: The Greek Revolution in Its International Dimension]. Athens: Pedio.

Kennedy, J. 1830. Conversations on Religion with Lord Byron and Others, Held in Cephalonia, A Short Time Previous to His Lordship's Death. London: John Murray.

Kersel, M.M. 2010. The changing legal landscape for Middle Eastern archaeology in the colonial era, 1800–1930. In Pioneers to the Past: American Archaeologists in the Middle East, 1919–1920, edited by G. Emberling, 85–90. Oriental Institute Museum Publications 30. Chicago: Oriental Institute.

Kessel, D. 1994. Η Ελλάδα του 1944 [Greece in 1944]. Athens: Ammos.

Khazoom, A. 2003. The great chain of orientalism: Jewish identity, stigma management, and ethnic exclusion in Israel. American Sociological Review 68.4: 481–510.

Kiilerich, B. 2006. Making sense of the spolia in the Little Metropolis in Athens. Arte Medievale 4.2: 95–114.

Kipperman, M. 1991. History and ideality: The politics of Shelley's Hellas. Studies in Romanticism 30.2: 147–168.

References

Kitromilides, P. 1989. "Imagined communities" and the origin of the national question in the Balkans. *European History Quarterly* 19: 149–194.

Kletter, R. 2006. *Just Past? The Making of Israeli Archaeology*. London: Routledge.

Kokkonas, Y. 2018. *Έγρεο Φίλα Μάτερ: Προσωποποιήσεις της Ελλάδας στα Χρόνια της Τουρκοκρατίας* [Rise up, Beloved Mother: Personifications of Greece in the Years of the Ottoman Rule]. Athens: Morfotiko Idryma Ethnikis Trapezas.

Kolovos, I., Ilıcak, S. and Shariat-Panahi, M. 2021. *Η Οργή του Σουλτάνου: Αυτόγραφα Διατάγματα του Μαχμούτ Β το 1821* [The Rage of the Sultan: Autograph Decrees by Mahmud II in 1821]. Athens: Elliniko Anoikto Panepistimio Press.

Kontiadis, X. 2021. *Η Περιπετειώδης Ιστορία των Επαναστατικών Συνταγμάτων του 1821* [The Adventurous History of the Revolutionary Constitutions of 1821]. Athens: Kastaniotis.

van Kooy, D. 2009. Improvising on the borders: Hellenism, history, and tragedy in Shelley's Hellas. In *Transnational England: Home and Abroad, 1780–1860*, edited by M. Class and T.F. Robinson, 41–57. Cambridge: Cambridge Scholars.

Korres, M. 2002. Αποκατάσταση και τελική διαμόρφωση των εδαφών της Ακρόπολης [Restoration and final shaping of the grounds of the Acropolis]. In *5η Διεθνής Συνάντηση για την Αποκατάσταση των Μνημείων της Ακρόπολης* [5th International Meeting for the Restoration of the Monuments of the Acropolis], edited by F. Mallouchou-Tufano, 413–438. Athens: Ministry of Culture, Committee for the Conservation of the Monuments of the Acropolis.

Kostopoulos, T. 2016. *Κόκκινος Δεκέμβρης: Το Ζήτημα της Επαναστατικής Βίας* [Red December: The Issue of Revolutionary Violence]. Athens: Vivliorama.

Kotsonis, Y. 2020. *Η Ελληνική Επανάσταση και οι Αυτοκρατορίες: Η Γαλλία και οι Έλληνες, 1797–1830* [The Greek Revolution and the Empires: France and the Greeks, 1797–1830]. Athens: Alexandria.

Koulouri, Ch. 2020. *Φουστανέλες και Χλαμύδες: Ιστορική Μνήμη και Εθνική Ταυτότητα 1821–1930* [Fustanellas and Gowns: Historical Memory and National Identity 1821–1930]. Athens: Alexandria.

Koumbourlis, I. 1998. Εννοιολογικές πολυσημίες και πολιτικό πρόταγμα. Ένα παράδειγμα από τον Κ. Παπαρρηγόπουλο [Conceptual Polysemy and Political Imperatives. An Example from K. Paparrigopoulos' Work]. *HISTORICA* 28/29: 31–58.

Krige, J. and Rausch, H. (eds.) 2012. *American Foundations and the Coproduction of World Order in the Twentieth Century*. Göttingen: Vandenhoeck and Ruprecht.

Kyramargiou, E., Papakondylis, Y., Scalora, F., and Dimitropoulos, D. 2020. Changing the map in Greece and Italy: place-name changes in the nineteenth century. *The Historical Review* 17: 205–250.

Laluk, N.C. 2017. The invisibility of land and mind: indigenous knowledge and collaborative archaeology within Apache contexts. *Journal of Social Archaeology* 17.1: 92–112.

Lambropoulos, V. 1993. *The Rise of Eurocentrism: Anatomy of Interpretation*. Princeton: Princeton University Press.

Latour, B. 1993. *We Have Never Been Modern*. Translated by Catharine Porter. Cambridge, MA: Harvard University Press.

Latour, B. 2013. *An Inquiry into Modes of Existence: An Anthropology of the Moderns*. Translated by Catharine Porter. Cambridge, MA: Harvard University Press.

Lazaridis, I., Mittnik, A., Patterson, N., Mallick, S., Rohland, N., Pfrengle, S., Furtwängler, A., Peltzer, A., Posth, C., Vasilakis, A., McGeorge, P. J. P., Konsolaki-Yannopoulou, E., Korres, G., Martlew, H., Michalodimitrakis, M., Özsait, M., Özsait, N., Papathanasiou, N., Richards, M., Alpaslan Roodenberg, S., Tzedakis, Y., Arnott, R., Fernandes, D.M., Hughey, J.R., Lotakis, D.M., Navas, P.A., Maniatis, Y., Stamatoyannopoulos, J.A., Stewardson, K., Stockhammer, P., Pinhasi, R., Reich, D., Krause, J., and Stamatoyannopoulos, G. 2017. Genetic origins of the Minoans and Mycenaeans. *Nature* 548 (7666): 214–218.

League of Nations 1922. Mandate for Palestine. https://ecf.org.il/media_items/291

Leake, W.M. 1830. *Travels in the Morea*, vol. 1. John Murray: London.

Lefkaditou, A. 2017. Observations on race and racism in Greece. *Journal of Anthropological Sciences* 95: 329–338.

Leontis, A. 1995. *Topographies of Hellenism: Mapping the Homeland*. Ithaca, NY: Cornell University Press.

Leoussi, A.S. 1998. *Nationalism and Classicism: The Classical Body as National Symbol in England and France*. Houndmills: Macmillan.

Leoussi, A.S. and Aberbach, D. 2002. Hellenism and Jewish nationalism: ambivalence and its ancient roots. *Ethnic and Racial Studies* 25.5: 755–777.

Levine-Rasky, C. 2008. White privilege: Jewish women's writing and the instability of categories. *Journal of Modern Jewish Studies* 7.1: 51–66.

Levy, A. 2003. Notes on Jewish-Muslim relationships: revisiting the vanishing Moroccan Jewish community. *Cultural Anthropology* 18.3: 365–397.

Lewis-Kraus, G. 2019. Is ancient DNA research revealing old truths – or falling into old traps? *New York Times Magazine*, January 17, 2019.

Liakos, A. 2019. *Ο Ελληνικός Εικοστός Αιώνας [The Greek 20th Century]*. Athens: Polis.

Lignadis, T. 2020 [1975]. *Η Ξενική Εξάρτησις κατά την Διαδρομήν του Νεοελληνικού Κράτους (1821–1945) [The Foreign Dependence during*

References

the Course of the Neohellenic State (1821–1945)]. Athens: Enallaktikes Ekdosis.
Lydon, J. and Rizvi, U. 2010 (eds). *Handbook of Postcolonial Archaeology*. Walnut Creek, CA: Left Coast Press.
Mackridge, P. 2010. *Language and National Identity in Greece, 1766–1976*. Oxford: Oxford University Press.
Magness, J., Kisilevitz, S., Grey, M., Mizzi, D., Schindler, D., Wells, M., Britt, K., Boustan, R., O'Connel, S., Hubbard, E., George, J., Ramsay, J., Boaretto, E., and Chazan, M. 2018. The Huqoq excavation project: 2014–2017 interim report. *Bulletin of the American Schools of Oriental Research* 380: 61–131.
Makdisi, S. 1998. *Romantic Imperialists: Universal Empire and the Culture of Modernity*. Cambridge: Cambridge University Press.
Marks, J. 2017. *Is Science Racist?* Cambridge: Polity.
Marks, R. 1982. Legitimating industrial capitalism: philanthropy and individual differences. In *Philanthropy and Cultural Imperialism: The Foundations at Home and Abroad*, edited by R.F. Arnove, 87–122. Bloomington: Indiana University Press.
Matalas, P. 2002. *Έθνος και Ορθοδοξία: Οι Περιπέτειες μιας Σχέσης*. [*Nation and Orthodoxy: the Adventures of a Relationship*]. Iraklio: Crete University Press.
Mavrogordatos, G. 2003. Orthodoxy and nationalism in the Greek case. *West European Politics* 26.1: 117–136.
Mazower, M. 1997. Policing the anti-communist state in Greece, 1922–1974. In *The Policing of Politics in the Twentieth Century: Historical Perspectives*, edited by M. Mazower, 129–150. Providence and Oxford: Berghahn.
Mbembe, A. 2019. *Necropolitics*. Durham, NC: Duke University Press.
McEnroe, J.C. 2002. Cretan questions: politics and archaeology 1898-1913. In *Labyrinth Revisited: Rethinking "Minoan" Archaeology*, edited by Y. Hamilakis, 59–72. Oxford: Oxbow.
McGeough, K. 2015. *The Ancient Near East in the 19th Century: Appreciations and Appropriations*, Vol. I: Claiming and Conquering. Sheffield: Phoenix Press.
Melman, B. 2020. *Empires of Antiquities: Modernity and the Rediscovery of the Ancient Near East, 1914–1950*. Oxford: Oxford University Press.
Mezzadra, S. and Neilson, B. 2013. *Border as Method: Or the Multiplication of Labor*. Durham, NC: Duke University Press.
Mignolo, W. 2009. Epistemic disobedience, independent thought and decolonial freedom. *Theory, Culture and Society* 26.7–8: 159–181.
Mignolo, W. 2011. Epistemic disobedience and the decolonial option: a manifesto. *Transmodernity: Journal of Peripheral Cultural Production of the Luso-Hispanic World* 1.2: 44–66.
Mizrachi, Y. 2017. *The Temple Mount/Haram ash-Sharif – Archaeology in a Political Context*. Jerusalem: Emek Shaveh.

Moiras, L. 2020. *Η Ελληνική Επανάσταση μέσα από τα Μάτια των Οθωμανών* [The Greek Revolution through the Eyes of the Ottomans]. Athens: Topos.

Moose, G. 1995. Racism and nationalism. *Nations and Nationalism* 1.2: 163–173.

Motzkin, G. 2011. Lamarck, Darwin, and the contemporary debate about levels of selection. In *Transformations of Lamarckism: From Subtle Fluids to Molecular Biology*, edited by S.B. Gissis and E. Jablonka, 3–8. Cambridge, MA: Massachusetts Institute of Technology Press.

Nathan, E. and Topolski, A. 2016. The myth of a Judeo-Christian tradition: introducing a European perspective. In *Is There a Judeo-Christian Tradition? A European Perspective*, edited by E. Nathan and A. Topolski, 1–16. Berlin and Boston: De Gruyter.

Nativ, A. and Lucas, G. 2020. Archaeology without antiquity. *Antiquity* 376: 852–863.

Navaro-Yashin, Y. 2009. Affective spaces, melancholic objects: ruination and the production of anthropological knowledge. *Journal of the Royal Anthropological Institute* 15.1: 1–18.

Nelson, A. 2016. *The Social Life of DNA: Race, Reparations, and Reconciliation after the Genome*. Boston: Beacon.

Nietzsche, F. 1997 [1876]. *Untimely Meditations*. Translated by R.Jh. Hollingdale. Cambridge: Cambridge University Press.

Nordau, M. 1898. *Degeneration*. London: William Heineman.

Ohana, D. 2012. *The Origins of Israeli Mythology: Neither Canaanites nor Crusaders*. Translated by D. Maisel. Cambridge: Cambridge University Press.

Ohana, D. 2017. *Nationalizing Judaism: Zionism as a Theological Ideology*. Lanham, MD: Lexington Books.

Omilade Flewellen, A. Dunnavant, J.P., Odewale, A., Jones, A., Wolde-Michael, T., Crossland, Z. and Maria Franklin. 2021. "The future of archaeology is anti-racist": archaeology in the time of Black Lives Matter. *American Antiquity* 86.2: 224–243.

Palmié, S. 2007. Genomics, divination, "racecraft." *American Ethnologist* 34.2: 205–222.

Papadopoulos, J.K. 2005. Inventing the Minoans: archaeology, modernity, and the quest for European identity. *Journal of Mediterranean Archaeology* 18.1: 87–149.

Papageorgiou-Venetas, A. 2001 [1994]. *Αθήνα, Ένα Όραμα του Κλασικισμού* [Athens: A Vision of Classicism]. Athens: Kapon.

Papagiannopoulos, I. 2019. *Ο Φρόυντ στην Ακρόπολη: Μια Ατοπογραφία* [Freud on the Acropolis: an Atopography]. Athens: Perispomeni.

Papagiannopoulos, I. 2020. On a *stasis* of memory or disrupting the Postliminium. In *Theology and World Politics: Metaphysics,*

Genealogies, Political Theologies, edited by V. Paipais, 211–233. Basingstoke: Palgrave-Macmillan.

Papanikolopoulos, D. 2021. *Το 1821 ως Επανάσταση. Γιατί Ξέσπασε και Γιατί Πέτυχε [1821 as Revolution: Why It Started and Why It Succeeded]*. Athens: Instítouto Enallaktikon Politikon.

Parmar, I. 2012. *Foundations of the American Century: The Ford, Carnegie, and Rockefeller Foundations in the Rise of American Power*. New York: Columbia University Press.

Pashley, R. 1837. *Travels in Crete v. 1*. Cambridge and London: Pitt Press and John Murray.

Pavli, K. 2014. *Εις το Όνομα του Πολιτισμού: Η Ιδεολογία των Ανασκαφών στη Μικρά Ασία κατά την μικρασιατικήν Κατοχήν υπό της Ελλάδος (1919–1922) [In the Name of Civilization: The Ideology of Excavations in Asia Minor during the Greek Occupation (1919–1922)]*. Ioannina: Isnafi.

Peckham, R.S. 2001. *National Histories, Natural States: Nationalism and the Politics of Place in Greece*. London: I.B. Tauris.

Petrakos, V.Ch. 2013. *Πρόχειρον Αρχαιολογικόν 1828–2012, Μέρος I. [Archaeological Draft 1828–2012, Part I]*. Athens: The Athens Archaeological Society.

Petrie, W.M.F. 1904. *Methods and Aims in Archaeology*. London: Macmillan.

Pizzato, F. 2017. How landscapes make science: Italian national narrative, the Great Mediterranean, and Giuseppe Sergi's biological myth. In *Mediterranean Identities: Environment, Society, Culture*, edited by B. Fuerst-Bjelis, 79–96. Rijeka: Intech.

Plantzos, D. 2011. Behold the raking geison: the new Acropolis museum and its context-free archaeologies. *Antiquity* 85: 613–625.

Plantzos, D. 2016. *Το Πρόσφατο Μέλλον: Η Κλασική Αρχαιότητα ως Βιοπολιτικό Εργαλείο [The Recent Future: Classical Antiquity as a Biopolitical Tool]*. Athens: Nefeli.

Ploumidis, S. 2012. Η έννοια του «θανάτου» στην Ελληνική Επανάσταση (1821–1832): Ιδεολογικές προσλήψεις και πολιτική πρακτική. [The Concept of "Death" in the Greek War of Independence, 1821–1832: Ideological Understandings and Political Practice]. *Mnimon* 32: 59–88.

Potts, A. 2000. *Flesh and the Ideal: Winckelmann and the Origins of Art History*. New Haven: Yale University Press.

Presner, T.S 2007. *Muscular Judaism: The Jewish Body and the Politics of Regeneration*. London and New York: Routledge.

Quirke, S. 2010. *Hidden Hands: Egyptian Workforces in Petrie Excavation Archives, 1880–1924*. London: Duckworth.

Reich, D. 2018. *Who are We and How We Got Here: Ancient DNA and the New Science of the Human Past*. Oxford: Oxford University Press.

Roche, H. 2013. *Sparta's German Children*. Swansea: Classical Press of Wales.

Roitman, A. 2001. Exhibiting the Dead Sea scrolls: some historical and theoretical considerations. In *Archaeology and Society in the 21st Century: The Dead Sea Scrolls and Other Case Studies*, edited by N.A. Silberman and E.S. Frerichs, 41–66. Jerusalem: Israel Exploration Society.

Rojas, F. 2019. *The Pasts of Roman Anatolia: Interpreters, Traces, Horizons*. Cambridge: Cambridge University Press.

Rosaldo, R. 1989. Imperialist nostalgia. *Representations* 26: 107–122.

Sabbagh-Khoury, A. 2018. Settler colonialism, the indigenous perspective, and the sociology of knowledge production in Israel. *Theory and Criticism* 50: 391–418 (in Hebrew).

Sahlins, M. 2012. *What Kinship Is…And Is Not*. Chicago: Chicago University Press.

Sakka, N. 2008. The excavation of the ancient Agora of Athens: the politics of commissioning and managing the project. In *A Singular Antiquity: Archaeology and Hellenic Identity in Twentieth Century Greece*, edited by D. Damaskos and D. Plantzos, 111–124. Athens: The Benaki Museum.

Sakka, N. 2021. Archaeology and politics in the interwar period: the Swedish excavations at Asine. In *Contested Antiquity: Archaeological Heritage and Social Conflict in Modern Greece and Cyprus*, edited by E. Solomon, 80–107. Bloomington: Indiana University Press.

Sakorafas, A. 2019. *The presence of the African slaves in Ottoman Greece and the transition to the independent Kingdom of Greece, with a special reference to Athens*. Post-graduate research paper, Free University of Berlin.

Sasson-Levy, O. 2013. A different kind of whiteness: marking and unmarking of social boundaries in the construction of hegemonic ethnicity. *Sociological Forum* 28.1: 27–50.

Schnapp, A. 1996 *The Discovery of the Past: The Origins of Archaeology*. Translated by I. A. Kinnes and G. Varndell. London: British Museum.

Scholem, G. 2003 [1959]. *Ο Ιουδαϊκός Μεσσιανισμός [The Judaic Messianism]*. Introduction and translation by N. Sevastakis. Athens: Erasmos.

Schulte, J. 2013. From Greek to Hebrew: Saul Tchernikhovsky and the translation of classical antiquity. *Simon Dubnow Institute Yearbook* 12: 15–36.

Sfikas, Th. 1994. *The British Labour Government and The Greek Civil War: The Imperialism of "Non Intervention."* Keele: Keele University Press.

Shavit, Y. 1987. *The New Hebrew Nation: A Study in Israeli Heresy and Fantasy*. London: F. Cass.

References

Shavit, Y. 1997a. *Athens in Jerusalem: Classical Antiquity and Hellenism in the Making of the Modern Secular Jew*. London: Littman Library of Jewish Civilization.
Shavit, Y. 1997b. Archaeology, political culture, and culture in Israel. In *The Archaeology of Israel. Constructing the Past, Interpreting the Present*, edited by N. A. Silberman and D. Small, 48–61. Sheffield: Sheffield Academic Press.
Shelley, P.B. 1886[1822]. *Hellas: A Lyrical Drama*. Edited by T.J. Wise. London: The Shelley Society.
Shenhav, Y. and Yonah, Y. (eds.). 2008. *Racism in Israel*. Jerusalem and Tel Aviv, Israel: Van Leer Institute and Hakibbutz Hameuchad (in Hebrew).
Silberman, N.A. 1982. *Digging for God and Country: Exploration, Archaeology and the Secret Struggle for the Holy Land, 1700–1917*. New York: Anchor Books Doubleday.
Silberman, N.A. 1990. *Between Past and Present: Archaeology, Ideology, and Nationalism in Modern Middle East*. New York: Henry Holt.
Silberman, N.A. 1993. *A Prophet from Amongst You: The Life of Yigael Yadin*. Reading, MA: Addison-Wesley.
Silk, M. 1984. Notes on the Judeo-Christian Tradition in America. *American Quarterly* 36.1: 65–85.
Skopetea, E. 1988. *Το "Πρότυπο Βασίλειο" και η Μεγάλη Ιδέα: Όψεις του Εθνικού Προβλήματος στην Ελλάδα (1830–1880)* [*The Model Kingdom and the Great Idea: Aspects of the National Issue in Greece (1830–1880)*]. Athens: Polytypo.
Skopetea, E. 1997. *Φαλμεράυερ: Τεχνάσματα του Αντίπαλου Δέους* [*Fallmerayer: Tricks of the Rival*]. Athens: Themelio.
Smith, A.D. 1997. Nation and ethnoscape. *Oxford International Review* 8: 8–16. [Repr. In *Myths and Memories of the Nation*, 149–159. Oxford: Oxford University Press (1999)].
Smith, A.D. 1998. *Nationalism and Modernism: A Critical Survey of Recent Theories of Nations and Nationalism*. London and New York: Routledge.
Smith, G.A. 1907. *Jerusalem: The Topography, Economics and History from the Earliest Times to A.D. 70*, vol. I. London: Hodder and Stoughton.
Smith, H. 2021. Acropolis now: Greeks outraged at concreting of ancient Site. *The Guardian*, June 10, 2021.
Smith, L. 2013. Discussion. In *Heritage Regimes and the State* (2nd ed) edited by R. F. Bendix, A. Eggert, and A. Peselmann, 389–398. Göttingen Studies in Cultural Property 6. Göttingen: Göttingen University.
Solomon, E. (ed.) 2021. *Contested Antiquity: Archaeological Heritage and Social Conflict in Modern Greece and Cyprus*. Bloomington: Indiana University Press.

Sotiris, P. 2021. Νέα αντιπαράθεση για τα έργα στην Ακρόπολη [New Clashes for the Works on the Acropolis]. www.in.gr, February 27, 2021.
Spector, S.A. 2010. *Byron and the Jews*. Detroit: Washington State University Press.
Spratt, T.A.B. 1865. *Travels and Researches in Crete v. 1*. London: John van Voorst.
Spyropoulos, Y. 2010. The creation of a homogeneous collective identity: towards a history of the Black people in the Ottoman Empire. *International Journal of Turkish Studies* 16.1–2: 25–46.
Spyropoulos, Y. 2015. Slaves and freedmen in the 17th- and early-18th century Ottoman Crete. *Turcica* 46: 177–204.
St. Clair, W. 2008. *That Greece Might Still Be Free: The Philhellens in the War of Independence* (revised edition). Cambridge: Open Book.
Stähler, A. 2013. Constructions of Jewish identity and the spectre of colonialism: of white skin and black masks in early Zionist discourse. *German Life and Letters* 66.3: 254–276.
Stanhope, L. 1824. *Greece in 1823 and 1824: Being a Series of Letters and Other Documents on the Greek Revolution Written during a Visit to That Country by the Honourable Colonel Leicester Stanhope*. London: Sherwood, Jones & co.
Starzmann, M.T. 2013. Occupying the past: colonial rule and archaeological practice in Israel/Palestine. *Archaeologies* 9: 546–570.
Stefanou, E. and Antoniadou, I. 2021. Eptapyrgio, a modern prison inside a World Heritage Monument: raw memories in the margins of archaeology. In *Contested Antiquity: Archaeological Heritage and Social Conflict in Modern Greece and Cyprus*, edited by E. Solomon, 272–296. Bloomington: Indiana University Press.
Stewart, C. 2017. *Dreaming and Historical Consciousness in Island Greece*. Chicago: Chicago University Press.
Stoler, A.L. 2016. *Duress: Imperial Durabilities in Our Times*. Durham, NC and London: Duke University Press.
Strauss, B. 2005. *The Battle of Salamis: The Naval Encounter that Saved Greece – and Western Civilization*. New York: Simon and Schuster.
Sutton, D. 1997. Local names, foreign claims: family inheritance and national heritage on a Greek island. *American Ethnologist* 24.2: 415–437.
Sutton, D. 2014. *The Concealed and the revealed: buried treasures as sense of place in neoliberal Greece*. Paper presented at the invited workshop "The Economic and the Political: Locating the Greek Crisis within History and Anthropology." Durham, UK, 20 December.
Svoronos, N. 1992. Ο Σπυρίδων Ζαμπέλιος [Spyridon Zambelios]. *Mnimon* 14: 11–20.
Szegedy-Maszak, A. 2001. Félix Bonfils and the traveller's trail through Athens. *History of Photography* 25.1: 13–22.

References

TallBear, K. 2013. *Native American DNA: Tribal Belonging and the False Promise of Genetic Science*. Minneapolis, MN: University of Minnesota Press.

Tamari, S. 2009. Lepers, lunatics and saints: the nativist ethnography of Tawfiq Canaan and his Jerusalem circle. In *Mountain against the Sea: Essays on Palestinian Society and Culture*, 93–112. Berkeley: University of California Press.

Taneja, A.V. 2013. Jinnealogy: everyday life and Islamic theology in post-partition Delhi. *Hau: Journal of Ethnographic Theory* 3.3: 139–165.

Tanoulas, T. 1997. *Τα Προπύλαια της Αθηναϊκής Ακρόπολης κατά το Μεσαίωνα* [*The Propylaia of the Athenian Acropolis in Medieval Times*]. Athens: The Athens Archaeological Society.

Theotokas, N. 1992. Παράδοση και νεοτερικότητα. Σχόλια για το Εικοσιένα. [Tradition and Modernity: Comments on 1821]. *HISTORICA* 17: 345–370.

Theotokas, N. 2021. Η επανάσταση του έθνους και το ορθόδοξο γένος: σχόλια για τις ιδεολογίες στο Εικοσιένα [The Revolution of the Nation and the Orthodox Genos: Comments on Ideology in 1821]. In *Πως Προσεγγίζουμε το 1821? Πολιτική, Κοινωνία, και Ιδεολογία στην Ελληνική Επανάσταση* [*How Do We Approach 1821? Politics, Society, and Ideology in the Greek Revolution*], edited by I. Kolovos and D. Dimitropoulos, 107–148. Athens: Efimerida ton Syntakton.

Thomas, J. 2004. *Archaeology and Modernity*. London: Routledge.

Todd, Z. 2016. An indigenous feminist's take on the ontological turn: "ontology" is just another word for colonialism. *Journal of Historical Sociology* 29.1: 4–22.

Todorova, M. 1997. *Imagining the Balkans*. New York: Oxford University Press.

Tolias, G. 2016. The resilience of Philhellenism. *The Historical Review* 13: 51–70.

Tosh, J. 2005. *Manliness and Masculinities in Nineteenth Century Britain Essays on Gender, Family and Empire*. Harlow: Pearson Longman.

Travlos, J. 2005 [1960]. *Πολεοδομική εξέλιξις των Αθηνών* [*Urban Development of Athens*]. Athens: Kapon.

Trubeta, S. 2013. *Physical Anthropology, Race and Eugenics in Greece (1880s–1970s)*. Leiden: Brill.

Tsiomis, Y. 2021 [2017]. *Η Αθήνα Ξένη στον Εαυτό της: Η Γέννηση μιας Νεοκλασικής Πρωτεύουσας* [*Athens, Foreign to Itself: The Birth of a Neoclassical Capital*]. Translated by T. Tsiatsika. Iraklio: Crete University Press.

Tsitselikis, K. 2021. *Σύνορα, Κυριαρχία, Γραμματόσημα: Οι Μεταβολές του Ελληνικού Εδάφους 1830–1947* [*Borders, Sovereignty, Postal Stamps: Changes in Greek Territory 1830–1947*]. Athens: The Laskaridis Foundation.

Tunali, G. 2019. An 18th century take on ancient Greece: Mahmud Efendi and the creation of the Tarih-i Medinetü'l-Hukema. In *Ottoman*

Athens: Archaeology, Topography, and History, edited by M. Georgopoulou and K. Thanasakis, 97–121. Athens: Gennadius Library and Aikaterini Laskaridis Foundation.

Ucko, P. J. 1998. The biography of a collection: the Sir Flinders Petrie Palestinian collection and the role of university museums. *Museum Management and Curatorship* 17.4: 351–399.

Vaad Leumi 1947. *Three Historical Memoranda. Submitted to the United Nations Special Committee on Palestine. 5707/1947.* Jerusalem: General Council (Vaad Leumi) of the Jewish Community of Palestine.

Vallianos, P.S. 2018. The ways of the nation: messianic and universalist nationalism in Renieris, Zambelios and Paparrigopoulos. *The Historical Review* 15: 163–194.

Varouchakis, V. 2017. Indigenous archaeologies of Crete, 1898–1913. *Public Archaeology* 16.1: 42–66.

Velianitis, T.Th. 1993. *Η Φιλόμουσος Εταιρεία των Αθηνών [The Athens Society for the Promotion of the Arts (Philomousos Etaireia)]*. Athens: Vasilopoulos.

Veloudis, G. 1982. *Ο Jakob Philipp Fallmerayer και η Γένεση του Ελληνικού Ιστορισμού [Jakob Philipp Fallmerayer and the Birth of Greek Historicism]*. Athens: EMNE-Mnimon.

Veracini, L. 2006. *Israel and Settler Society*. London and Ann Arbor: Pluto Press

Vogli, E.K. 2018. Ο ορισμός του πολίτη και οι αναμορφώσεις της ελληνικής ταυτότητας κατά τη διάρκεια της Επανάστασης [The definition of the citizen and the reshaping of Greek identity during the Revolution]. In *Έλλην, Ρωμιός, Γραικός: Συλλογικοί Προσδιορισμοί και Ταυτότητες [Ellin, Romios, Graikos: Collective Definitions and Identities]*, edited by O. Katsiardi-Hering, A. Papadia-Lala, K. Nikolaou, and V. Karamanolakis, 497–513. Athens: Eurasia.

Volpe, L. 2016. Embodying the octoroon: abolitionist performance at the London Crystal Palace, 1851. *Nineteenth-Century Art Worldwide* 15.2. www.19thc-artworldwide.org/summer16/volpe-on-abolitionist-performance-at-the-london-crystal-palace-1851.

Voudouri, D. 2010. Law and the politics of the past: legal protection of cultural heritage in Greece. *International Journal of Cultural Property* 17.3: 547–568.

Voudouri, D. 2017. The legal protection of antiquities in Greece and national identity. In *Ancient Monuments and Modern Identities: A Critical History of Archaeology in 19th and 20th century Greece*, edited by S. Voutsaki and P. Cartledge, 77–94. London: Routledge.

Vournelis, L. 2016. Alexander's great treasure: wonder and mistrust in neoliberal Greece. *History and Anthropology* 27.1: 121–133.

References

Warren, C. 1871. Excavations of Jerusalem. In *The Recovery of Jerusalem: A Narrative of Exploration and Discovery in the City and the Holy Land*, edited by C.W. Wilson and C. Warren, 26–260. New York: D. Appleton & Co.

Warren, C. 1875. *The Land of Promise or, Turkey's Guarantee*. London: George Bell and Sons.

Weizman, E. 2002. The Politics of Verticality. www.opendemocracy.net/en/article_801jsp/

Wheler, G. 1682. *A Journey into Greece in Company of Dr Spon of Lyons*. London: William Cademan, Robert Kettlewell and Awnsham Churchill.

Wilson, C.W. 1871. Ordnance Survey of Jerusalem. In *The Recovery of Jerusalem: A Narrative of Exploration and Discovery in the City and the Holy Land*, edited by C.W. Wilson and C. Warren, 1–25. New York: D. Appleton & Co.

Wilson, C.W. and Warren, C. 1871. *The Recovery of Jerusalem: A Narrative of Exploration and Discovery in the City and the Holy Land*. New York: D. Appleton & Co.

Winichakul, T. 1994. *Siam Mapped: A History of the Geo-Body of a Nation*. Honolulu: University of Hawaii Press.

Wright, G.E. and Filson, F.V. (eds). 1945. *The Westminster Historical Atlas to the Bible*. Philadelphia: Westminster Press.

Yahya, A. 2005. Archaeology and nationalism in the Holy Land. In *Archaeologies of the Middle East: Critical Perspectives*, edited by S. Pollock and R. Bernbeck, 66–77. Oxford: Wiley-Blackwell.

Yakovaki, N. 2006. *Ευρώπη Μέσω Ελλάδας: Μια Καμπή στην Ευρωπαϊκή Αυτοσυνείδηση, 17ος -18ος Αιώνας [Europe via Greece: A Turning Point in European Self-Consciousness, 17th–18th c.]*. Athens: Estia.

Yakovaki, N. 2014. The Filiki Etaireia revisited: in search of contexts, national and international. *The Historical Review* 11: 171–187.

Yalouri, E. 2001. *The Acropolis: Global Fame, Local Claim*. Berg: Oxford.

Yalouri, E. 2004. When the new world meets the ancient. American and Greek experiences of the 1896 "revival" of the Olympic Games. In *Athens, Olympic City 1896–1906*, edited by Ch. Koulouri, 297–335. Athens: International Olympic Committee.

Zacharia, K. 2015. Nelly's iconography of Greece. In *Camera Graeca: Photographs, Narratives, Materialities*, edited by Ph. Carabott, Y. Hamilakis, and E. Papargyriou, 233–256. London: Routledge.

Zahavi, Y. 2009. Archaeology, *Stamps and Coins of the State of Israel*. https://books.google.co.il/books?id=f_MM5-ucPWMC&printsec=frontcover&hl=iw&source=gbs_ge_summary_r&cad=0#v=onepage&q&f=false (accessed April 17, 2021).

Zalmona, Y. and Manor-Friedman, T. 1998. *To the East: Orientalism in the Arts in Israel*. Jerusalem: Israel Museum.

Zambelios, S. 1852. Άσματα Δημοτικά της Ελλάδος, Εκδοθέντα μετά Μελέτης Ιστορικής περί Μεσαιωνικού Ελληνισμού [Folk Songs of Greece, Issued Together with a Historical Study of Medieval Hellenism]. Corfu: Ermis.

Zanou, K. 2018. *Transnational Patriotism in the Mediterranean, 1800–1850: Stammering the Nation*. Oxford: Oxford University Press.

Zerubavel, Y. 1995. *Recovered Roots: Collective Memory and the Making of the Israeli National Tradition*. Chicago: University of Chicago Press.

Zerubavel, Y. 2008. Memory, the rebirth of the native, and the "Hebrew bedouin" identity. *Social Research* 75.1: 315–352.

Zevgos, Y. 2021[1945]. Η Λαϊκή Αντίσταση του Δεκέμβρη και το Νεοελληνικό Πρόβλημα [The Popular Resistance of December and the Problem of Modern Greece]. Athens: Efimerida ton Syntakton [originally published by "Rigas" Publishers].

Ziadeh-Seely, G. 2007. An Archaeology of Palestine: Mourning a Dream. In *Selective Remembrances: Archaeology in the Construction, Commemoration, and Consecration of National Pasts*, edited by P.L. Kohl, M. Kozelsky, and N. Ben-Yehuda, 326–345. Chicago: University of Chicago Press.

Index

Aberbach, D. 34, 36
Abu El-Haj, Nadia 6, 80
Acciaiuoli 95
Acropolis, Acropolis Museum see Athens
Aeschylus' *Persians* 46
affordances 175
Afro-centrists 137
Afro-Greek 117
agency 18, 89, 91, 173, 175
Agora see *Athens*
Alexander the Great 23–24, 35, 139
Al-Houdalieh, Salah 90
allochronization 15
American School of Classical Studies at Athens see *foreign schools*
  see also Agora
Amphipolis see *Greece*
Anatolia 23, 67, 70, 135
ancient DNA see *archaeogenetics and ancient DNA*
Anderson, Ben 16, 90
Andronikos, Manolis 9, 23, 26
  see also Vergina
animality 92–93, 95–97

Antetokounmpo, Giannis Ugo 117
  see also Afro-Greek
anthropocentrism 92, 95, 97
anthropology 5, 60, 77, 147, 153
  see also racial anthropology
Anthropos 88
antiquarianism 15, 90
antiquarians 11, 91, 118
  proto-scientific 15
  Western 11, 14, 16–17, 93
Antiquities, Laws of/archaeological law 22, 25, 28–29, 55, 69, 80, 154–155, 157
antiquities, restitution of 63
apodimos ellinismos 100
  see also Hellenism: diasporic Hellenism
Arab 86, 113, 118–119
Arabim 118
Arapi (Αράπη) (*Arap* in Turkish) 118
  see also Arabim
archaeogenetics and ancient DNA 61, 109, 114, 140–148, 157, 182
archaeological ethnography 5, 7 n.7, 168–169

archaeology
    biblical 11, 26, 32–33, 59, 62–63, 105, 144, 170–171
    classical 4, 32, 63, 126
    colonialist 10
    community 3, 103, 168
    contemporary 159, 165, 171–172
    crypto-colonial 169
    modernist 21, 88, 90, 152–153
    nationalist 55, 97
    salvage 2, 62
archaeophilia 90–91
Artemision Zeus 145
    see also Poseidon; New York World's Fair
Asia Minor 68–70
Aspasie 134
    see also Delacroix, Eugène; Greece on the Ruins of Missolonghi
assemblages of life 91–92
atheism, Soviet 73 n.53
Athens
    Acropolis 22, 25, 28, 31, 39 n.6, 49–51, 66, 93–98, 102, 118, 173–174
    Acropolis Museum 102
    Agora 29, 56–57, 60, 93
    Mosque 167
    Parthenon 12–13, 15, 49, 94, 97, 161, 167
Athens Archaeological Society 29, 57, 93–94
autochthony 116
Avi-Yonah, Michael 32

Babri Masjid mosque 108 n.65
Bakalakis, Georgios 49
Balkanism 136

Balkans 17, 136–137
    Jews of 137
Bar Kokhba rebellion 30–31, 33, 39
Battle of Athens (December 1944) 48, 72 n.34
    see also Dekemvriana
Battle of Salamis 47, 52
    see also Aeschylus' *Persians*; Persians
Battle of Thermopylai 72 n.34
Bavaria 21–22
Bavarians 28, 53, 55, 154
Beaton, R. 45
Bembo 119–120
    see also Candia; Greece
Ben Gurion, David 27, 106
Benvenisti, Meron 106
Bergson, Henri 88, 172–173
Berlin 22
Bernal, Martin 136–137
biblical archaeology see *archaeology*
biopolitics 37
Black Athena 136
Black Lives Matter Movement 109
body, Aryan 37
Boer War 51
Bolsheviks 51
Bonfils, Félix 19, 94
    see also Propylaia
border crossers 52, 163–164
    see also migrants
Boyarin, Daniel 38–39
Boyer, J.-P. 130
    see also Haiti; Haitian revolution
British School at Athens see *foreign schools*
Bronze Age 3, 5, 6, 29, 112, 136, 139, 145, 147, 161

Index

buffering 44–46, 49, 52
  buffer area/country 47, 131
  buffer role 116, 149 n.48, 161
  buffer state/s 58, 110
  buffer zone/s 42–43, 44, 47, 52, 164, 181
Butler, Beverley 169
Byron 44–47
Byzantine period (Greece)
  Byzantine art 4
  Byzantine Hellenism see *Hellenism*
  Byzantine heritage 55, 99
  Byzantine legacy 88
  Byzantine monuments 100
  Byzantine museum 100
  See also Palestine, Byzantine
Byzantium 23, 66, 135

Canaan, Canaanites 27, 33–34, 36, 39, 140, 143
  see also Zionism: Hebrew/Canaanite identity
Candia see *Greece*
  see also Bembo
capitalism 21, 57, 65, 114, 161, 168
Cephalonia see *Greece*
Chateaubriand, François-René de 21, 130, 149 n.48
Choiseul-Gouffier, M.-G.-A.-F. de 93
Christianity, Orthodox 55, 88, 99–101
Christians 16, 18, 20, 40 n.20, 22, 33, 62, 82, 86, 95, 98–99, 116, 119, 122, 125, 128, 130–131, 134, 148 n.21
Christian nationalism 86
Churchill, W. 48
Civil War, Greek 47–48, 57

classical antiquity 15, 101, 116, 161, 163
colonialism
  and racism 3
  and nationalism 11, 42, 109, 182
  settler 58, 182
  financial 42
coloniality 5, 88, 130–132, 153, 155, 181
colonization
  and decolonization 91
  archaeological 54, 68, 75
  colonialism and 5
  process of 11
  of imagination 156
  of the ideal 11
  Western 15
Colophon 68
  see also Asia Minor
Committee for the Conservation of the Monuments of the Acropolis 95
community archaeology see *archaeology*
Conder, Claude 111
Constantinople 14, 16, 22, 39, 99–100, 156
contemporary archaeology see *archaeology*
Cook, J. M. 49
  see also British School of Classical Studies at Athens
Crete 3–6, 23, 56, 100, 117, 119–120, 146–147
crisis, financial 24, 42, 65, 85
crypto-coloniality 153
crypto-colonization 1, 47, 49, 52–53, 55, 75, 156, 164
crypto-colony 1, 43–44, 58–59, 65, 71, 157–158

Crystal Palace 128
  see also Powers, Hiram; The Greek Slave
Cyprus 139, 147

Davis, Jack 73 n.44
Daʻadli, Tawfiq 159–160
Dayan, Moshe 34
decolonization 1, 91, 151–153, 155–156, 158–159, 161–162, 168, 182
Dekemvriana 48
  see also Battle of Athens
Delacroix, Eugène 125, 132–134
Deleuze, Gilles 88, 172
Delphi see Greece
determinism
  biological 125
  environmental 4, 126
  geographic 60
Diamantis, Dimitrios 49
dictatorship (1967–1974), military 57
dirt 2, 81, 93
Dodecanese 43, 165
Dodwell, E. 118
Dragoumis, Ion 71 n.2
dreaming 46, 71 n.2, 107, n.19
Douglas, Mary 75, 77
Du Bois, W.E.B. 48
duration 172, 175

ELAS see *National Liberation Army*
Elon, Amos 34
elliniki fili 122
Ellino-Christianikos see *Helleno-Christian*
Emperor Constantine, Byzantine 66

Empire
  Helleno-Christian 23
  Ottoman 8, 16–18, 45, 56, 99, 117, 128, 155
  Russian 16
Enlightenment 16, 123
En Touto Nika 66
Epirus, Northern 66
Essay on the Inequality of the Human Races 135
  see also Gobineau, Arthur de
ethnicity 109, 110, 112, 117, 121, 141, 147
Eurocentrism 15
Europeanness 125, 131
European Economic Community 58, 135
European Union 52, 58, 135
evangelical Christians 33, 62, 86
Evans, Arthur 6, 146
exceptionalism, national 64

Feige, Michael 26, 114
Fallmerayer, J.P. 134, 145, 149, n.56
Farnoux, Alexandre 73 n.44
Feraios, Rigas 122
figurines, Cycladic 136
Filiki Etaireia see *Society of Friends*
Filomousos Etaireia see *Society for the Friends of the Arts*
folklorists 89
foreign (archaeological) schools 29, 53–55, 154–155, 157
  American School of Classical Studies at Athens 56–57, 68–69, 73 n.44, 157
  British school at Athens 16, 49, 157

Index

French School at Athens 68, 73 n.44
Jerusalem 60, 157
Swedish Institute at Athens 73 n.44
Franklin, C. 45
French Revolution 122
Freud, Sigmund 98, 107 n.49
Foucault, M. 121

Gastouni see *Greece*
Gaza 84, 138
Gazi, Efi 71 n.2
gentrification 76, 78
geo-body 69–70
Gerola, Giussepe 119
  see also Bembo; Candia
Gissis, Snait 144
Goldman, Hetty 69
Great Idea 22, 66, 70, 139
  see also Asia Minor; Hellenicity; Hellenism
Great Powers 21, 53
Germany 9, 19, 37–38, 42, 58
Gobineau, Arthur de 135
Golden Ages 23, 30, 154, 182
Golden Dawn 116, 145–146
Greece
  Amphipolis 24, 85
  Candia 119–120
  Cephalonia 45
  Delphi 29, 56
  Gastouni 118
  Knossos 29, 56
  Koroni 118
  Larissa 118
  Nafplio 105
  Mothoni/Metheni 118
  Olympia 29, 37, 56
  Patras 118
  Preveza 118
  Salamis, island of 66
  Vergina 23
Greece on the ruins of Missolonghi 132–134
  see also Delacroix, Eugène
Greek Communist party 70
  see also KKE
Greek Revival 22
Greek Slave, The
  see also Powers, Hiram; *Virginian Slave, The*
Grigsby, Darcy Grimaldo 128, 134

Hagia Sophia 70
  see also Constantinople; Istanbul
Haiti 130
Haitian Revolution 130–131
  see also Boyer
Hasluck, F.W. 119
Hasmoneans (Maccabees) 25, 30, 33, 39, 82
Hazor 26–27, 111–112
Hellenicity 68
Hellenism
  Ancient 23
  and the body 36–37
  and Judaism 34, 180–181
  Byzantine 23
  diasporic 100
  indigenous 55, 66, 88, 92, 95, 100–101, 181
  modern 22–23
  Western 11, 14, 16–18, 46, 53, 55, 65–66, 88, 100–101, 135, 161, 167, 181
Hellenization 16, 23, 66
Helleno-Christian 100
Helleno-Christian synthesis 66, 100

Hellas 1, 12–18, 23, 40 n.22, 46, 66, 116, 122–123, 126
Heng, Geraldine 121
Herzfeld, Michael 42–43, 72 n.8
Herzl, Theodore 39
Hess, Moses 19
Hill, B.H. 69
Hitler 37
Holland, Henry 118
Holy Rock 102
Huqoq synagogue 35

Ibn Khaldun 89
Ibrahim Pasha 130
imperialism
  American 37
  19th-century 9
indigenous archaeology see *archaeology*
indigenous ontologies 175
Ionian Islands 43, 47, 71 n.3
Ireland 44, 55
Islam 18, 46, 82, 98, 110, 115, 154, 165, 167
  Islamic fundamentalism 73 n.53
  Islamophobia 86, 122, 135
See also minarets; Muslims
Israel
  and Mediterranean identity 137–138
  Antiquities Authority (IAA) 2–3
  archaeology and antiquities 2, 6, 11, 26–28, 30–31, 33–34, 61–62, 80, 103–104, 114, 138, 143–144
  as crypto-colony 48, 58–59, 63–64, 65–66, 110, 157–158
  as settler colony 64, 70, 158
  decolonized archaeology in 158–161, 171–172, 175–178
  popular music 137
  race and racialization in 109–115, 143–144
  sacralization and ethnoscape 82–83, 103–104, 105–106
  see also Antiquities, laws of; Jerusalem; Zionism
Israel Exploration Society 26, 114
Istanbul 18, 37, 70

Jerusalem 3, 10, 14–15, 19, 20, 31, 35, 79, 86, 175
  Archaeological Schools in 60, 157
  Old City 1, 79, 92
  Shrine of the Book 103
  Silwan 3, 76–79, 81
  Temple Mount/Haram ash-Sharif 31–32, 78, 82, 103
  tunnels and vertical separation 80, 83–86, 103
  water supply 78–79, 92
Jews 9, 19, 24–25, 31, 36, 38–39, 44–45, 82, 103, 110, 112, 113–115, 116, 125, 131, 137, 140
Josephus, Flavius 25–26, 30, 32
Judaism 33–36, 82, 180–181
Judeo-Christian tradition/ethic 11, 59, 62–63, 65, 76, 86, 110–111, 115
Judeo-Christianity 65, 115
jure sanguinis 116

Kaftantzoglou, Lyssandros 93
Kalaureia 73 n.44 *see also* foreign schools: Swedish Institute
Kambouroglou, D. 148 n.21
Karamanlis, Konstantinos 135
katharevoussa 98
King Otto 22

Index

KKE 72 n.34 *see also* Greek Communist party
Klenze, Leo von 22, 28, 107 n.44
Knossos see *Greece*
 see also Crete
Korais, Adamantios 123–124, 131
Koran 130
Koroni see *Greece*
Korres, Manolis 95–97
Kossinna, Gustav 141
Kotsonis, Y. 18, 118
Kourouniotis, Konstantinos 69

laografi see *folklorists*
laografia 89
Larissa see *Greece*
Latour, Bruno 76, 81, 87–88
Lausanne Treaty 105, 165
Leake, W.M. 118
Leonidases 47
Leoussi, Athena 34, 36
Levantine identity 110, 114–115, 143
Lignadis, Tasos 71 n.2
Lilien, Moses 38–39
Lucas, G. 155
Ludd, al- 159–160

Macedonia
 Ancient 23
 Republic of North 23
Macedonians 17, 23
Macridy Bey, Theodor 68
Mahmud Efendi 15
Makronisos
 camp of 48
 The New Parthenon 48, 51
malicide 122
 see also Heng, Geraldine

Massacre at Chios, The 126, 131–132
 see also Delacroix, Eugène
Masada 26, 31, 61–62
material melancholia 104
 see also Navaro-Yashin, Yael
Mavrogordatos, G. 100
Mazower, Mark 51
Mbembe, Achille 81, 121
Mediterraneanness 138–139
Megiddo 60
Melman, Billie 28
Metaxas 145
migrants 1, 52, 116–117, 136, 138, 143, 164
Migration crisis 52, 116, 163
millet 98
minarets 61, 104–105, 167
Minoans 6, 139–141, 145–146, 161
Moria (refugee camp) 165–166
Mosque (Athens) see *Athens*
Mothoni/Metheni see *Greece*
Motzkin, Gabriel 140
muezzin 104
multi-temporality 152, 175–176
Munich 22
musalla 148, 21
museums 63, 69, 91–92, 95, 102, 157, 165
 see also Acropolis museum
Muslims 18, 21, 82–83, 98, 117, 119, 123, 125, 148 n.21
Mycenaeans 139–141, 145–147, 161

Nafplio see *Greece*
Napoleon Bonaparte 123, 125
Napoli 139
national imagination 4, 23, 30, 31, 70, 100–101, 135, 167
National Liberation Army (ELAS) 48

nationalism
  as a derivative discourse 11
  Christian 86
  colonialism and 42, 109, 182
  Greek 9, 16–17, 55
  Hellenic and Zionist 8
  Israeli 30
  religious 32, 121, 138
  Turkish, Kemalist 33
  Western Hellenism and 66
  Western modernity and 3
  white 3
Nativ, A. 155
Navaro-Yashin, Yael 104
Nazi regime 37
necro-politics 121
Nelly, the photographer 145
neoclassicism 22, 126
New York World's Fair 145
  see also Artemision Zeus; Poseidon
North Africa 24, 89, 111–112, 125, 137, 139
  imperial ambitions in 139
  Jews of 24, 111–112, 125, 137
Notion 68
  see also Asia Minor

occidentality 61, 131
  see also whiteness
occult economy 85
Odessa 17
Olympia see Greece
Olympics 37
Oriental Institute (University of Chicago) 60–61, 111
orientalism 9, 20–21, 43–44, 46, 54, 97–98, 125, 131–135, 157, 182
Orthodox Christians 16, 40 n.20, 22, 116

paganism 15, 34
Palestine
  and Mediterranean identity 137–138
  archaeology and antiquities 6, 10–11, 24, 29, 32, 58–60, 77, 79–80, 89–90, 156
  as Holy Land 9–11, 19, 61, 82, 170–171
  British interest in 24, 59, 105, 111
  Byzantine 32, 35–36
  colonialism in 58, 110, 156–159
  decolonized archaeology in 159–160, 170–172, 175–178
  Jewish indigeneity in 110–115
  Mandate 25–26, 28–29, 60, 79–81, 157
  Muslims in 10, 18–19, 82–83, 86
  Ottomans in 10–11, 18–20, 25, 54, 79, 81, 86, 111, 120, 155, 160
  racialization in 111, 120
  West Bank 26, 70, 84, 106, 158, 182
  see also Jerusalem; Israel
Palmié, Stephan 141
Papagiannopoulos, I. 71 n.7, 107, 49
Paparrigopoulos, Konstantinos 135
Paris 17, 22, 124
Parthenon see Athens
Parthenon marbles 63, 102
PASOK 139
Patras see Greece
Patriarchate 18, 40 n.20, 99–100
Pausanias 12
Pericles 15
Persians 21, 47, 52, 95, 125
Petrie, W.M.F. 29, 111
Philhellenes 20, 44, 47, 128
Philhellenism 39, 45

Index

Philip II 23
Phoenicians 33, 36, 140–141, 143
physiognomy and craniometrics 147
  see also racism and antiracism
Pittakis, Kyriakos 22
pollution 75–77, 79, 81–83, 92–93, 97–98, 101, 104, 106 n.6
Poseidon 145
  see also Artemision Zeus; New York World's Fair
Powers, Hiram 126–127
  see also Greek Slave, The
prehistory 4, 33, 63
Presner, Todd 38–39
Preveza see *Greece*
Propylaia 49, 93–95
  see also Acropolis; Parthenon
psychoanalysis 84
Punch, magazine 128 See also *Virginian Slave, The*
purification 1, 36, 71, 75–82, 86–88, 92–93, 96, 98, 101, 103–105, 173, 182
Pyramid, Cheops's 97

Qadas, village of 176–178

racecraft 141
racial anthropology 147
  see also anthropology
racism and anti-racism 3, 37–38, 120, 130, 135–136, 143, 152
  see also Israel, race and racialization; Palestine, racialization; white supremacy
Reich, David 140–141
religion 6, 34, 82–83, 98–100, 106, 109, 116–117, 121, 123, 130, 135

Rockefeller, John D. Jr. 57, 60
Rojas, Felipe 90
Romans 25, 30, 138
romanticism 97
Royal Ulster Constabulary 51
ruins and ruination 3, 9–10, 12–15, 23, 25, 49, 81, 118–120, 130, 132–134, 164, 173–174, 177, 180–182
Rum 40 n.22
Russia 17, 21, 45–46, 51, 56, 135

sacralization 31, 71, 101, 103, 105
  see also classical antiquity
Sahlins, Marshall 142
Saint-Domingue 130
  see also Haiti
Saint Louis 37
  see also Olympics
Saint-Simon 47
saints' tombs 82–83, 105
Salamis, island of see *Greece*
salvage archaeology see *archaeology*
Sardis 68
  see also Asia Minor
Schliemann, Heinrich 94, 146
Schnapp, Alain 90
self-colonization 181–182
sensorial perception 173
Shakespeare 131
Shelley, Percy Bysshe 46
Silberman, Neil 6
Silwan see *Jerusalem: Silwan*
slavery 121, 128, 130, 149 n.43
  Atlantic 131
  black 130
  Ottoman empire 128
  transatlantic 128
  white 128, 130

slaves 44, 117, 118, 128
    black 118
    in Ottoman times 117
    see also Virginian Slave, The;
        Greek slave, The
Slavic presence in Greece 135
Smith, George Adam 10, 12, 20
Smith, Laurajane 159
Smyrna 68, 70
Society for the Friends of the Arts 17
Society of Friends 17, 98
Souvenirs of the Orient 20
    see also Bonfils, Félix
Soviet Republics 136
    Soviet East 48, 139
    Soviet influence 51, 57
Sparta, legacy of 37
sphragis, practice of 105
    see also Byzantine period
Stanhope, L. 47
symbolic capital 15, 28, 53, 161–163, 170

Tosh, John 54
travellers, Western 11–14, 20–21, 92, 119
Truman Doctrine 57
Tsirivakou-Neumann, Ch. 97
Tenniel, John 129
    see also Virginian Slave, The
Thomas, Julian 84
Thrace 66, 67, 165

UNESCO 102, 154, 159
University of Crete 4–5
USA 37, 56–59, 62, 109, 145, 175

Valide mosque 11
Venice 16
Vergina see Greece
    see also Andronikos, Manolis

Vienna 16–17
Virginian Slave, The 128–129
    see also Tenniel, John; Punch;
        Greek slave, The

War of Independence (Greek) 8, 20, 22, 44, 46, 98–99, 116, 121–123, 125–126, 128, 182
War, Greco-Turkish 22, 57, 139
Warren, Charles 24, 86
Wheler, George 12–13
white supremacy 37, 117, 131, 152, 161, 182
whiteness 39, 97, 110, 117, 122, 125–136, 147, 164
Wickham, Charles 51
Winckelmann, Johann Joachim 4, 6, 3, 126
Winichakul, Thongchai 69
Wilson, Charles 84, 86

Yadin, Yigael 9, 26–27, 31, 61–62, 111–112
Yunanistan 40 n.22

Zambelios, Spyridon 100–101
Zeus, Olympian 118
Zevgos, Yannis 72 n.34
Zionism
    and antiquities 9, 25, 31
    and colonialism 58
    and indigeneity 112, 115
    and purification 82
    and the Jewish body 36–39
    Balfour declaration 25
    Christian 24, 45, 125
    emergence of 9, 18–19
    Hebrew/Canaanite identity 33, 36, 113–114